THE AMERICAN NEGRO

HIS HISTORY AND LITERATURE

OUT OF THE
HOUSE OF BONDAGE

Kelly Miller

ARNO PRESS and THE NEW YORK TIMES

NEW YORK 1969

General Editor
WILLIAM LOREN KATZ

KELLY MILLER, PROFESSOR OF SOCIOLOGY AND Dean of the College of Liberal Arts at Howard University, was a felicitous and perceptive essayist and commentator, whose articles, published in leading white journals, were widely read by the educated of both races during the first quarter of the nineteenth century. The son of a South Carolina cash-renting cotton farmer, Miller had secured his undergraduate degree from Howard University, and after two years of advanced mathematics at Johns Hopkins University, had been awarded a professorship at his alma mater in 1890. He gradually shifted his interests from mathematics to social commentary and sociology; even after his appointment as dean in 1907, he remained best known for his lucid analyses, his thoughtful probing of the nature of race relations in the United States.

Miller reached intellectual maturity at the turn of the century, at a time of increasing racial proscription. It was a period of disfranchisement and Jim Crow laws in the southern states; of sharecropping for the majority of black men who lived in the rural South; of the apogee of mob violence in the form of lynchings and anti-Negro race riots; of growing indifference and hostility on the part of the white North. Not unnaturally, therefore, it was a time when an ideology of accommodation, epitomized in the philosophy and leadership of Booker T. Washington, secured the ascendancy in Negro thought and action. Yet the protest tradition retained vitality, and a small band of articulate black intellectuals, led by W. E. B. Du Bois, articulated a philosophy of protest. They organized the short-lived Niagara Movement in 1905, and a few years later were influential in forming the NAACP, which became the dominant race-advancement group by the end of World War I. Miller, reflecting a broad spectrum of thought among the Negro middle and upper classes, stood between these two points of view, and attempted to synthesize elements from the thoughts of both Washington and Du Bois.

The volume of essays reprinted here is a typical sampling of Miller's writing, drawn from a number of magazines. It appeared in 1914, six years after the publication of Miller's first and most celebrated volume of essays, *Race Adjustment*. The items Miller chose for *Out of the House of Bondage* were written mostly in 1912 and 1913, and reflected his evaluation of the race's position half a century after the issuance of the Emancipation Proclamation.

Several themes stand out in these essays. Especially significant is the substantial sampling of Miller's writings on education. Though an admirer of Booker T. Washington, the apostle of vocational or industrial education and "working with the hands" at the expense of higher education and the professions, Miller himself had received an excellent college and graduate school education and throughout this period, when the Negro colleges were under severe attack, remained, like Du Bois, their staunch defender. Miller conceded that both types of education were necessary, but he maintained that for the preservation of the race's manhood and self-respect, and for the creation of what Du Bois called the "talented tenth," higher education was an absolute necessity.

In these essays is Miller's protest against American racism and discrimination—expressed in moderate, though explicit terms, as befitted a man who essayed to harmonize the views of the accommodators and the protesters. There is Miller's defense of the Negro race from charges of inferiority, criminality, and lack of historic achievement. Here, as a moderate, Miller conceded something to the popular white prejudices of his time, by agreeing that at the period in which he was writing, Anglo-Saxon civilization was superior to any other, while Africans had an inferior and backward culture; but he explicitly denied that such cultural differences were based on any innate racial differences. In tune with the retrospective nature of the volume, which appeared around the fiftieth anniversary of Emancipation, is Miller's concern with the ultimate destiny of the race. This is exhibited both in his discussion of race mixture and the long-range possibility of the disappearance of Negroes as a distinct race in the United States, and, in his emphasis on the race's remarkable progress in spite of handicaps, and his optimistic encouragement to black youth to strive for further progress by avoiding bitterness and working for success in accordance with standard white middle-class American values.

Today Miller's views sound quaint, if not largely irrelevant. The significance of these essays is that they mirrored so well the thinking of the vast majority of articulate and educated American Negroes half a century ago.

August Meier
DEPARTMENT OF HISTORY
KENT STATE UNIVERSITY

OUT OF THE
HOUSE OF BONDAGE

OUT OF THE HOUSE OF BONDAGE

A DISCUSSION OF THE RACE PROBLEM

BY

KELLY MILLER

DEAN OF THE COLLEGE OF ARTS AND SCIENCES, HOWARD UNIVERSITY; AUTHOR
OF "RACE ADJUSTMENT: ESSAYS ON THE NEGRO IN AMERICA,"

NEW YORK
THOMAS Y. CROWELL COMPANY
PUBLISHERS

PREFACE

The essays herein collected have appeared during the past few years in such magazines as *The Independent, The Atlantic Monthly, The Dial, The Nineteenth Century and After, The Educational Review, The Annals of the Academy of Political and Social Science, The Popular Science Monthly,* and *Neale's Monthly.* Acknowledgment and thanks are hereby rendered the above named publications for permission to use these papers in the present form. The titular essay appeared in *Neale's Monthly* for October, 1913.

While these essays do not pretend to offer a formal solution of the Race problem, yet it is believed that they deal with fundamental principles, and with issues that must be involved in any proposed scheme of solution.

K. M.

Howard University, Washington, D. C.

OATH OF AFRO-AMERICAN YOUTH

I will never bring disgrace upon my race by any unworthy deed or dishonorable act. I will live a clean, decent, manly life; and will ever respect and defend the virtue and honor of womanhood; I will uphold and obey the just laws of my country and of the community in which I live, and will encourage others to do likewise; I will not allow prejudice, injustice, insult or outrage to cower my spirit or sour my soul; but will ever preserve the inner freedom of heart and conscience; I will not allow myself to be overcome of evil; but will strive to overcome evil with good; I will endeavor to develop and exert the best powers within me for my own personal improvement, and will strive unceasingly to quicken the sense of racial duty and responsibility; I will in all these ways aim to uplift my race so that, to everyone bound to it by ties of blood, it shall become a bond of ennoblement and not a byword of reproach.

TABLE OF CONTENTS

A MORAL AXIOM

Which constitutes the Foreword as well as
the Final Word of this volume.

I hate a cat. The very sight
    Of the feline form evokes my wrath;
    Whene'er one goes across my path,
I shiver with instinctive fright.

And yet there is one little kit
    I treat with tender kindliness,
    The fondled pet of my darling, Bess;
For I love her and she loves it.

In earth beneath, as Heaven above,
    It satisfies the reasoning,
    That those who love the self-same thing
Must also one another love.

Then if our Father loveth all
    Mankind, of every clime and hue,
    Who loveth Him must love them, too;
It cannot otherwise befall.

OUT OF THE HOUSE OF BONDAGE

The story of the African on the American continent possesses both the painful reality of truth and the pleasing fascination of fiction. Although this story has been so frequently repeated as to become a wearisome recital, yet no sooner does the flagging public mind tire of the rehearsal than some accentuating feature demands it anew. This narrative will ever be fresh with perennial interest, not only because of the ever recurring dramatic incidents and episodes, but because its motif touches the hidden springs of the deepest human solicitude and passion. The continued performance of this never ending drama has already stretched through well-nigh three centuries, with not a hint of termination. The Emancipation Problem may be regarded as the close of the first act. The Golden Jubilee of this event justifies a moment's pause for a cursory glance at the past, a glimpse of the present, and, if it might be vouchsafed, an inkling of the future.

Three centuries ago two streams of population began to flow to the newer from the older continents of the world. The European component was but the natural overflow of the fountain of civilization, while the African confluent was forced upward from the lowest level of savagery. The confluence of these two streams has constituted our present population of some hundred million souls, divided into the approximate ratio of ten to one. Here we have the most gigantic instance in history of the hemispheric transference of population. The closest intimacy of contact of markedly dissimilar races gives the world its acutest and most interesting object lesson in race relationship. We are easily convinced that the whole movement must have been under the direction of a guiding hand higher than human intelligence or foresight. The deep cried unto the deep, and the nations heard and heeded the cry, although they little understood its far reaching meaning and import. The negro was introduced into this land by the European lord of creation, not as a fellow creature, but as a thing apart, destined to a lower range and scope by eternal and unalterable decree. This *tertium quid* was deemed a little more than animal and a little less than human. He was endowed with certain animal and mechanical powers which might justly be utilized and exploited for the glorification of the self-centred over-lord, to whom had been ordained dominion and power and glory forever. The exploitation of one race or individual for the aggrandization of another was the universally received and accepted doctrine of the age. Immediate economic advantage was the controlling motive. Greed for gain and glory takes little counsel of ultimate philosophy. Even so eminent an authority as Sir Harry Johnston tells us that "there is sufficient of the devil still left in the white man for the 300 years' cruelties of negro (or other) slavery to be repeated, if it were worth the white man's while." Although the devil may still be dominant in the white man's breast, and it might seem, for the time being, profitable to reënact the iniquitous industrial régime of the past, yet the present state of knowledge of the far reaching consequences of economic and social laws would effectually forbid. Had there been three hundred years ago the faintest conception that this new-caught child of the tropics was endowed with human powers and aspirations that must ere long demand full satisfaction and acknowledgment, and had the enslavers been vouchsafed a glimpse of the tangled web of intricate issues involved in his enslavement, the tale of two continents would now be different to relate. The incident evils that have grown out of the historic contact of these two races is but the logical outcome of a shortsighted and fatuous philosophy. The concomitant benefit to human civilization now flowing, and destined to flow from this contact, illustrates the sure teaching of history, that an over-ruling Providence makes the wrath of man to praise him, while holding the remainder of wrath in restraint.

All rational discussion must have a point of departure. Before we can make any just appraisement of the negro's progress during the past fifty years we must project his achievements against the background of his inherent' or acquired capacities and equipment at the beginning of this period. Actual attainment must be evaluated in terms of coincident helps and hindrances. The significance of the crop must be adjudged in light of the quality and culture of the soil. It is wholly needless for our purpose to discuss the native endowment of the native African at the time of his transplantation in America. It is finally sufficient to describe his undisputed attainments gained in the household of bondage, and his marvelous development since his release.

Slavery was an institution of learning as

well as labor. The negro's taskmaster was also his schoolmaster. In order that he might accomplish the crude tasks imposed upon him, it was necessary that he should be instructed in the rudimentary principles and crude methods of its accomplishment. Efficiency as a tool depended upon his aptness as a pupil. Had the negro been inapt in understanding and inept in performance, he would have been unprofitable and, therefore, undesirable as a servant. The red Indian was not satisfactorily reduced to a condition of slavery, not merely because of the pugnaciousness of his spirit but also by reason of the stolidity of his understanding. He seemed to be hopelessly incapable of comprehending the white man's ways of doing things and the reason therefor. He lacked the negro's aptitude of mind and docility of disposition.

Slavery was always under the paradoxical necessity of developing the slave as an instrument while suppressing him as a person. Without a certain degree of intelligence the slave became useless; with too much intelligence he became dangerous. The fundamental fallacy of the institution lay in the supposition that one race or individual was predetermined for servile relationship to another. The biologists tell us that there is not found within the sphere

of created things a single species with purposely altruistic function. Each species and individual is endowed with powers and prowess
calculated to promote advancement after its
kind. The predestined end and way of every
creature is to advance its own well-being, the
welfare of others being subserved incidentally
and indirectly, if at all. Efficiency is not an
altruistic virtue. The individual exerts his
best powers only when he can visualize the
efforts of his toil translated into terms of his
own personal or tribal weal. To exploit human endeavor on any other hypothesis is to
sin against the eternal cause. With a secret
suspicion of this far sweeping truth, the master felt forced to limit the black man's activity
to the crudest tasks, not because he was incapable of performing any other, but rather
because he must not be initiated into the ulterior meaning and aim of the gospel of work.
He must be kept in ignorance of the hidden
meaning of things, lest he become restive under
restraint and assert his human prerogative.
There was a tinge of that primeval apprehension for fear the under man might stretch
forth his hand and partake of the tree of
knowledge and become as one of us. Nevertheless the negro became domesticated, if not
educated, in the University of slavery, whose

diploma admitted him to practice in the wide
arena of the world's work. The narrator of
the story of the negro is prone to touch too
lightly upon the tutelage of servitude as being
among the regrettable delenda of his experience in the household of bondage. But this
discipline and experience formed his initiation
into the civilizaton of the new world. All subsequent progress is based upon the foundation
here laid.

Under the tuition of slavery the negro
gained acquaintance with the English language,
which is the most effective agency of civilization now operating on the face of the earth. All
of the secrets of knowledge and culture are hidden in written and oral speech. There is nothing hidden that shall not be revealed to people
who form acquaintance with the English
tongue. The European child devotes the
greater part of his time and effort to the acquisition of language because this is the key
that unlocks the storehouse of the accumulated
culture of the race. This is the gateway
through which individuals and races must enter
into the inheritance of the ages. The forms of
language communicated to the negro under slavery were of the crudest and most imperfect
character. The ear alone was initiated while
the eye remained illiterate. Oral symbols of

ideas might be imparted to the ear, but must
not be presented to the eye or reproduced by
hand. The process was limited to the short circuit of ear and tongue but the longer and more
involved circuit of eye and finger was forbidden. The slave must be ear-minded alone; the
master alone must be eye-minded. The black
man was permitted to hear and speak but not to
read and write. Even within the permitted
range there were sharp and severe limitations.
Only the simplest possible ideas were communicated in the most rudimentary terms. The recipient was supposed to understand only so
much as he was expected immediately to execute. Not only must the higher ideas and ideals
be withholden but also their forms of verbal expression. The negro knew nothing of the syntactical arrangement of the parts of speech nor
the rules governing their meaning and use. The
noun and the verb did not usually find themselves in agreement, nor was there any dis-
coverable plan of grammatical law and order.
Nevertheless he gained the essential function
and power of the English language as a vehicle
through which ideas are received and conveyed.

It was through slavery also that the negro
was brought in touch with the Christian religion. The whole race, as if by magic, embraced this spiritual cult which appeals so

powerfully to its own inner longings. Christianity affects the negro's spiritual nature as
the sunlight writes its impression on the sen-
sitized plate in photography. While the institution of slavery does not deserve the credit,
it nevertheless afforded the occasion for the
evangelization of the race. There was no adequate agency for this gigantic achievement. It
doubtless would have taken centuries under
ordinary missionary auspices to accomplish so
great a result. The whole race, following the
infallible logic of feeling, on first suggestion,
embraced the new gospel which appealed at
once to its inner disposition and outward situation.

The institution of slavery, as such, was necessarily averse to the evangelization of a subject race; for the mission of Christianity is to
quicken the sense of inherent divinity easily
translated into the more concrete terms of
manhood. The desideratum of slavery was to
inculcate a satisfied and complaisant servitude. The evangelization of the negro was accomplished through the stealthy process, so
aptly described in that soul melting melody:
"Steal away to Jesus." The humble slave with
overtaxed body and overburdened soul, after
the onerous task of the day's work, literally
stole away to the low grounds and desolate

places, in the loneliness of the midnight hour, and poured out his soul in anguish, where master might not molest, and none but God was near. Let the proud and haughty religionists, worshiping in marble temple, sitting before gilded altars in polished pews, and performing formal genuflections on cushioned knee-rests, disdain, if they will, these wild, incoherent spiritual longings of these despised and rejected creatures; but the sure satisfaction of their yearnings is the highest proof that our age affords that God still hears and answers prayer.

It is not necessary to say that the negro's religion was imperfect. People of imperfect development cannot have perfect accomplishments in any department of human excellence. Christianity found the negro in his humble and lowly estate, and appealed to his nature, just as he was, without one plea. Ignorance did not instantaneously give way to knowledge, corruption did not at once put on incorruption, nor did grossness immediately clothe itself with decorum and dignity of life. Unless the heavenly treasure were placed in earthen vessels, Christianity would find no lodgment among the frail children of men. If the test of perfection were to be applied, there would not be found a single Christian nation or race on the face of the earth, and indeed but few individuals. But the embracement of religion has been the chief factor in the progress of the negro race on this continent, and represents the highest gain that has come to it out of three centuries of contact with the Western world. This is the strongest tie that binds the negro in the ennobling bond of spiritual kinship to the fellowship of humanity.

The highest evidence of the essential quality of the negro's racial nature appears in his folk songs. Nowhere else does one find such perfect embodiment of the Christian graces of meekness, humility and forgiveness of spirit. Although subject to crushing conditions that would have caused any other race to vent its spirit in malediction, yet this race uttered the burden of its soul in these songs of sorrow, without the slightest tinge of bitterness, animosity or revenge. Such underlying soul-stuff is surely material meet for the kingdom of heaven.

Another inimitable quality which slavery developed out of the negro nature was manifested in the "black mammy." We search in vain the records of the human race for like indication of altruistic endowment and wealth of maternal affection. This crude, uncouth negro woman could take the child of her mistress

on one knee and her own offspring on another
and satisfy both out of the storehouse of her
mother love. By sheer force of this endowment, she was able to take the child of her cultivated mistress and foster for herself an attachment and endearment beyond that it bore
its own mother after the flesh. The undevi-
ating devotion of man-servant to master grew
out of the same spirit. Such instances of vicariousness on part of the race indicate the underlying soul quality of which they were but
fragmentary croppings. It is sometimes asserted that these qualities have not been transmitted to the new issue which seems prone to
display the opposite extreme of bumptious con-
ceitedness. The first effect of release from any
condition is apt to lead to its opposite. When
the pendulum is freed from one extreme of its
amplitude, it moves swiftly to the opposite
limit of its range. These are, however, but
fluctuating conditions due to shifting circumstances. Benevolence is essentially an altruistic virtue. Self-sacrifice is an inalienable co-
efficient of negro blood. The specific devotion
of maid-servant and man-servant under the
former régime is not destroyed by the overthrow of that régime, but is perpetuated and
carried forward to be manifested, it may be, in
other forms of outgiving. The South does well

to build a monument to the black mammy whose altruistic devotion is worthy to be perpetuated through all time. But let it never be forgotten that this memorial is not to her disinterested and detached devotion alone, but will stand as a perpetual reminder of the vicarious virtues of a sacrificial race.

The negroes were brought to America as disjected and expatriated individuals. The imported slaves represented the conquered and subdued, the despised and outcast of their own country and race. Taken from widely separated sections of the African continent, representing tribes divided by dialect, custom and feudal strife, there was naturally enough no common bond of union among the scattered fragments that were thrown together in a new and strange land. They were held together only by the outward compulsion of a common bondage and the facial compulsion of a common color. There was neither a common spirit, purpose nor impulse. Surprise is sometimes expressed that the American negro shows such little regard for the welfare of his native continent and for his parent racial stock. He was literally cut out off from the land of the living with a complete severance of ties. No ennobling or endearing stream of influence followed him across the sea. He was sustained by no

comforting recollections of his native land.
Had the first penal colonists of Georgia been
permanently severed from the ennobling influence of their native England, and abandoned
to the brooding recollection of their hard
prison lot in the land from which they had es-
caped, we should hardly expect them to culti-
vate much reverential regard for the country
or the people of their origin.

The negro had to develop as best he might
a race consciousness, although it was the prudent policy and fixed purpose of the institution of slavery to frustrate its orderly and
effective formation. Forbidden freedom of motion, means of intercommunication and the
privilege of unconstrained assemblage, there
was nevertheless the emergence of a crude race
consciousness which was necessarily too feeble
for effective service in the making of a race.

It should be added also that slavery contributed to the negro race a considerable infusion
of white blood with whatever modifying or
transforming power may be ascribed to the
prepotency of that blood which is now dominant throughout the world. The American negro at the time of his emancipation, therefore,
did not represent the African pure and simple, but the African plus a modifying modicum
of European infusion and reinforcement.

The negro proved to be an apt pupil in taking on the general culture, manners and methods of his master. He quickly fell into his bias of mind and habits of thought, so much so that the psychic kinship of the negro and the Aryan seems much closer than that of breeds of nearer blood relationship. Imitation is the essential process by which culture is transmitted from age to age and from race to race. The imitator shows an appreciation of and a predilection toward the imitated attainment. Thus the negro, snatched from the wilds of savagery and plunged into the midst of a mighty civilization, received his preliminary preparation for his physical emancipation destined to come in the fullness of time.

The Emancipation Proclamation, demanded by the exigencies of war, destroyed, at one stroke, the institution of slavery which had been a thorn in the flesh of the nation from the time of its foundation. The remission of sin was not accomplished without the shedding of blood. This document is universally regarded as the world's greatest charter of liberty. A wave of altruistic ardor swept over the nation. The anti-slavery crusade showed as high a test of the Christ's spirit as has been afforded in all the list of Christian years. When the great deed had been done the whole nation burst forth in one triumphant song of moral elation, "Mine eyes have seen the glory of the coming of the Lord." Statesmanship and philanthropy vied with each other in their ministration to the new made freed-man. He was clothed with the full prerogative of citizenship and placed in competition with the strongest and most aggressive people on the face of the earth. The experience was indeed a stupendous one. But the African was not left alone in his upward struggle. A generous philanthropy furnished him schools and colleges in which the choice youth of his blood might partake of the secret and method of civilization and show them unto their more benighted brethren. A wise and discerning statemanship furnished schools for the education of the young. He was invited to partake of the tree of knowledge which he had neither planted nor watered. The current of public sentiment ran high in his favor. It was worth the price of public favor for anyone in high place to say harsh or unkind words against the least of these. Privilege and prerogative were accorded him which others had purchased at great price. No other submerged race ever enjoyed so profuse a measure of public favor as did the negro for a season. He proved to be an apt pupil and showed surprising acquisitive and inquisitive power. It seemed for a time that he would be the perpetual recipient of this favor. But the tide of public sentiment ebbs and flows like the waves of the sea. The black man has been both the beneficiary and victim of its sportive caprice. If to-day the current against him seems to be running cold and chilly, to-morrow it may be tempered again with the general warmth of human kindliness and sympathy. Any hopelessly submerged people entrapped in an environment such as his must depend largely upon the force of public sentiment.

The upward progress of the negro since his emancipation has not been a smooth and unhindered path. Indeed, the pathway of progress has never been a straight line, but always a zigzag course between the forces of right and wrong, justice and injustice, goodness and evil, cruelty and mercy. The journey from Egyptian bondage to the promised land beyond the Jordan could not be made by steam and electricity, but must be accomplished by the slowly moving caravan amidst the dangers and vicissitudes of the desert. While the negro has manifested the virtues of his status he has also shown the imperfection of his lot. His follies and frailties have been such as usually attach themselves to his class and condition. He is neither angelic nor diabolic, but simply human, with vice and virtues, excellences and imperfections such as befall the lot of man laboring under such burdens.

The advancement of the race during the past fifty years has been the marvel of the world. By universal agreement it is conceded that no people in the similar interval of time has made such wonderful strides in the ways of civilization. This progress is as unique as the contrasted helps and hindrances amidst which it has been attained have been striking. Progress cannot be finally evaluated in the terms of material units. Such standards do not constitute the best gauge of advancement toward the goal of human striving. The essential thing is to determine how far the postulant people have acquired the capacity, the equipment, appreciation and the purpose to become not merely recipients but partakers of the life and spirit and power of that civilization of which they would constitute a part. Material substances and outward forms of progress are but manifestations of the inner attitude and spirit.

Fifty years is entirely too short a time to measure the potency and promise of the race. In the economy of racial life a half century is scarcely more than a single year in the experience of an individual. It is the preparation period for rooting and grounding itself in the fundamental understanding and appreciation of the underlying principle of things. The things already accomplished or achieved should be regarded as but the first fruit and the earnest of larger things to come.

Rather than describe the progress of the race in terms of definite data and tabular array of ascertained facts after the manner of the statistician, let us, if we may, clothe the dry bones of bare facts with the vital power of the living truth.

Physical persistence is the fundamental test of civilization. If the red Indian does not live he cannot become civilized. On the other hand, if the negro continues to live and multiply he cannot escape the happy lot. It is small wonder that the social philosophers of a generation ago prophesied that the negro would speedily disappear under the stress of Aryan competition and arrogance, for what other weaker race can stand and withstand contact and attrition of the dauntless Teuton, and live? After the lapse of a half century of freedom, four and one half million slaves have doubled their number, under the strain and stress of conditions that would have caused almost any other of the weaker breeds of men to pine away and die. Eliminating foreign reinforce-

ment, the negro outstrides the European element of our population in the natural rate of
increase. The presence and promise of the negro race in the Western world is a clear fulfillment of that beatitude of promise, "Blessed
are the meek for they shall inherit the earth."
There are twenty-five millions of negroes on
the Western hemisphere, who through physical
persistence and a spirit of meekness have multiplied and thriven and are destined to inherit
all of the accumulated and transmitted civilization and culture of the ages. It requires no
gift of prophecy to predict that the American
negro will enter into this inheritance as heir
and joint-heir in the patrimony of mankind.

The discipline of slavery, though valuable as
a preliminary training, was, nevertheless, subject to such severe limitations that it illy fitted
the recipient for the competitive life of the
freeman. In the very nature of the case it
would impart only the passive and inert virtues. It made no appeal to the spirit of thrift,
economy, independence, enterprise and initiative. These virtues, essential in the freeman,
were discouraged in the slave. The method of
slavery was that of domestication as distin-
guished from the process of education, as that
term is nowadays wont to be interpreted.
Through domestication certain fundamental

and easily communicable qualities were transmitted by familiarity, association and contact
with the surcharged environment. This process necessarily preceded the formal method of
pedagogy in the experience of both the individual and the race. Under slavery the negro was
given the process without the principle, the
knack without the knowledge. The essential
basis of education is that it leads the recipient
to an understanding of the underlying principle, use and function of things. The slave was
told the relative distance between two rows of
cotton or hills of corn as a working formula,
but knew nothing of the laws controlling the
growth and culture of plants, nor the rules of
the market governing their distribution. Indeed he was not supposed to understand the
ultimate meaning and purpose of a single feature of life, but was directed to do things for
the ulterior benefit of the director. Education
had to begin where domestication left off. The
effort of the past fifty years on the part of this
race has been largely devoted to education in
the sense of understanding and making definite
the meaning and purpose of the formulas acquired under slavery. The rapidity with which
this race has become literalized is considered
its most marvelous attainment during the past
half century. In a period of fifty years a con-

siderable majority of its numbers have learned the use of letters. This is a much larger per cent. than is shown by many of the historic races of the older world. The mere technical acquisition of the use of letters is from one standpoint a very simple attainment. A few months' schooling is sufficient to communicate to the individual the symbols of knowledge and the method of combining them into written and spoken speech. But, unless this attainment is built upon a previous conception of the meaning and aim of the accumulated body of knowledge to which it leads, it is a comparatively useless attainment. The key to the storehouse of accumulated wisdom and experience of mankind is useless unless the wielder has a previous appreciation for the values which that storehouse contains. The red Indian might acquire the ability to read and write within a single generation, but if he still clings to his ancestral ways, and without the curiosity to understand the secret and method of civilization or the desire to avail himself of them, his technical acquisition would be little more than a curious intellectual gymnastic. But the negro had already had a foretaste of the white man's civilization vouchsafed through the institution of slavery. This simply whetted his appetite for the fuller understanding of the things

which had been withholden. Just as the child
does not gain from the school his first conception of the meaning and use of things, but
merely learns to correlate ear and tongue, eye
and finger in speech facility and general understanding, so the negro, who has already received his initial tuition through slavery,
grasped eagerly the opportunity to strengthen
and enlarge his acquisition through the process
of literalization. His schooling so far has
mainly strengthened and confirmed what had
already been acquired by contact and use, and
laid the basis for still greater accomplishment. The first effect of knowledge is potential
rather than practical. The application to actual
life conditions comes only after the knowledge
is absorbed and assimilated. So far, the energy of the race has been absorbed in the process of acquisition. The period of application
has just begun. It is noticeable that any element of the white population makes a much
greater use of a given amount of knowledge
than does the negro at the present time. The
ways of knowledge are comparatively new to
him, and a larger part of his energy is consumed in grasping its meaning and, therefore,
the dynamic residue is correspondingly dim-
inished. On the other hand, the white race already possesses the meaning and spirit and

power of civilization, even though the individual man be illiterate. Within the next fifty years we may expect to see the negro apply his knowledge to things concrete to a degree not yet dreamed of. This is more than a question of industrial or technical training, but involves the larger issue of applying thought to things. The thought must precede the application. The Anglo-Saxon race never needs any particular kind of education to accomplish any desired task. It comprehends the nature and purpose of the task and quickly devises means of its accomplishment. "To do with your might what your hands find to do" is a mistaken and inverted motto. The proper form should run, "To do with your hands what your mind finds to do." The material accumulation of the negro, marvelous as it seems, is but an incident of his general education. The great value of the knowledge which he has received is that it has indoctrinated him into the ideas and spirit of the world around him. This indoctrination cannot but shortly bear adequate fruit in terms of concrete attainment.

Whenever a single individual of the race becomes literate, he has gained an everlasting acquisition which in all probability will be handed down from generation to generation, and become more effective with each transmission. It is hardly conceivable that literate parents will ever rear illiterate offspring. A race with the curiosity and ambition of the negro, which has once gained possession of the golden key of knowledge with its twenty-six notches unlocking all of the secrets of things, can hardly be held back from full realization of all that there is in store.

The accumulation of houses and lands and material goods on the part of the negro has been commendable and encouraging. If his landed possessions could be formed into one continuous area, it would make a territory larger than many a far famed principality in ancient and modern annals.

In industry he has pushed his way into every line of listed occupation and contributes his full share to the nation's industrial equation.

He has developed a professional class who sprang into existence suddenly like Melchisedeck of old, without antecedent or beginning of days. This professional class must stand in the high places of leadership and guidance of the masses and direct them aright amid the stress and strain of a strenuous civilization. It is easy to predict the speedy undoing of a race that fails to produce its own competent leaders. A people that can produce safe and sagacious leadership can never be undone.

In religion, the race has developed a priesthood whose increasing power and piety will enable them to hold this vast Christian constituency in definite organic relation to the great religious movements of the age.

In morals, manners, social customs and habits he conforms to the prevailing standards, with no greater variation than grows out of his status in the general scheme. The negro shows his near kinship to the great body of white Americans by speaking the same language, worshiping the same God, striving after the same ideals, longing for the same destiny. None but the most confirmed pessimist can say that that past half century has not given a satisfactory indication that he will be able to meet every exaction that the coming years may impose upon him.

The case of the negro in America, though of striking and unique interest, is but a part of the great problem of contact, attrition and adjustment of the various races of man which has filled the pages of history, is now operating in all the ends of the earth, and is projected to the ages yet to be.

The function of the prophet is to tell us of the future. He peeps over the horizon of the present and gives his fellowmen, of duller vision, a hint of coming events. He does not see any particular isolated future occurrence, but his deeper insight enables him to forecast the drift and tendency of things. The true poet is gifted with clairvoyant power. He visualizes future events with unerring certainty. The prophet Isaiah deserves the highest rank in this class. The messianic appropriation of his prophecy has robbed it of the universality of its application. All true prophecies apply to universal human conditions, and the unfolding of human experience will furnish their perpetual fulfilment. The prophet embodies the feeling and aspiration of those who suffer and gives prophetic utterance of their hope of relief. He voices the eternal utterings of the man farthest down, who will ever find in the circumstances of his lot perennial fulfilment of prophecy. The Hebrew prophet's utterances apply with all but absolute accuracy, even in detail and minutia, to the relative circumstances and situation of the white race and the negro of the American soil. Not a line, scarcely a word, can be omitted from the description without seriously impairing the analogy.

Isaiah, 53rd Chapter:

For he shall grow up before him as a tender plant, and as a root out of dry ground; he hath no form nor comeliness; and when we shall see him, there is no beauty that we should desire him.

He is despised and rejected of men; a man of sorrow and acquainted with grief; and we hid as it were our faces from him; he was despised, and we esteemed him not.

Surely he hath borne our grief, and carried our sorrow: yet we did not esteem him stricken, smitten of God and afflicted.

But he was wounded for our transgressions, he was bruised for our iniquities; the chastisement of our peace was upon him; and with his stripes we are healed.

All we, like sheep, have gone astray; we have turned every one to his own way; and the Lord hath laid on him the iniquity of us all.

He was oppressed, and he was afflicted, yet he opened not his mouth; he is brought as a lamb to the slaughter, and as a sheep before her shearers is dumb, so he openeth not his mouth.

He was taken from prison and from judgment; and who shall declare his generation? for he was cut off out of the land of the living: for the transgressions of my people was he stricken.

And he made his grave with the wicked, and with the rich in his death, because he had done no violence, neither was any deceit in his mouth.

Yet it pleased the Lord to bruise him; he hath put him to grief: when thou shalt make his soul an offering for sin, he shall see his seed, he shall prolong his days, and the pleasure of the Lord shall prosper in his hand.

He shall see of the travail of his soul, and shall be satisfied: by his knowledge shall my righteous servant justify many; for he shall bear their iniquities.

Therefore will I divide him a portion with the great,

and he shall divide the spoil with the strong; because he
hath poured out his soul unto death: and he was num-
bered with the transgressors; and he bore the sin of many,
and made intercession for the transgressors.

The hardships and tribulation and vicarious
function of this prophecy have already been
fulfilled on the part of the negro by three centuries of toil and anguish; the triumph and
glorification of it are now fulfilling and seem
clearly destined to be wholly fulfilled. When
the white race awakens to a quickening sense
of the sacrificial function of this transplanted
race; how it has done the rough work of the
nation; how it has relieved their own sons and
daughters from the lower range of toil and
released them for thee.

THE PHYSICAL DESTINY OF THE
AMERICAN NEGRO

America has been called the universal melt
ing pot, in which the various nationalities of
Europe are to be fused into one homogeneous
type. This alembic, however, is supposed to
affect only the different branches of the Aryan
race. The accepted assimilative process is not
universal in its scope, but is limited to the continent of Europe. The white races alone are
deemed eligible components of the desired com-
pound. The polychrome races and sub-races of
Asia, Africa, and the scattered islands of the
seas are not considered as contributory factors to the forthcoming composite American
type.

The primal passion of mankind recognizes
no ethnic limitations or physical barriers of
race, but results in fusion of blood wherever
it has unconstrained exercise and scope. Racial antipathies real or alleged, political pro-
nouncements, religious inhibition, social proscription, all break down in face of the cosmic

urge to multiply and replenish the earth. The
sons of God, in their supercilious security,
never fail to look lustfully upon the daughters
of men, while shielding their own sisters from
the embraces of the lower order of males. The
composite progeny is the offspring of the male
sex of the stronger race and the female sex
of the weaker; but, in the final fetching up of
things, the same results will be accomplished.
Wherever different racial elements are brought
into proximity, physical separation can be safeguarded only by legislative enactment, religious sanction, and the excitation of race antipathy by artificial stimulus. Universal experience shows that natural aversion of races does
not possess strength and stubbornness to preserve purity of breed.

The white race in America is put to its wit's
end to keep its racial stock free from the taint
of Asiatic and African blood. A monochrome
civilization presents the prevalent ideal. At
present it presents the spell and power of religious frenzy. Under the sanction of this
craze, it is considered more blessed to be white
than to be right. A polychrome social scheme
is deemed abominable to God and man. An
inspirited race consciousness is growing
keener and keener with the passing years.
This consciousness is based upon physical

rather than psychical likeness. The bond of brotherhood includes those who are born of the flesh rather than those who are born of the spirit. Superficial distinction of color counts for more than cult or creed.

Patriotic fervor or emotional zeal may beget emotional solidarity which entirely overleaps the cleavage of race or color. The triumph of Islam is a concrete, living embodiment of this principle. The ideal of Christianity is that all of its devotees, regardless of ethnic deviation, are baptized into one spirit, in which there is neither Jew nor Greek, Barbarian, Scythian, bond or free. The Christian creed is absolutely incompatible with the caste of color. Spiritual kinship transcends all other relations among men. The proclaimed purpose of this religion is to establish peace and good will on earth, but there is a wide margin between the proclaimed purpose and practical operation of this religion, especially as it relates itself to the Teutonic branch of the white race. Its chief beneficial effect is seen in the minor merciful ministrations of charity, but nowhere has it dominated the tough Teutonic spirit of race intolerance. The Protestant Christian in dealing with other races of men, passively acquiesces in the doctrine of the equality of the soul, but stubbornly balks at social equality. A continuance of this exclusive spirit on the part of the dominant race in America is as certain as any other calculable force concerning which we have predictive data. If the undesirable element be black, like the negro, it is excluded from the social scheme on the ground of inferiority. If it be yellow, like the Japanese, it meets with a like fate because of suspected superiority. So feeble is the force of logic against the dominating purpose of an arrogant race!

It must be taken for granted in the final outcome of things that the color line will be wholly obliterated. While blood may be thicker than water, it does not possess the spissitude or inherency of everlasting principle. The brotherhood of man is more fundamental than the fellowship of race. A physical and spiritual identity of all peoples occupying common territory is a logical necessity of thought. The clear seeing mind refuses to yield or give its assent to any other ultimate conclusion. This consummation, however, is far too removed from the sphere of present probability to have decisive influence upon practical procedure. It runs parallel with the prophecy that every valley shall be exalted and every hill shall be brought low. This is a physical necessity. Under the continuing law of gravitation, every stream that trickles down the mountain side, every downpour of rain, and every passing gust of wind removes infinite particles and shifts them from a higher to a lower level. This tendency to lower the one and lift the other will continue everlastingly until equality has been established as the final condition of stable equilibrium. In the meantime, however, the human race must adjust itself to the existence of mountain and valley as a lasting, if not everlasting, reality. Likewise, perpetual attrition of races must ultimately wear away all distinction and result in a universal blend. But the approximation of this goal is too slow and imperceptible to have any effect upon the present plan of race adjustment. We are concerned with persistent, stubborn realities which we have the power neither to influence nor affect, and must deal with conditions as they are in our day and generation, and not as we may vainly or vaguely imagine them in the ages yet to be. The time-server is often considered as a designation of reproach, but finite comprehension can only serve its day and generation. It requires omniscience to serve eternity.

The absence of the brown, the rapid extermination of the red, and the forced exclusion of the yellow leave the white and black races

as residuary constituents in the drama of race
adjustment on this continent.   The rapid as-
similation of European nationalities into one
homogeneous type proceeds apace without
noise or notice.   The negro element, too, is
slowly developing an ethnic solidarity which
indicates its immediate, if not ultimate, physical destiny in this land.

In current discussion the term "negro" is
used loosely to designate those people whose
maternal ancestors were imported as slaves
from the continent of Africa.   While the term
ordinarily denotes color, it also connotes condition.   The social segregation of the colored
race is based no less upon its traditional servile status than upon ethnic characteristics.

The American negro, as he is called, does
not constitute a race in the sense of a compact,
ethnic group, imbued with a common spirit and
impelled by a common impulse.   There is no
solidified physical basis as a background for
the emergence of a common consciousness with
a strength and stubbornness to compel a co-
ordinate policy of persistent procedure.   There
is rather a promiscuous assortment of individuals with diverse physical and spiritual dispo-
sitions and actuated by the antagonistic instinct
of the Ishmaelite.   Psychologists tell us that
a collective soul emerges most easily from a

basis of physical likeness either through its inherent predisposition or by force of external compulsion. The imported slaves were disjected and expatriated individuals snatched from wide apart geographical areas, and captured from tribes differing widely in cult, custom and color.

The white race has never failed to infuse its blood into the veins of inferior races with whom it has come in contact. We are told in Greek mythology that Father Chronos devoured the offspring of his lust as soon as they were born, in order to avoid future complications of a troublesome issue. The Teutonic races seek to accomplish the same end by relegating their composite progeny to the lower status of the mother race. This policy is intended to preserve the purity of the stronger race while it mixes the blood of the weaker. The prepotent influence of the male progenitor upon the progeny is left out of account. The Latin races, on the other hand, incorporate the offspring of the dominant male and the dominated female, thus affecting a mixture of the white while preserving the purity of the darker breed. The immediate effect of the Teutonic policy may be agreeable, for the time being, to its Aryan arrogance, but there must, at some time, come a reckoning for the awful conse-

quences of visiting the lustful burden of one
race upon another.

The negro woman has been made to bear the
brunt of the evil passions of all the races of
men living or sojourning in this country.
Within the veins of the so-called negro race
there course traces of the blood of every known
variety or sub-variety of the human family.
Not only within the limits of the race itself,
but even within the veins of the same individuals, the strains of blood are mingled and
blended in inextricable confusion. Indeed, if
there be such a thing as natural race antipathy,
the negro, both as a race and as an individual, would be confronted by fightings within
and fires without. The task of fusing these
people into a common ethnic unity constitutes
its primary problem. The institution of slavery fostered a spirit of internal antagonism.
Every safeguard was taken to prevent the
emergence of an effective social consciousness.
Wherever two or three negroes were gathered
together, a white man was set in the midst of
them to frustrate any attempt at coördinate
purposes.

The Jewish race has preserved its physical
identity for two thousand years, albeit the
overflow of its blood has been transfused into

all nations among which the Jew has sojourned. The integrity of this race, however, has been preserved through spiritual sanction rather than by physical or racial proclivity.

It must be conceded that the quickest solution of the American race problem would be the immediate physical absorption of the negro element in the white race; but this is not possible, due to the universal attitude of the dominant race toward miscegenation.

The weaker race cannot force itself upon the stronger except through universal prostitution, a policy which is too repugnant to the moral sense to be contemplated as a racial policy. The American negro will be compelled to preserve his social and physical solidarity for many years to come through force of external compulsion. He is subject to conditions which he did not create and cannot control. The negro race in this country must become one with itself before it can become one with the American people.

The Federal Census shows unmistakably the drift of the negro population toward the formation of a new sub-race. This coming race will be composed of African-European blood, and its color will not be black, but a yellowish brown.

Negro and mulatto population of the U. S. from 1850 to 1910:

Year	Tot. Colored	Black	Mulatto	Per Cent. Mulatto
1850	3,638,808	3,233,057	405,751	11.2
1860	4,441,830	3,853,467	588,363	13.2
1870	4,880,009	4,295,960	583,049	12.0
1890	7,470,040	6,337,980	1,132,060	15.2
1910	9,828,294	7,766,894	2,051,400	20.9

Strictly speaking, the term mulatto includes only the first offspring of white and black parents, but, in the census sense of the term, it contemplates all persons who show some perceptible trace of negro blood. Due allowance must also be made for discrepant definitions of the terms at the several census decades. The well known inaccuracies of the census of 1870 are clearly disclosed in this table. But, after making all possible allowances, there is a persistent tendency toward a wider and wider distribution of the white blood already injected into the negro race. This tendency will inevitably continue until there has been an equable diffusion throughout the entire mass. During the past twenty years the so-called mulatto element increased 82 per cent., while the blacks increased only 23 per cent. The rapid relative increase of the mixed element indicates clearly the physical destiny of the race. This increase is maintained in every Southern state. In the Northern and Western states the black element has gained somewhat on the mulatto during the past twenty years. During the days of slavery many slaves were freed by their father-masters, or, as more frequently happened, were given opportunity to work out their freedom on easy terms, and were either sent or voluntarily migrated to the free states. The blacks rarely enjoyed such privileges. In 1850 there were more mulattoes than blacks in Maine, New Hampshire, Michigan, Wisconsin and Ohio. In every instance, however, the blacks predominated in the census of 1910. Since emancipation there has been a constant stream of emigration to the free states composed largely of blacks.

The rapid growth of the mulatto element is not due in any great degree to its inherent fecundity. The mulatto birth-rate is probably considerably lower and the death-rate higher than that of the blacks under similar conditions of living. This conclusion is forced by the fact that the mulattoes are found mainly in the Northern states and in the cities and towns where the birth-rate is lower and the death-rate higher than in the rural communities where the blacks predominate.

Every fresh infusion of white blood increases

the mulatto element at the expense of the black. The black woman who has a number of children by a white father would probably have borne as many or more had she yoked with a black spouse instead of a white paramour. The rise and spread of the mixed element has not in any degree increased the numerical strength of the colored race. They have merely over-lapped a like number of blacks. The lighter color gains upon the darker, like the illuminant upon the darkened surface of the waxing moon, without increasing the total surface of the lunar orb. The mulatto offspring of a white parentage may be regarded as a continuing though rapidly diminishing factor in the equation of the negro population. There is not likely to be much further direct infusion of white blood into the negro race.

Under the institution of slavery the negro was suppressed below the level of self-respect. The black woman often felt her superior importance by becoming the mother of a tawny child. The white master or overseer felt no legal, social, or conscientious constraint in victimizing the female chattel. Had this institution continued for another hundred years without further importation of blacks from the continent of Africa, the race would probably have been well bleached through this libidinous

process. But the growing sense of self-respect
and decency on the part of the black, as well
as restraints of law and conscience on the part
of the white man, has checked, if not halted,
this outrageous procedure. The establishment
of domestic ties and social standards in colored
society effectively forbids such illicit relationship and makes outcasts of all such issue.

The laws of the Southern states forbidding
intermarriage and social proximity of the races
will absolutely prevent legitimate mulatto offspring. The social sensibilities of both races
are at present so delicate on this issue that intermarriage would be exceedingly rare even if
there were no forbidding laws. In the North,
where there is no such restrictive law, the il-
legitimate offspring is so small as to be a negligible factor. The over-zealous quest of the
negro prize-fighter for a white spouse so
aroused the emotional frenzy of her race that
it caused a half dozen state legislatures to
contemplate enacting miscegenation laws.

Whatever illicit intercourse may still continue between the races at the present day, it
is not likely to result in issue, as it was once
wont to do. It partakes rather of the nature
of the vice of the city slums and of the red
light district, and it is an entirely different
process from the old order of complaisant con-

cubinage. The rise of the "sage femme" and the practice of race suicide tend to the same conclusion.

The segregation of the races, both in cities and in the rural districts, will lessen the opportunity for illicit offspring. In the large cities the negroes are segregated in wards and sections. In the Southern states, where they reside in greatest numbers, the black belts and sections are growing blacker and the white communities are growing whiter, indicating the metes and bounds of racial residence. This segregative tendency is wholly apart from and independent of the recent attempt to fix the bounds of the negro's habitation by law. In the sections where the negro resides the presence of the white man is not expected except in a purely business capacity. Illicit relationship will decrease in proportion to the separation of the areas of domicile.

As an illustration of the infrequency of the direct mulatto progeny, the student body of Howard University, about fifteen hundred in number, is composed largely of the mixed element. There are probably not a half dozen children of white parents in this entire number. On the other hand, the first pupils in this institution, a generation ago, were very largely the offspring of such parentage. The ones who are of lighest hue and show closest physical similarity to the white race are known to be the legitimate children of a colored co-parency. Of the more than two million so-called mulattoes in the colored race, an overwhelming number, especially of the younger generation, are offspring of colored fathers and mothers. It is safe to say that they average about one-fourth of the full measure of white blood. This would be equivalent to a half million full blooded white men who have become absorbed in the colored race. This European blood cannot remain in any one compartment of the race, but will tend to diffuse itself throughout the entire mass until it has assumed an approximate oneness in color and physical likeness. The process of diffusion will be facilitated by the well known tendency of the male to mate with the female of lighter hue. The poet Dunbar speaks of the swarthy maid with her swarthier swain as typical of this tendency.

In the census of 1890 some attempt was made to differentiate the mulatto element according to the degree of blood composition. The results showed that there were 105,136 quadroons, and 69,936 octoroons, and 967,988 mulattoes. The proportion of negro blood in the quadroon and octoroon elements represents over 30,000 full blooded negroes. Many of this

class have crossed or are likely to cross the
social divide and incorporate themselves into
the white race, in order to escape the nether
status of the despised blood. In some states a
person with only one-eighth negro blood in
his veins is given legal status with the white
race. These racial transmigrants carry with
them as much of negro blood as can easily be
concealed under an albicant skin and unkinked
hair. The white race will take only such homeopathic dashes of negro blood as to remain substantially pure. It is reasonable to assume that
the equivalent of 50,000 full blooded blacks
have or are likely to be thus incorporated into
the white race. The transition of the quadroon
and octoroon classes will tend to widen the
physical margin between the two races.

There is unmistakable evidence that, in the
birth-rate of the mulatto element, the female
offspring is more numerous than the male.
The octoroon and quadroon male can more
easily conceal their negroid origin and clandestinely pass over to the white race than the
corresponding female. These factors leave a
considerable surplus of female mulattoes over
the corresponding male element. This gives
the darker male a wider area for his well
known propensity to mate with the lighter fe-

male, and will thus facilitate the rapid diffusion of this blood throughout the race.

A careful observation of negro schools, churches and miscellaneous gatherings in all parts of the country convinces the writer that fully three-fourths of the rising generation of the race have some traceable measure of white blood in their veins. The negro school, especially in the cities and towns, has about as many children of the unadulterated negro type as of the other extremes which cannot be easily detected from white. Both extremes, however, are a rapidly diminishing quantity, while the average of the race is approaching a medium of yellowish brown rather than black. We must take into account, also, the fact that a considerable portion of white blood can be wholly concealed under a negro exterior, which may reappear in the next generation. Within the next three or four generations the pure negro will be hard to find outside of the black belts and rural portions of the South and a new race will have arisen.

Science is of value to man only in proportion as it becomes predictive and enables him to adjust himself in harmony with foreseen events which he can neither alter nor control. The Weather Bureau at Washington forecasts the coming of frost and storm, so that the prudent farmer may cover his crop and the sailor seek shelter on the shore. A clear indication of the physical destiny of the colored race ought to enable us to deal more effectively with the complicated features of this perplexing problem and, at the same time, free the white man from the frantic dread of amalgamation which now harasses his waking hours and haunts him in his dreams.

EDUCATION FOR MANHOOD

The well known and well worn maxim of the poet, Lowell:

> "New occasions teach new duties,
>   Time makes ancient good uncouth,"

expressed, with practical shrewdness, a transient phase, rather than the permanent form of truth. Good in the positive, or even in the comparative, degree may, indeed, be limited by circumstances, time and place; but superlative good is of the nature and essence of things eternal. A shallow philosophy emphasizes the evanescent phase of things rather than their permanent and enduring quality. To the superficial observer the world would seem to be one continuous panorama of evanescent issues. Practical wisdom would seem to be the only effective wisdom.

Opportuneness seems to be the controlling virtue. The man who is wise in his day and generation must catch the manners living as they rise, or they will forever elude his grasp.

The wisdom of one age becomes the folly of the next. The schoolboy of to-day laughs at the erudition of the ancient sage. The theories which passed as marvels of knowledge a generation ago are now regarded as curious survivals of the intellectual dark ages. Celebrated works on science, philosophy and social polity which once held the world under the dominion of their dogma are now relegated to the moth and dust of oblivion. The path of progress is strewn with the derelict of discarded and discredited theories. The science of yesterday, to-day, is science but falsely socalled.

"We call our fathers fools, so wise we grow,
Our wiser sons, no doubt, will call us so."

But a deeper philosophy gives a more comprehensive and far reaching vision. Essential truth transcends the mutation of time and the vicissitude of condition, and perdures from everlasting to everlasting. The waves of the sea may fluctuate with the shifting phases of the moon; the lunar orb herself may wax and wane in her periodic relations to earth, sun and stars; but our solar system sweeps on forever along its trackless path through space. According to the laws of grammar, everlasting fact and unchangeable truth is not subject to

syntactical variations, but is always expressed
in the present tense and active voice. It is the
voice of truth issuing eternally from the burning bush: "Before Abraham was, I am." The
educational philosopher must have a clear understanding of the relative place and importance of things incidental and things essential,
of things timely and things timeless, of things
transient and things eternal.

Education has two clearly differentiable
functions, (1) to develop and perfect the human qualities of the individual, as a personality, and (2) to render him a willing and competent participant, as an instrumentality, in the
federation of the world's work. The one in-
heres in the nature of man and is conditioned
only by the innate economy of human nature;
the other is responsive to contemporary social
demands. The one is independent of time,
place and circumstances; the other is adjusta-
ble to these various elements. The one represents a pedagogical constant; the other presents the widest margin of variation. The one
is generic in its embracement of all mankind;
the other is specific in its application to the
peculiar needs and requirements of each individual. Failure to grasp, with tight seizure,
this dual aim of education leads to much con-

fusion of thought and obfuscation of counsel in our pedagogical discussions.

In the lower orders of creation the process, in both of its aspects, is all but spontaneous. The individual swiftly attains to the perfection of qualities, with little or no guidance and direction, and acquires the requisite experience and method, through the operation of instinct which instantaneously hands down to each, alike, the full patrimony of the race. With man, this must be accomplished by the slower and more uncertain processes of human pedagogy.

Education is not an end in itself, but is conditioned upon the nature of man and upon his place in the social scheme; it is not an independent and self-contained entity, but is conducive to the fulfilment of ulterior aims. The pedagogical ideal and method will always depend upon the queries—"What is the chief end of man?" and "What does society require of him?"

Man as a Personality

The old idea of education derived its aim from the conception of the origin and destiny of man. Under this conception, man was regarded as the son of heaven—a creature made a little lower than the angels, only that he might rise to the higher level by conscious effort. His present state and lot were regarded as a lapse from his pristine happiness, and his highest concern was to regain the blissful seat. Man was created in the image of God, Who breathed into his nostrils the breath of life, when he became a living soul. He was considered to be essentially a personality—a self-conscious, moral agent, who longed for the higher satisfaction of his nature, as the thirsty hart panteth for the water brook. The highest concern of this school of pedagogy was to develop man as a rational being—a creature capable of thinking, hoping, loving, believing, craving, striving for higher things. Shakespeare has given us perhaps the clearest definition from this point of view:

> "What a piece of work is man!
> How noble in reason! how infinite in faculty!
> In form and moving how express and admirable!
> In action how like an angel!
> In apprehension how like a God!"

History, philosophy and theology agreed substantially to this definition of man as the crown and climax of creation. The old definition of education, namely, "The process of unfolding the seed of immortality which God has implanted in men,'' was perfectly consistent with this idea. However the form of statement might be modified or multiplied, this was the essential meaning which underlay them all. The programs and subject matter of instruction were but incidental to this one controlling purpose. Books, libraries, laboratories, schedules, appliances, were but the scaffolding for the structure. Discipline, culture, knowledge, exact or refined, belles-lettres, poetry, music, art, were all considered as incidental means of developing in man the higher appreciation of and reverence for himself as a conscious personality.

Man as an Instrumentality

Under the dominion of the Darwinian theory, the present day conception of man is that he represents the higher section of biology, rather than the direct descendant of heaven. He is of the earth, earthy. In origin, development, purpose and destiny he is subject to the same conditions as the beasts that perish. His fundamental concern, therefore, is to provide what he shall eat, what he shall drink, wherewithal he shall be clothed, and how he may derive creature comforts and temporary satisfaction as the days go by.

Under modern requirements, the demands of living make such a heavy draft upon human faculties that political economy, which Carlyle characterizes as a dismal science, is wont to embrace the entire sphere of social endeavor. The invention of machinery lies at the basis of modern industrial methods. The practical activities of the age are organized upon the basis of machinery in which the assembled parts coöperate in the accomplishment of the required task. Transition from the hand process to the factory process was made inevitable under the stimulus of inventive genius. The great industrial establishments of the modern world are as much a machine as a well built watch, in which all parts are incidental and coöperant to a single end. The human element is placed on the same footing as mechanical attachments. The individual, so far as he represents a conscious personality, is wholly submerged as a part of the machine to which he is attached. The contractor advertises for so many "hands" because the hand is often the only part of the individual called into requisition to accomplish the desired task. No demand is made upon the higher powers and faculties, and therefore they are wholly ignored in the designation. The term "typewriter" means either the machine which makes the impression upon paper, or the young woman who operates it. They are both considered as mere parts of the apparatus which transmits the author's thought to paper without modifying it. It is entirely conceivable that in the process of invention the human element in this psycho-physical process may be wholly eliminated. The stenographer, the telegraph operator, the printer, the messenger merely serve as mechanical mediaries, or pure instrumentalities, in the process of transmission of intelligence. The engineer, the brakeman, the mortorman, the chauffeur take their designation from their mechanical function. When we fly through the air on the limited express at the rate of sixty miles an hour, the engineer and the engine are alike but parts of the process of transportation. The "hello girl" who sits all day as part of the machinery of transmission of the human voice is but an attachment of the telephonic mechanism. Indeed, inventive genius has made the connective process automatic, so that the human element is no longer an indispensability. We need not, therefore, be surprised at the long standing feud between man and the machine. The working world has always opposed the invention of new machinery on the ground that it displaced the human element by mere mechanism. Man

is justly jealous of his human prerogative. In
the mere pronunciation of such words as "fire
man," "salesman," "plowman," "workman,"
the penultimate accent plainly shows that the
function, and not the performer, receives the
stress of emphasis and consideration. Man
thus becomes a mere tool, or implement, in the
process of industrial advance. Human instrumentality is necessary to carry on the process
of the world's work. Agriculture, the mechanical activities, manufacture, trade and
transportation must be carried on through
such an agency or the social fabric must fail.
If, then, the exploitation of this side of man
must continue for all time to come, it is simply a matter of prudence to provide that he
should be made proficient as an instrument in
the performance of this mechanical mission.
Herein consist the basis and justification of
the modern claim for industrial education. If
man is, and of necessity must be, utilized as an
instrumentality in the production and distribution of wealth, then it is easy to conclude that
he should be trained to the highest degree of
efficiency in the accomplishment of such tasks.
Industrial education and occupational training
are hereby justified and made inevitable. The
captains of industry must be greatly concerned
in the perfecting of the tools, animate or in-

animate, that contribute to the efficient operation of their projects. The invention of a
safety device or economic contrivance adds
not so much to the efficiency of operation as
improvement of their workmen as human instruments. As corporations have no souls,
they have little regard for the higher personality of their work people. They can utilize
on perfected instrumentalities. While it is
true that life is more than meat, yet man must
devote a large part of his powers to the procurement of meat; not for meat's sake, but in
order that he might, through meat, attain to
larger life. If meat and raiment were the end
and aim of life, then man would needs be limited to an instrumentality to procure these
things.

The old idea that man was a personality pure
and simple disregarded almost wholly his incidental function as an instrumentality. In fact,
man is of twofold nature. He is both instrumentality and personality. The two functions
inhere in every human creature. Each represents complementary factors of a full development. The old idea, in order to escape the
illogicality of its own philosophy, made of some
men, the favored few, pure personalities; while
the great bulk of mankind was worked to the
lower level of beasts of burden, and was thus

excluded from the highest sphere of human consideration. History in its records, even down to comparatively recent times, is concerned mainly with the deeds and doings of kings and noblemen, with persons of position and power and prestige. The people, in mass, had no voice or part in the process except as instruments to be utilized and exploited by the lordly pretensions of the higher class.

There is a constant duel between the process of machinery and the spirit of democracy— the one tending to subordinate the human element to the mechanical process; the other insisting upon the higher rights and powers of man. Democracy banishes distinction between classes, and gives all men the same right to develop and exploit the higher powers and susceptibilities with which they may be endowed. Our educational system to-day is between the upper and nether stress of these conflicting influences. If we keep clearly in mind the twofold development of man as an instrumentality and as a personality, we shall, thereby, get a clear understanding of the relative place and importance of the so-called practical and liberal education. The essential, immediate aim of industrial education is to develop man as an instrumentality. The chief end of the so-called liberal education is to develop man as a personality. These two features are not antagonistic nor mutually exclusive, but are joint factors of a common product. The industrial advocates would claim that their ultimate aim is the development of man as a personality through instrumentality. The higher education presumes instrumentality as a corollary of personality.

The great bulk of mankind, even under the best ordered conditions, are so circumstanced that they are, perforce, compelled to devote most of their time and strength as human tools. The miner who must toil underground half of the day, and thereby so exhaust his physical energies that he must needs spend the other half in recuperative rest, becomes almost as much a tool of production as the pick he uses to extract the coal from the ground. The ox which pulls the plow and the plowman who guides, or rather who follows it, are part and partners in the general agricultural process. If, however, the plowman leaves room for the exercise of his human powers which transmute the products of agriculture into higher values, he thereby vindicates his claim to be lord of creation. The man with the hoe aptly fulfills this illustration:

> "Bowed by the weight of centuries he leans
> Upon his hoe and gazes on the ground:

> The emptiness of ages in his face,
> And on his back the burden of the world.
> Who made him dead to rapture and despair?
> Stolid, yet stunned, a brother to the ox."

This man with the hoe is of all men most miserable, unless, forsooth, he has a hope which bridges "the gulfs between him and the seraphim" and puts him *en rapport* with "Plato and the swing of the Pleiades, the long reaches of the peaks of song; the rift of dawn, the reddening of the rose." Unless, indeed, "this monstrous thing distorted and soul-quenched" can be touched with a quickening sense of personality, the ends of creation are defeated and we may as well welcome Thomas Huxley's friendly comet to blot mankind out of existence.

Under our present dispensation, most men must devote the larger part of their powers to processes of producing and distributing wealth, while a smaller number, either through natural or artificial selection, are set apart to the higher intellectual, moral, and spiritual tasks; but, however exacting the present necessities may be, it is incumbent upon each individual to have in view his best development as a personality.

The highest decree of the Godhead was— "Let us make man." The true end of education is to develop man, the average man, as a self-conscious personality. This can be done not by imparting information to the mind or facility to the fingers, but felicity to the feelings and inspiration to the soul. Develop the man; the rest will follow. The final expression of education is not in terms of discipline, culture, efficiency, service, or specific virtues, but in terms of manhood, which is the substance and summation of them all. The whole is greater than any of its parts.

When electricity has been developed and controlled, it can be given out in any desired form of manifestation. It may be transmuted into heat, light, tractive power or the more mysterious form resulting in ethereal transmission or the marvelous manifestation of the Roentgen rays. And so, when the manhood has been quickened, it may express itself in terms of character, efficiency, initiative, service or enjoyment, as that occasion may require. None of these things represent final values in themselves, but are incidental manifestations of manhood from which they are derived and to which they conduce.

CHARACTER

Character, as ordinarily defined, is the chief thing in our educational philosophy; but this is merely the mark, the image, the superscription, the impression from which to judge the inherent quality of the object upon which it is made. Manhood is the underlying substance which manifests itself through character. The sculptor cannot work as well on mud as on marble, because it lacks the inherent quality to hold and reflect the impression made upon it. Character is but the guinea's stamp; the man is the "gowd for a' that." Character issues from manhood as light from the sun or as fragrance from the flower.

Efficiency

The watchword of the practical world is "Efficiency." The economic application of effort to task is the industrial desideratum of the age. Under the slovenly system, half of the effort put forth is without beneficial effect. Efficiency consists in the economy of human energy in the accomplishment of personal or social tasks. It is an essential pedagogical fallacy to suppose that efficiency can be taught as an isolated quality. You must first develop the man before you can make a workman. The master and the man may wield the same instrument; the one proceeds with higher efficiency

because he has the vision to foresee the fruits
of his labor transmuted into higher human values. On the other hand, the man is a mere
eye-servant, whose vision cannot reach beyond
the time and the hour. The history of the
world emphasizes the disastrousness of this
fallacy. Labor, in order to be efficient, must be
directed to some ulterior end, namely, the fulfillment of the human aspirations of the laborer. In order that man may become an efficient instrumentality, he must first be developed as a conscious personality. Serfdom,
slavery and peonage, which seek to exploit man
as a purely mechanical or animal asset, are
shown to be a fatuous philosophy.

No human creature is ever at his best in any
field of endeavor unless he is quickened by a
conscious sense of his own individuality. For
this reason democracy is almost synonymous
with progress. To suppress the higher crav-
ings of a human being, in order to make of him
an easily controlled and contented instrument,
has been exploited and proved to be a self-
defeating policy. Slave labor is slothful labor.
Neither the slave, nor yet the semi-slave, can
compete in efficiency with the freeman; for the
one represents mindless muscle, while the other
represents muscle under the dominion of the
mind. Whenever the conscious sense of indi-

viduality is aroused in a single individual, a new power is added to the social equation. Any scheme of education which is focused upon specific educational preparation, without a broader basis of appeal, is as ineffectual as to substitute symptomatic for systematic treatment in therapeutics.

To make bricklayers men is a hundredfold more difficult than to make men bricklayers; for, if there be men, they will make bricks, even without straw, if bricks must needs be made. Consciousness of personality energizes all of the faculties and powers and gives them facility and adaptability as nothing else can do. The wise procedure is to develop personality, which easily results in efficient instrumentality.

INITIATIVE

Elbert Hubbard, with Philistine philosophy, defines initiative as the ability to do the right thing without being told. It is the direct expression of manhood in terms of the thing which needs to be done. Manhood, therefore, perceiving the thing needful, proceeds to its accomplishment without exterior direction. If initiative is the ability to do the right thing, efficiency is the ability to do the thing right. Both of these flow from the common fountain.

Neither can be taught as isolated qualities, but both issue from the higher fountain of manhood.

Service

Service, according to current cant, is considered the ultimate end of education. The whole drift of our educational scheme is tending in this direction; but the slightest reflection will convince the average intelligence that service is not an end in itself, but merely a means of developing the qualities of manhood on the part of those deprived of equal opportunity. The ultimate expression of service, therefore, is in terms of manhood. "Culture for service" has become a sing-song motto in our educational polity. Like all such mottoes, whose constant dinging wears off the fresh luster of the original significance, it has become sickled o'er with a pale cast of thought. If by culture we mean the perfection of human faculties, then the form of motto should be inverted so as to read "Service through culture." Experience proves that the developed personality not only becomes an effective instrumentality to meet its own personal needs of life, but will also utilize the larger powers to assist the less fortunate. Altruistic service justly receives our highest meed of praise. The actuating motive is the sure impulse of a highly developed personality to lift others to its own exalted plane of manhood. A prurient, eleemosynary disposition, which merely obeys the prevalent fashion or fancy, like the meritorious almsgiving of the Pharisees, has its own reward. It was this superficial vicariousness which the Apostle Paul deplored when he said, "Though I give my substance to the poor and my body to be burned, and have not love, I am become as a tinkling cymbal and sounding brass." True benevolence is the desire to assist each of God's human creatures to develop his fullest personality. There is neither natural satisfaction nor ultimate reward in mere feeding the hungry and clothing the naked. A little girl, dressing her doll-baby alone, has a self-justifying delight in clothing the naked, as the sausage grinder in the perpetual feeding process. Carlyle says, "That anyone should die ignorant who had capacity for knowledge is a tragedy." In order to avert these human tragedies which are occurring all around us, the true man puts forth his best endeavor that no one shall live or die ignorant who has capacity for knowledge, or vicious who has capacity for virtue, or sinful who may receive the saving knowledge of the truth. True manhood responds to the imperative force of the mandate, ''Go ye into all the world and preach the gospel (of innate manhood), to every creature. He that believeth shall be saved and he that believeth not shall be damned.'' When these glad tidings are brought to the individual with the opportunity to embrace them, if he does not believe in his own essential manhood, deep down in the very cells and fibers of his nature, he is condemned already; nor is there any greater condemnation than this.

The missionary who cheerfully sacrifices every creature comfort in order that the humblest of human creatures may have the opportunity to develop the God-implanted norms of personality touches the highest level of true manhood. It is here that the motto, ''Service through culture,'' finds the highest expression and justification.

Enjoyment

Just as electricity is not limited in its manifestation to heat and power alone, but sometimes gives itself out as light, so manhood cannot be confined in its outgivings to discipline or efficiency or sacrificial service, but at times and on occasions expresses itself in enjoyment and

in personal elation. It concerns itself as much
with things beautiful as with things useful or
with things good. The hard utilitarian and
vicarious theory of education is advocated only
by the self-denying or the unreflecting. Each
individual must spend a large fraction of his
time in pursuit of personal satisfaction, along
ways that are neither utilitarian nor vicarious.
Indeed, this is, perhaps, the highest outlet of
manhood; as the poet Whitman would say, it
is sufficient justification "to merely be."
Keenness of appreciation for intellectual, social, esthetic, moral and spiritual value is one
of the essential ends aimed at in education.
Faulty, indeed, would be that pedagogic scheme
which left this element out of account. Indeed,
on final analysis, the joy of service will be
found to be closely akin to other forms of personal gratification. Some of our educational
theories would educate people only for the factory and charity organizations. All else is regarded as selfish or unworthy gratification.
Banish from the world all literature, poetry,
music, art, architecture, and the beauties of
flowers, and the glories of the sky; take all
sculpture from the mantels and pictures from
the walls; put under ban the graces and
charms of pleasurable intercourse and social
satisfaction—and a man becomes a little more

than the wild savage of the forest. A comprehensive scheme of education, therefore, must give scope and play for exercise of the many-sided features of manhood. It must involve discipline, initiative, culture, personal and altruistic service and rational enjoyment.

The charge is often made that the so-called higher education has no direct practical aim. A sufficient response would be that its aim is to develop manhood. Merely this and nothing more. Manhood is its own justification and needs no ulterior policy or sanction. When this is developed, as we have already seen, it readily transmutes itself into the requisite mode of manifestation, whether it be efficiency, initiative, culture, vicarious service, or the joy of existence.

Someone asked a New Englander what did they grow in the rocky hills of that barren section. The quick reply was, "We grow men here." New England has, indeed, been the breeding ground for men. This manhood has manifested itself at times in industry, as seen in the exploitation of the resources of this continent. Wherever you see a railroad or a factory or any of the gigantic business and industrial organizations which characterize our economic system, the underlying basis can easily be traced back to New England manhood.

Hill, Rockefeller, Morgan, Harriman are examples of this manhood devoting itself to the making of money; in Emerson, Longfellow, Lowell, Russell we see the same manhood transmuting itself into culture; Edison and Morse devote their powers to the unraveling of the mysteries of nature; Garrison, Phillips and Sumner express their manhood in terms of moral and social reforms; Howard, Armstrong, Cravath and Ware express it in terms of altruistic service; but there is the selfsame manhood that worketh in all and through all.

It can be seen that human values are but the various outgivings of manhood. Man is more than industry, trade, commerce, politics, government, science, art, literature or religion, all of which grow out of his inherent needs and necessities. The fundamental aim of education, therefore, should be manhood rather than mechanism. The ideal is not a working man, but a man working; not a business man, but a man doing business; not a school man, but a man teaching school; not a statesman, but a man handling the affairs of state; not a medicine man, but a man practising medicine; not a clergyman, but a man devoted to the things of the soul.

Application to the Colored Race

In the foregoing discussion I have laid down the general proposition disengaged from the meshes of racial incidents. It now remains to point out their pertinency to the present situation and circumstances of the colored race of the United States.

We must keep clearly in mind that the educational process is always under domination of contemporary opinion. The education prescribed for any class is likely to be conditioned upon the presumed relationship of that class to the social body. When woman was regarded as an inferior creature, whose destiny was to serve as a tool and plaything of man, she was accorded only such education as would fit her for this subsidiary function. Any other training was regarded as unnecessary and mischievous. It is only within comparatively recent times, when man began to realize the essential human quality and powers of the female sex, and deemed it not mockery to place her on the same footing with himself, that the comprehensive education of woman has become a possibility.

The traditional relation of the American negro to the society of which he forms a part is too well known to need extensive treatment in this connection.   The African slave was introduced into this country as a pure animal instrumentality to perform the rougher work under dominion of his white lord and master. There was not the remotest thought of his human personality.   No more account was taken of his higher qualities than of the higher susceptibilities of the lower animals.   His mission was considered to be as purely mechanical as that of the ox which pulls the plough.   Indeed, his human capabilities were emphatically denied.   It was stoutly contended that he did not possess a soul to be saved in the world to come nor a mind to be enlightened in the world that now is.   Under the dominion of this dogma, education was absolutely forbidden him.   It became a crime even to attempt to educate this *tertium quid,* which was regarded as little more than brute and little less than human.   The white race, in its arrogant conceit, constituted the personalities and the negroes the instrumentalities.   Man may be defined as a distinction-making animal.   He is ever prone to set up barriers between members of his own species and to deny one part of God's human creatures the inalienable birthright vouchsafed to all alike.   But the process was entirely logical and consistent with the prevailing philosophy.

Northern Philanthropy

The anti-slavery struggle stimulated the moral energy of the American people in a manner that perhaps has never had a parallel in the history of vicarious endeavor. "One touch of nature makes the whole world kin." In dealing with fundamental principles of human rights and human wrongs involved in the issue of slavery, these moral reformers found that the negro was a human being, endowed with heart and mind and conscience like themselves; albeit these powers of personality had long been smothered and imbruted by centuries of suppression and hard usage. These philanthropists believed in the essential manhood of the negro. This belief was the chief dynamic of their endeavor. Upon this foundation they not only broke the negro's chain, but clothed him with political and civic prerogative as an American citizen. They established schools and colleges and universities for him because they believed in his higher susceptibilities. To-day we are almost astounded at the audacity of their faith. They projected a scheme of education comparable with the standards set up for the choicest European youth for a race which had hitherto been submerged below the zero point of intelligence. These schools and colleges, founded and fostered on this basis, were the beginning of the best that there is in the race and the highest which it can hope to be.

But, alas, as the passion engendered by the war grew weaker and weaker, the corresponding belief in the negro has also declined, and the old dogma concerning his mission as a human tool has begun to reassert itself. In certain sections the white race has always claimed that the negro should not be encouraged in the development of personality. The denial of the designation "mister" is suggestive of this disposition. With them the term "mister" is made to mean a direct designation of personality. There is no objection to such titles as "doctor," "reverend" or "professor," as these connote professional rather than personal quality.

Our whole educational activities are under the thrall of this retrograde spirit. We are marking time rather than moving forward. The work is being carried on rather than up. Our bepuzzled pedagogs are seriously reflecting over the query, *Cui bono?*—Is it worth while? Few, indeed, are left who have the intensity of belief and the intrepidity of spirit to defend the higher pretensions of the negro without apology or equivocation. The old form of appeal has become insipid and uninspiring. The ear has become dull to its dinning. The old blade has become blunt and needs a new sharpness of point and keenness of edge. Where now is heard the tocsin call whose keynote a generation ago resounded from the highlands of Kentucky and Tennessee to the plains of the Carolinas calling the black youths, whose hopes ran high within their bosoms, to rise and make for higher things? This clarion note, though still for the nonce, shall not become a lost chord. Its inspiring tones must again appeal to the youth to arise to their higher assertion and exertion. If you wish to reach and inspire the life of the people, the approach must be made not to the intellect, nor yet to the feelings, as the final basis of appeal, but to the manhood that lies back of these. That education of youth, especially the suppressed class, that does not make insistent and incessant appeals to the smothered manhood (I had almost said godhood) within will prove to be but vanity and vexation of spirit. What boots a few chapters in Chemistry, or pages in History, or paragraphs in Philosophy, unless they result in an enlarged appreciation of one's own manhood? Those who are to stand in the high places of intellectual, moral and spiritual leadership of such a people in

such a time must be made to feel deep down
in their own souls their own essential manhood.
They must believe that they are created in the
image of God and that nothing clothed in human guise is a more faithful likeness of that
original. This must be the dominant note in
the education of the negro. If the note itself
is not new, there must at least be a newness of
emphasis and insistence. The negro must learn
in school what the white boy learns from association and environment. The American white
man in his ordinary state is supremely conscious of his manhood prerogative. He may be
ignorant or poor or vicious; yet he never for-
gets that he is a man. But every feature of
our civilization is calculated to impress upon
the negro a sense of his inferiority and to make
him feel and believe that he is good for nothing
but to be cast out and trodden under foot of
other men. A race, like an individual, that
compromises its own self-respect paralyzes
and enfeebles its own energies. The motto
which should be engraved upon the conscience
of every American negro is that which Milton
places in the mouth of His Satanic Majesty:
"The mind is its own place and of itself can
make a heaven of hell; a hell of heaven." To
inculcate this principle is the highest mission
of the higher education. The old theologians

used to insist upon the freedom of the will, but the demand of the negro to-day is the freedom and independence of his own spirit. Destroy this and all is lost; preserve it, and though political rights, civil privileges, industrial opportunities be taken away for the time, they will all be regained.

By the development of manhood on the part of the negro nothing is farther from my thought than the inculcation of that pugnacious, defiant disposition which vents itself in wild ejaculations and impotent screaming against the evils of society. I mean the full appreciation of essential human qualities and claims, and the firm, unyielding determination to press forward to the mark of this high calling, and not to be swerved from its pursuit by doubt, denial, danger, rebuff, ridicule, insult and contemptuous treatment. While the negro may not have it within his power to resist or overcome these things, he must preserve the integrity of his own soul.

The higher education of the negro up to this point has been very largely under the direction and control of philanthropy. The support has come almost wholly from that source. The development of this sense of manhood should be the highest concern of a wise, discriminating philanthropy, for if this is once developed the negro will be able to handle his own situation and relieve his philanthropic friends from further consideration or concern; but, if he fails to develop this spirit of 'manhood, he will be but a drag upon the resources of philanthropy for all time to come.

The negro must develop courage and self-confidence. A grasp upon the principles of knowledge gives the possessor the requisite spirit of confidence. To the timid, the world is full of mystery manipulated and controlled by forces and powers beyond their ken to comprehend. But knowledge convinces us that there is no mystery in civilization. The railroad, the steamship and the practical projects that loom so large to the unreflecting are but the result of the application of thought to things. The mechanical powers and forces of nature are open secrets for all who will undertake to unravel the mystery. And so it is with essential and moral principles. The one who would have himself rooted and grounded in the fundamental principles of things can look with complacence upon the panorama of the world's progress. The negro should plant one foot on the Ten Commandments and the other on the Binomial Theorem: he can then stand steadfast and immovable, however the rain of racial

wrath may fall or the angry winds of prejudice
may blow and beat upon him.

The educated negro must learn to state his
own case and to plead his own cause before the
bar of public opinion. No people who raise
up from out their midst a cultivated class, who
can plead their own cause and state their own
case, will fail of a hearing before the just judgment of mankind.

The educated negro to-day represents the
first generation grown to the fullness of the
stature of manhood under the influence and
power of education. They are the first ripened
fruit of philanthropy, and by them alone will
the wisdom or folly of that philanthropy be
justified. The hope of the race is focused in
them. They are the headlight to direct the
pathway through the dangers and vicissitudes
of the wilderness. For want of vision, the
people perish. For want of wise direction,
they stumble and fall. There is no body of
men in the world to-day, nor in the history of
the world, who have, or ever have had, greater
responsibilities or more coveted opportunities
than devolve upon the educated negro to-day.
It is, indeed, a privilege to be a negro of light
and leading in such a time as this. The incidental embarrassments and disadvantages
which for the time being must be endured are

not to be compared with the far more exceeding weight of privileges and glory which awaits him if he rises to these high demands. For such a privilege well may he forego the pleasure of civilization for a season.

His world consists of ten million souls, who have wrapped up in them all of the needs and necessities, powers and possibilities of human nature; they contain all of the norms of civilization, from its roots to its florescence. His is the task to develop and vitalize these smothered faculties and potentialities. His education will prove to be but vanity and vexation of spirit, unless it ultimates in this task. He is the salt of the earth, and, if the salt lose its savor, wherewith shall it be salted? If the light within the racial world be darkness, how great is that darkness?

The highest call of the civilization of the world of to-day is to the educated young men of the belated races. The educated young manhood of Japan, China, India, Egypt, Turkey must lift their own people up to the level of their own high conception. They must partake of the best things in the civilization of Europe and show them unto their own people. The task of the educated American negro is the same as theirs, intensified, perhaps, by the more difficult and intricate tangle of circum-

stances and conditions with which he has to
deal.

He cannot afford to slink into slothful satisfaction and enjoy a tasteless leisure or with
inane self-deception hide his head under the
shadows of his wings, like the foolish bird,
which thereby hopes to escape the wrath to
come. The white race, through philanthropy,
has done much; but its vicarious task cul-
minated when it developed the first generation
of educated men and women. They must do
the rest. These philanthropists spoke for us
when our tongues were tied. They pleaded
our cause when we were speechless; but now
our faculties have been unloosed. We must
stand upon our own footing. In buffeting the
tempestuous torrents of the world we must
either swim on the surface or else sink out of
sight. The greatest gratitude that the beneficiary can show to the benefactor is, as soon as
possible, to do without his benefaction. The
task of race statesmanship and reclamation de-
volves upon the educated negro of this day and
generation. Moral energy must be brought to
bear upon the task, whether the negro be engaged in the production of wealth or in the
more recondite pursuits which minister to the
higher needs of man.

The white race is fast losing faith in the

negro as an efficient and suitable factor in the equation of our civilization. Curtailment of political, civil and religious privilege and opportunity is but the outward expression of this apostasy. As the white man's faith decreases, our belief in ourselves must increase. Every negro in America should utter this prayer, with his face turned toward the light: "Lord, I believe in my own inherent manhood; help Thou my unbelief." The educated negro must express his manhood in terms of courage, in the active as well as in the passive voice: courage to do, as well as to endure; courage to contend for the right while suffering wrong; the courage of self-belief that is always commensurate with the imposed task. The world believes in a race that believes in itself; but justly despises the self-bemeaned. Such is the mark,—such is the high calling to which the educated negro of to-day is called. May he rise to the high level of it. Never was there a field whiter unto harvest; never was there louder cry for laborers in the vineyard of the Lord.

CRIME AMONG NEGROES

The criminal status of the negro race is a matter that should be carefully weighed and investigated, and cautious and reasoned conclusion deduced therefrom. The anti-negro doctrinaires are ever prone to seize upon the surface appearance of things criminal and utilize them to blacken and blast the reputation of the race.

The census of 1890 made a study of criminal statistics. Although the Twelfth Census made no such investigation, there was a special bulletin issued in 1904, which made a partial examination of criminal statistics.

The one essential fact, so far as the negro race is concerned, is that twelve per cent. of the population contributed thirty-two per cent. of the crimes of the United States. This ratio was practically the same for 1890 and 1904. During the interval of fourteen years there has been no absolute increase in negro crime, but in some instances there was a relative increase, as compared with that of the white population.

In 1890 there were 24,227 negro prisoners in the United States. In 1904 there were 26,870 such prisoners. Although there was some discrepancy in the methods of return at the two census periods, the underlying fact remains that the criminal status of the race had made no notable increase, as compared with the growth of the negro population during the intervening fourteen years.

The sociologist first ascertains the facts. Then he accounts for and interprets them. Finally, he generalizes upon them and points out their prophetic import. The orator, on the other hand, first generalizes and prophesies, and afterwards finds it necessary to ascertain the facts lying at the basis of his generalization and prophecy. Now the fact is that the negro has a criminal record about three times as great as his numbers entitle him to. How shall we account for this? If one should go to England or to any other part of the earth and study the condition of the people who live in poverty in the crowded cities, he would find an overwhelming preponderance of crime among the submerged elements as compared with the general population. The negro shows this high criminal rating because he constitutes, in the United States and especially in the large cities, the submerged stratum where the bulk of actionable crime is found the world over. Crime is a question of condition, not of color.

Another reason, in my judgment, which contributes to the seeming increase in negro crime is the fact that during the last fifteen years there has grown up, on the part of the white race, a spirit of racial exclusiveness and intolerance. This is outwardly manifested in the public provisions for the sharp separation of the races in all matters where there is likely to be anything like intimacy of contact. Formerly there was a kindly personal and patriarchal relation between the races, but in these latter days it is becoming hard and business like. "If the negro offends against the law, let him perish by the law," is the prevailing motto and method. A famous English writer some time ago said: "If you wish to destroy a feeble race, you can do so more easily by the law than without it. Make the laws as rigid as possible and enforce them rigidly." Those who watch events closely must have noticed the application of this principle in certain parts of the country.

I believe, from observation and examination, that, taking the Southern courts as a whole, the negro in some cases is treated unusually severely, and in others with unusual lenity. Bal-

ancing the two extremes, he gets substantial
justice; but there is a difference between fairness and justice. *Fairness* consists in equal
distribution of favor; *justice* in equal application of rights. The laborer in the parable,
who entered at the eleventh hour, was received
on terms of compensatory equality with the
one who had borne the heat and burden of the
day, but the more strenuous workman could
not accuse the master of the vineyard of injustice, but merely of unfairness. If the negro gets justice in the Southern courts, the
white man gets less than justice, and this
makes an unfair distribution of penalties.

When negroes commit crimes among themselves they are not apt to be punished with
undue severity, but when they commit crime
against the white race punishment is sure,
swift and severe. On the other hand, when the
white man commits an offense against the negro, acquittal is almost sure to follow; and
even if convicted he is released with a slight
fine and does not go to swell the prison record
of his race. Even where the white man commits an offence against his own race he is not
apt to receive the full rigor of the law. When
two races are living together, the race which
assumes superiority is wont to regard itself
as sacred in the eyes of the other, and is very

reluctant to humiliate any of its members, even by due process of law.

I believe that all will agree that a white person in Massachusetts is in every way as upright and as well behaved as the white person in any other place in the world, and yet, if we follow statistics, we find that the white people in Mississippi are angels of grace as compared with the white people of Massachusetts. In Massachusetts there are 5,477 whites in prison; in Mississippi only 114. The ingenuity of the Yankee sociologist can easily explain away this seeming discrepancy. By the same process of reasoning, the glaring criminal discrepancy between the races can be accounted for. There are probably no more white prisoners in Massachusetts than there ought to be, but no man in his senses, not even Senator Vardaman, will claim that only 114 white persons in Mississippi should be "in durance vile." By parity of reason, it is fair to say that probably in the South the number of white prisoners falls immensely below the number of white offenders against the law.

If the entire negro population should withdraw from the South and its place be supplied by whites occupying a similar status, the crime rate of the South would *not* be appreciably affected. In the United States as a whole there is an average of one prisoner to every one thousand of the population. In the South Atlantic states, where the negro is found in the largest numbers, the criminal rate is almost exactly the same as that of the nation at large. In the North Atlantic states, where there are few negroes, there is a still higher average, and in the Western states, where there are no negroes, comparatively speaking, the rate is highest of all. It is impossible to trace any connection between race and crime. If the negro in the North shows a much higher criminal rate than the negro in the South, it is also true that the white race in the North shows a greater ratio of crime over that same race in the South.

The negro in this country is the sacrificial race. He is the burden bearer of the white race. He constitutes the mud sill of society and suffers the ills of that lowly place. He performs the rough work of society. He suffers the affliction and even commits the crimes which always fall to the lot of his status. Were it not for him the white race would suffer corresponding ills. The Caucasian should appreciate the vicariousness of the black man's lot and not strive by false reasoning and force argument to make his burdens greater than they are.

Just as the negro death rate, three times as great as that of the whites, is clearly due to his condition, so his crime rate, bearing the same disproportion, is also attributable to the same cause.

What should be the attitude of negro men and women of light and learning toward this high criminal record and the interpretation just placed upon it? In the first place, they should strive insistently and incessantly to reduce this rate. It is always more satisfactory, from a sociological point of view, to remove an evil than to explain the cause of its existence. Laws are made for the protection of the weak. It makes my heart bleed when I see a negro violating the law, which is his only safeguard and protection under our scheme of civilization. This Samsonian folly pulls down the pillars of the temple of justice, the only asylum for the weak. Colored men should use their best offices to persuade those who are in control of the lawmaking agencies in the States and in the nation to enact only such laws as can be cheerfully upheld and obeyed by all, without compromise of becoming dignity and self-respect. The white race should enact laws of such equity and fairness that the negroes will have no cause to complain of their unrighteousness and injustice. For if the laws themselves are unrighteous, where shall we look for righteousness?

Let the negro obey the Ten Commandments and the white man the Golden Rule. Then all will be well. Ephraim will not envy Judah, and Judah will not vex Ephraim.

THE AMERICAN NEGRO AS A POLITI-
CAL FACTOR

Professor E. A. Freeman once defined politics as present history, and history as past politics. With a greater proneness for picturesque language, John J. Ingalls described politics as "the metaphysics of force," in which none but the strenuous may expect to play a part. According to Webster's Dictionary, politics is "that part of ethics which has to do with the regulation and government of a nation or state, the defense of its existence and rights against foreign control and conquest, the augmentation of its strength and resources, and the protection of its citizens in their rights, with the preservation and improvement of their morals." According to this conception, it will be seen that politics is the chief concern of man in his associated relations, and conditions all other modes of activity, whether economic, industrial, educational or social.

The derivative, or secondary, meaning of

the word "politics" is the management of a political party and the advancement of candidates to office. Throughout our discussion it will be well to keep sharply in mind the distinction between politics as the science of government and politics as the art of partisan policy and manipulation. In a country like ours, where the functions of government are conducted through partisan organizations, the secondary meaning of the word is apt to obscure its primary significance in popular estimation. The vast majority of the people have no conception of the word aside from party contentions and the procurement of office. So great is the perversity of popular understanding that to refer to a public man as a politician is accounted an uncomplimentary designation.

In considering the negro as a political factor, reference is hardly ever had to the essential functions and purposes of government, but he is regarded merely as the sport, the jest and the riddle of party rivalry. Our political philosophers are inclined to ignore the negro as a constituent governmental factor by reason of the manner of his introduction into this country. The African was imported for the sole purpose of performing manual and menial labor. His bodily powers alone were called into requisition. His function was as purely mechanical as that of the ox which pulls the plow. He was a chattel, a part of the nation's material assets. There was no more thought of admitting him into the body politic than of thus ennobling the lower animals. The gulf that separated him from the proud Aryan was supposed to be so wide and deep that the two races could never be made amenable to the same moral, political and social *régime*.

But the transplanted African has manifested surprising capacities and aptitudes for the standards of his European captors, so that the races must now be separated, if at all, by purely artificial barriers. This upward struggle on the part of the African has been against continuous doubt, ridicule and contemptuous denial on the part of those who would profit by his inferior status. Those who once assumed the piety of their day and generation at one time stoutly declared that the negro did not possess a soul to be saved in the world to come, but was merely as the beasts that perish; but he is now considered the man of oversoul, as Emerson would say, by reason of his marvelous emotional characteristics. Then the wise ones maintained that he did not possess a mind to be enlightened according to the standards of European intellect, and hence he was forbidden a knowledge of letters. The same dogma affirmed that the black man would not work except under the stern compulsion of the white man's beneficent whip, and that he would die out under freedom. But all of these dogmas have been disproved by the progress of events.

The ancient doctrine of racial inferiority, however, now reasserts itself under a different guise. With a prudent generality it avers with great vehemence of spirit that the negro is inherently, unalterably and everlastingly inferior to the white race as a part of God's cosmic scheme of things, and, therefore, is an unfit factor for self-government, which is the highest human function. It is a shrewd and cunning controversialist who posits the universal negative and defies the world to disprove his thesis. His tactical method is to deny all things, and to ignore that which has been proved. But, in spite of it all, the negro is steadily and unmistakably moving toward the great free ocean of human privilege, and, like the mountain stream, though his progress here and there may be impeded and delayed, artificial barriers and obstructions can only retard but not stay his onward flow.

The white race in this country is ensnared in meshes of its own law. The negro has been, and is, the incidental beneficiary of this entanglement. Circumstances have forced him into a political scheme not designed for him. Universal principles have no ethnic quality. By the irony of history the white man's maxims have risen up to trouble him. The Ten Commandments will not budge, neither will the Declaration of Independence. It is said that the Anglo-Saxon race is noted for its bad logic, but good sense. The revolutionary fathers must have shut their eyes to the logical results of their own doctrine, or else they lacked the courage of their conscience. The negro has been the incidental beneficiary of the two waves of revolutionary feeling which have swept the current of popular sentiment beyond the limits of its accustomed channel. He moves up and down on the scale of national sentiment as the mercury in the thermometric tube, reaching blood-heat in periods of national stress and excitement and sinking to the freezing point in seasons of tranquillity and repose. In none other than revolutionary crises could the Declaration of Independence have been written or the last two amendments appended to our Federal Constitution. The former held out to the negro the hope of ultimate citizenship and political equality, while the latter was the first step toward this realization. These two milestones of promise and partial fulfilment were one hundred years apart. As the nation is becoming settled in its normal modes, the disposition is to relegate the negro to the state of political nullity.

But, despite this political apostasy, the negro constitutes a political factor which cannot be ignored without local and national peril. He constitutes one-ninth the numerical strength of the American people, and is promiscuously scattered over the whole geographical area of the United States, ranging in relative density from ten to one in the black belts of the South to less than one per cent. in the higher latitudes. He furnishes one-sixth of the wage-earning class, and is inextricably interwoven in the national, industrial, and economic fabric. He speaks the same language, conducts the same modes of activity, reads the same literature, worships God after the same ritual as his white fellow citizens. As the late Dr. W. T. Harris once said, he has acquired the Anglo Saxon consciousness and put on his spiritual clothing. He delights in his new habiliment. He appeals to his white brother in the language of Ruth to Naomi: ''Where thou goest I will go; and where thou lodgest I will lodge; thy people shall be my people, and thy God my God; where thou diest I will die, and there will I be buried.''

A nation consists of the people living in a prescribed territory who hold the same general belief, sentiment and aspiration. The negro is, therefore, not an alien, but an essential part of the body politic. He is not like the Red Indian, with whose corporeal presence alone we have to deal and who stands stolidly aloof from the great throbbing current of national thought, feeling and aspirations, but he is a vital part in the spirit and potency of the national life. The negro is not merely a recipient, but a partaker in all of the objects and aims of government. Is he not a vital element in every measure intended to preserve the national peace and prosperity, to augment the nation's strength and resources, for the protection of citizens in their rights, and the preservation and improvement of their morals? The negro may indeed be eliminated by force as a factor in party management and patronage, but he can no more be eliminated from politics, in the broader significance of that term, than we can eliminate one side from a triangle without destroying the figure.

In current political discussion the negro is ever referred to as a negligible public quantity. The term "southern people," by a strange twist of lexical usage, is intended to signify a part, and sometimes a smaller part, of the community, and yet the negro in the South, in some instances, constitutes the majority of the population and contributes the greater part of the industrial strength, and makes possible the larger proportion of the public powers and functions of the State. Whenever political exigency suggests the curtailment of the representative power resident in the black population by way of reducing representation in the national congress, the beneficiaries of this power interpose the most strenuous and vehement objections. The marble apex of a monument may indeed look with despite upon the grosser material of its foundation, but it cannot deny that the foundation is as essential an element of the structure as its more ornamental and pretentious capstone.

The present reactionary political tendency has produced a class of political leaders who base their motive on race hatred and strife. They are adepts in the use of the dynamic power of race animosity. Without philosophic insight or far-seeing wisdom, they appeal to the passion of their followers with utter recklessness of logic and conscience. That the negro is incapable of self-government is a maxim which springs spontaneously from the lips of every speaker and to the pen tip of every

writer who attempts to justify the unrighteous
and iniquitous political treatment which is accorded him. This assertion they relish and
roll under their tongues as a sweet morsel.
By hoary usage and glib recital it has become
a stereotyped motto. We are ever referred to
the failure of the native tribes in Africa, the
dismal experiments of Hayti and Liberia, and
the reconstruction régime of the Southern
States. These are always recounted in the
same order of recital, and set forth with the
same vehemence of rhetoric as the basis of the
same derogatory conclusion. The argument,
or alleged argument, has been repeated so often
that the indolent feel forced to accept it
through sheer weariness. It is dinned into
their dull understanding by unending and
never-varying repetition as the recurrent
chorus of a popular song. The unvaried repetition of hoary argument ordinarily damages
the intellectual reputation of its users as being
deficient in originality and resource; but those
who delight to belittle and condemn the negro are no whit abashed by such considerations
of moral and intellectual frugality.

What is self government? If by the power
of self-government we mean the ability of any
people to exist according to the requirements
of their stage of development under their own

autonomy, and to adjust themselves to that environment, then all of the people on the face of the earth are capable of self-government. If, on the other hand, it implies that the ability of the retarded races to regulate their affairs after the fashion of the most advanced section of the European people, then the question is not only unnecessary but preposterous. Ireland has for years been waging a gigantic struggle for the priceless boon of self-government, as the Englishman understands and exercises that function, but England, on the other hand, is determined to withhold it on the ground that the wild, hysteric Celt is not prepared to exercise so high a prerogative with safety to himself and to the British Empire. The masses of the population of Europe, with centuries of inherited freedom and civilization behind them, are not deemed fit for self-government in the exalted sense of that term. Indeed, it is only the Anglo-Saxon race that has as yet demonstrated the capacity to use this prerogative as a means of social and political progress. The revolutions and counter revolutions and rumors of revolutions which are almost daily occurring in South and Central American Republics show that the forms of government copied from Anglo-Saxon models are far in advance of the development of these

Latin copyists. Self-government is not an absolute but a relative term. The Red Indian
governed himself for centuries before the ad-
vent of the pale-face, and throve much better
under his own autonomy than under alien control. The negroes of Hayti under their own
form of government are as happy and contented, as thrifty and progressive, and are approaching the standards of European civilization as surely and as rapidly as the
corresponding number of blacks in Jamaica
under British control, or as a like number of
negroes in Georgia under the dominion of the
Stars and Stripes. If it be true that the negro has never shown any conspicuous capacity
for self-government after the European standard, it is also true that the white race has not
yet shown any conspicuous success in governing him.

The Republic of Hayti, contrary to prevailing belief, is the most marvelous illustration
of self-governing ability on the face of the
globe. Where else can be found a race of
slaves who rose up in their independence of
spirit and banished the ruling race to another
continent, set up free government, and maintained it for one hundred years in face of the
taunts and sneers and despiteful usage of a
frowning world? If there be imperfections,

internal dissensions, and repeated revolutions, it is merely a repetition of the experience of mankind in learning the lesson of self-government.

Liberia is held up to ridicule and scorn, and pointed to as an everlasting argument of the negro's governmental incapacity; and yet we have here a handful of ex-slaves who had only played for a while in the backyard of American civilization, and who, feeling the fires of freedom burning in their breasts, crossed the ocean and establishehd a government on the miasmatic coasts of Africa. This government has been maintained, however, feebly, for ninety years. For nearly a century a handful of American negroes have exercised a salutary control over two millions of natives, and have maintained themselves amid the intrigue and sinister design of great European powers. If the colony at Jamestown or at Plymouth had been forced to confront such an overwhelming number of savages as the Liberian colony has had to do, and had they been cut off from the constant stream of European reinforcement, sympathy and support fifty years after their foundation, they would have perished from savage onslaught and the vicissitudes of the wilderness of the new world.

But those who deny the political capacity

of the negro point to the reconstruction régime, and exclaim, "What need we of further
proof?" At the time of reconstruction ninety-
five per cent. of the negroes were densely illiterate, none of whom had had experience in
governmental affairs. This happened, too, at
a period of general political and social up-
heaval, when the country was overrun with
nondescript and renegade adventurers who
were going throughout the land seeking whom
they might devour. They seized upon the
newly enfranchised negro as their natural prey.
And yet these ignorant ex-slaves, amid all the
snares which beset them from without and
within, maintained governments for several
years, against which the only charge that has
ever been preferred is that they were grotesque
and extravagant. Grotesqueness is a matter
of taste. In many minds it is synonymous
with the unusual. If we are unaccustomed to
seeing negroes in places of political control,
the spectacle of the negro congressman or
judge would at first seem incongruous and
grotesque, but as a part of the usual order it
would become normal and seemly in our eyes.
If we may believe the rumors of municipal
mismanagement, it is doubtful whether any of
the Southern States, in their palmiest reconstruction days, could equal New York, Phil-

adelphia, San Francisco, or St. Louis in the quality or extent of public corruption. The corrupting influence and practice, be it understood, were not due to the initiative of the negro, but of the white carpetbagger and native scalawag who exploited him in his weakness. These much-abused "negro governments," as they are called, changed the oligarchy of the conquered States into true democracies, inaugurated a system of public instruction for all classes, and the general character of their constitutions was regarded as so excellent that many of them have not been altered up to the present time, except for the worse. As documents of human liberty they stand out bold and pronounced as compared with the tricky instruments that have supplanted them. They passed no laws against human liberty, or at variance with the Constitution of the United States. They denied no man the God given right of liberty, or the constitutionally vouchsafed privilege of participating in the government under which he must live. The failure of these governments was inevitable. To expect ignorant and inexperienced slaves to maintain a government not merely for themselves, but also for a greater number of Anglo-Saxons with trained faculty for leadership and inborn power of dominion, is a proposition too

preposterous for the present generation to entertain. The marvel is not that they succeeded
so poorly, but that they proceeded at all. It
is not to the negro's discredit that he did not
accomplish the impossible.

It is time to lay aside the animosities of by-
gone reconstruction and consider the situation
in the light of changed conditions. The question of the present day is not whether the negro can govern himself, but how far, with increasing intelligence and substance, he can co-
operate with the white race in maintaining
good government for all; and whether he can
be effectually ignored as a governmental factor by any section of the country without ac-
cumulating serious peril, not only for that
section, but for the nation at large.

That the participation of the negro in governmental affairs constitutes a menace both to
himself and the community is a dogma which
has attained wide currency and general acceptance in present day discussion; but, like other
damaging dogmas of which he from time im-
memorial has been made the victim, this proposition is not justly upheld by facts or argument; and yet it has been proclaimed or as-
severated with such positiveness of assertion
and rhetorical vehemence as almost to deceive
his erstwhile friends, who once championed his

cause as being entitled to the full measure of
the prerogative and privilege of an American
citizen. The former enthusiastic and aggressive attitude toward the rights of this race
has given way to a feeble, apathetic and apol-
ogetic avowal of faith in the abstract principle
of human rights, but there is a sinister indifference to practical application and concrete
sanction. Such defenders of the negro's cause

> Damn with faint praise, assent with civil leer:
> And without sneering teach the rest to sneer.

This radical change of attitude has been due
to a studied and deliberate policy on the part
of the more rabid and rancorous anti-negro
agitators, who study to make this race odious
and offensive in the eyes of the civilized world.
They have seized upon the evil deeds of the
dastardly wrongdoer, and exploited them to the
everlasting detriment of a whole race. Their
chief delight consists in learning that some negro, in some part of the land, has committed
a flagrant and outrageous crime. They count
that day a sad one when the morning's paper
does not reveal that some one out of ten millions has been apprehended for a grave and
nefarious offense. With ghoulish glee they
revel in the hideous manifestations of human

nature if the culprit happens to be of the despised blood.

Such a deliberate and calculated propaganda to exploit and magnify the moral and criminal imperfections of any other element of our population would blast and blacken the reputation of the race held in despite, and make it odious in the estimation of their fellow-men. If every offense committed by an Italian wrongdoer should be magnified in its heinous and hideous features, and proclaimed in flaming headlines all over America as portraying the bestial traits and tendencies of the diabolical "dago," that race would soon be deemed unfit to form a constituent and participating factor in the equation of national life. The negro race is daily subjected to microscopic search for shortcomings and imperfections to be exploited for political ends. The negro is the victim of the iniquitous propaganda that portrays and magnifies repugnant imperfections which in the case of other races are attributed to human frailty. This political philosophy is clearly expressed in one of the homely maxims of its chief philosopher: "The negro is a frozen serpent, and we propose to keep him frozen." His facts are erroneous and his philosophy is false. The negro is in no sense a menace to America or to any part of it except in so far as ignorance is a menace to knowledge, vice to virtue, degradation to decency; and the only effective way to relieve the menace of the situation is by removing the cause and not perpetuating it under the spell of any fancied dread. If the negro is to be kept "frozen" under such frenzied philosophy, the white race, too, may become frost-bitten by the resulting frigidity of the atmosphere.

On the other hand, the negro has evinced amazing patriotic devotion. As soon as the first pangs of grief at severance from his native land faded away, he fell completely in love with his new environment. He soon forgot the "sunny clime and palmy wine" of his native land for the "cotton, corn and sweet potatoes" of old Virginia. The negro is unsurpassed in the strength and intensity of his local attachment. Herein consists the true quality of patriotism. It is not to be found merely in the achievements of renowned warriors and statesmen, which indeed are their own reward. In this sense only a few conspicuous names in any country could be accounted patriotic, but rather the duties and endearments of the common people make the deeper and more lasting impression upon the human heart. Robert Burns, the national poet of Scotland, has seized upon the endearments and local attachments of the lowly life of Scotland and woven them into soulful song, and has thus rendered old Scotia ever dear to all mankind. If the human heart ever turns with a passionate longing to our own southland, it will not be in quest of traditions of their great warriors and statesmen, but rather to revel in the songs, the sorrows, the sighings, and the spiritual strivings as embodied in the plantation melodies. Which of her patriotic odes would America not willingly give away in exchange for "Swing low, sweet chariot," or "Steal away to Jesus?" Or where can be found a pathetic or patriotic appeal more racy of the soil and melting to the soul than "Way down upon the Suwanee River"? It is curious that the negro furnished the musical inspiration for the Southern Confederacy, for the famous song of *Dixie* merely expresses the longing of the slave to return to his native home "way down South in Dixie." It is claimed that this is a white man's country. This proposition is understandable when we consider that the white race constitutes eight-ninths of its population, and has absorbed a still larger proportion of its material and substantial strength; and, representing as they do the most populous and powerful factor, they are fairly entitled to, as they are in the habit of securing, all that justly belongs to them: but, according to any just and righteous standard, this country belongs to the negro as much as to any other, not only because he has helped to redeem it from the wilderness by the energy of his own arm, but because he has also bathed it with his blood and watered it with his tears, and hallowed it with the yearning of his soul.

Not only in local attachment, but also in devotion of spirit to American institutions and ideals, the negro has played a notable part. It was the negro slaves whose blood was first shed in the streets of Boston as an earnest of American independence. The statue of Crispus Attucks on Boston Common was doubtless intended to typify the spirit of the revolutionary war, but it has a deeper and muter meaning. It illustrates the self-sacrificing patriotism of a transplanted race. In every national crisis the negro has demonstrated his patriotism anew. It runs like a thread through every chapter of our national history from Boston Common to San Juan Hill. His soldierly service has not been that of the Hessian hireling peddling his prowess for pay, or the cowardly conscript forced to the front by the bayonet behind, but he has ever rushed to his country's battle line with his country's battle cry exultant on his lips. He was with Washington in the days of Valley Forge. He was with Jackson behind the fleecy breastwork of New Orleans. He responded two hundred thousand strong to the call of Father Abraham for the preservation of this Union; and it was his valor, as much as any other, that placed the American standards on the Spanish ramparts in the West Indies. Is it a political as it is a sacred principle that without the shedding of blood there is no remission of sins? If this be true, when we consider the blood of the captive making red the Atlantic current on his way to cruel bondage, the blood of a slave drawn by the lash, the blood of a soldier shed in behalf of his country, the blood of the victim of cruelty and outrage, we may exclaim, with Kipling:

> "If blood be the price of liberty,
> If blood be the price of liberty,
> If blood be the price of liberty,
> Lord God! he has paid in full."

It does seem remarkable that this crude, untutored race, without the inheritance of freedom, should display such an absorbing passion for free institutions. Throughout the whole range of sectional contention the negro has been on the side of liberty, law and national authority. On the whole he has advocated the party, men, measures and policies that were calculated to uphold the best traditions and the highest American ideals. He is passionately attached to party organization, which embodies principles too subtle to be grasped in the abstract. His attachment to the party of Lincoln and Sumner was characterized by blind hysteria verging on fanaticism. He did not regard it as an instrument to be used, but as a fetish to be worshiped. He bowed down before it with reverence and gratitude and awe, as Friday before the gun of Robinson Crusoe because it had once rescued him from circumstances of great peril. This is the manner in which the negro manifested patriotism. To him party signified all that there was noble and worthy in the country. All else was ruin and destruction. His ablest and most sagacious leader, Frederick Douglass, at that time counseled that the "Republican party is the ship; all else is the sea." The verdict of history will show that even this excessive party devotion was in the line of the highest and best patriotism, for the party of his love was, at that time, the exclusive party of progress and freedom. The political historian will seek in vain to find in any national or local crises that the negro has ever upheld unworthy local or national aim or ideal. The possibility of such patriotic devo-

tion ought to convince the nation that the
black race is a natural storehouse of loyalty
which it may yet be called upon to utilize in
the day of peril. No people of Anglo-Saxon
breed would, like the negro, practice civic and
political self-sacrifice, and say to their country, "Though you slay me, yet will I serve
you."

By what possible stretch of argument can a
race with such potential patriotic capacity be
construed into a menace to free institutions?
If there be any menaceful feature in the negro's political status, it is merely that he grows
out of poverty, ignorance and the resultant
degradation. These are only temporary and
incidental, and they endure only until adequate
means are put forward for their removal.
There are some who are blinded by the spirit
of racial animosity and hate, and with whom
racial passion is the only political stock-in-
trade, so that they will willingly create a racial
menace where none exists, or perpetuate it
though it might easily be removed. These are
the most unloyal, unpatriotic men in America,
and could profitably sit at the feet of the negro, whom they hold in despite, and learn the
fundamental principles of loyalty and devotion
to country and its cause.

That the negro is unfit to participate in any

degree in the affairs of government passes as
a political axiom in some sections of the country.   Whoever dares question the validity of
this axiom by that action puts himself outside
the pale of tolerant consideration.   Acquiescence is the one test of political and social san-
ity.   Men always resent the attempt to uproot
their fondly cherished dogmas, especially if
they inure to their benefit or appeal to their
vanity; but, like most passionate dogmas, this
one fails of substantiation when subjected to
practical test.   Its only support is a vehement
and intolerable spirit which is appealed to as
the first and last principles of argument.   Experience does not show that, where the negro
exercises the untrammeled right of franchise,
he ever votes for men or measures inimical to
the best welfare of the country at large or of
the community in which he resides.   In Missouri,
Kentucky,   West   Virginia,   and   Maryland,
where the negro vote represents a considerable
fraction of the total electorate, negro voters
uniformly support the best men and measures
put forward in their respective States.   The
men who, in these border States, have succeeded to office largely on the basis of negro
votes stand, and have always stood, for the
best local and national ideals.   If we take the
personnel of the Senators, Representatives,

and local officials with negro support, and
compare them with the corresponding officials,
on the basis of an exclusive white electorate,
the former would suffer no whit by comparison
either in ability, devotion or patriotic integrity. In a border State, where the negro vote
constitutes one-fifth of the total electorate,
desperate efforts have been made to eliminate
him from the franchise. The reasons urged
are mainly speculative and frenzied. The most
ardent eliminationist may be confidently chal-
lenged to point out where the negro vote in
that State has ever resulted in the choice of
unworthy or incompetent public servants, or
has promoted measures contrary to the peace,
progress and well being of the commonwealth.
Since reconstruction, numerous negroes have
filled official positions under the government,
both elective and appointive. They have usually
conducted the business committed to them to
the entire satisfaction of the people, and have
been subjected to the same test of competency
as white officials in like situations. The chief
federal official in a Southern State is a negro
who has filled the position for thirteen years,
and holds a record of efficiency comparable
with any official of his grade in the entire public service. Protest against such officials is not
because they are incompetent or undeserving,

but merely because, for racial reasons, they are considered undesirable. If the reasoning might be put in a logical formula, it would run thus: "The white man should rule: therefore, the negro is unfit to exercise any of the functions of government." Or, as a famous critic once said, "Shakespeare should not have painted Othello black, because a hero of a drama ought to be white."

The negro is now passing through the most distressing stage of his political experience. He stands listlessly by as his political rights are denied, his privileges curtailed, and the current of public feeling grows cold and chilly. The constitutional amendments in the reconstruction states have been and are inspired by the purpose to eliminate the black factor from the governmental equation. This is the overt or covert intention of them all. By the utmost stretch of ingenuity and strain of conscience the technical phrasing of the letter may seem to square with constitutional requirements, but there is no room to doubt the underlying spirit and purpose. It does not lessen the fraudulent quality of fraud by giving it legal sanction. These tricky and ingenious instruments may seem to do credit to the cunning of their devisers, but they portray a lamentable state of the conscience. If the offence must needs

come, it were far better that the wrongdoer
should sin against the law than that the seared
conscience of the State should enact an unrighteous code. President Taft has explained,
in extenuation of the devious devices to eliminate the negro, that statesmen in the individual States growing weary of individual fraud
and violence preferred that the State should
relieve the individual conscience by a legal
sanction. We condemn butchery and slaughter
in Turkey, not because they are more outrageous than the innumerable murders and lynchings in the United States, but because they have
the tacit or avowed sanction of constituted authority. Lynching is the outbreak of an evil
propensity which constituted authorities are
either unable or unwilling to check; but is it
not infinitely better that, if lynchings must
needs be, they should stand as an expression of
individual sin against the law rather than that
they should be sanctioned by law?

No law, whether enacted by God or man, has
ever been perfectly obeyed. The Ten Commandments have been violated hourly ever
since they were announced amid the thunder
and smoke of Mount Sinai. Should the Divine
Author, therefore, modify his law to accommodate human frailties and imperfections? Above
all things the organic laws of a State should

be fair and candid, and should recommend themselves to the conscientious approval of all honest and upright citizens. Great indeed is the condemnation of that commonwealth whose organic law rests upon the basis of a lie.

These disfranchisement measures, harsh and severe as they are in many features, meet with little or no opposition from the nation at large. Although the clear and unmistakable intent of the Federal Constitution is set at naught, yet the nation suffereth it to be so. There is no moral force in the nation at present that will lead to their undoing, and no political exigency seems to demand it. That they violate the spirit, if not the letter, of the Federal Constitution is notorious. Every fourteen year old child in America is fully aware of this fact, and yet the nation winks at the violation of its own fundamental law. Men of the highest patriotic and personal probity ignore their oath to execute the law, and condone its annulment. If there is a growing disrespect for law in the attitude of the American mind, the cause is not far to seek nor hard to find. If one portion of the organic law may be violated with impunity, why not another if it seems to conflict with our interests or with our prejudices?

The negro is impotent. He makes his puny

protest, but the nation heeds it not. It is like sheep proclaiming the law of righteousness to a congregation of wolves. A complaint is effective only in so far as there is power to enforce it. That individual, race or nation is considered cowardly, and justly so, that will not use all available means to enforce a proper recognition of its rights and prerogatives; while the world looks with contempt upon a people who allow themselves to suffer wrong and injustice without using the most effective protests at their command. It also despises a lachrymose race which possesses no language but a cry. The sufferer owes it to the wrong-doer, not less than to himself, not to remain impassive or indifferent under outrage or wrong. It lowers the moral status of the perpetrator, not less than the victim, to encourage him to continue in his career of evil-doing with none to molest or make afraid.

The Anglo-Saxon race boasts that it neither needs nor heeds a law in face of its imperial will. It is his imperturbable spirit

> That bids him flout the laws he makes,
> That bids him make the laws he flouts.

And yet this imperturbable race must be amenable to the ethic principles which operate regardless of ethnic proclivities. The question as to whether might makes right must be relegated to the realm of pure morals; but sensible men know that might is still the effective force in practical government. In spite of constitutional compacts or written pledges, the strong will rule the weak, the rich will control the poor, and the wise will dominate the simple. In such contingencies we can always foretell the outcome with the predictive decision of natural law, and we may rely upon the prediction with the same assurance as we expect sparks to fly upward, or water to seek its level. This may not be the written law nor the preached gospel, but in its effective sanction of the practical conduct of men it is stronger than either. Social forces work out their inevitable results as assuredly as natural causes. The laws of social evolution are not going to suspend their operation. No one expects that the earth will again stand and gaze like Joshua's moon on Ajalon until a feebler contestant wins a victory over a more powerful adversary. If history teaches any clear lesson it is to the effect that the developed races are superior in all practical tests of power to the backward ones. This is especially true in the political arena. It is in this sphere that the Anglo-Saxon race manifests its peculiar genius. World-wide dominion seems to be in

the line of its natural destiny. The Englishman has clearly manifested his political superiority over the Asiatic as did the old Ro-
man over the Gaul and Briton. A handful of
Englishmen control the destiny of two hundred
million dusky Hindoos with as much ease as
the legions of Cæsar controlled the nomads of
the forests of northern Europe. This political dominance is not due to an attribute of
blood, but rises from a practical efficiency
gained through the discipline of civilization.
Thirty thousand American co-Liberians are
able to keep under governmental control two
millions of native Africans by reason of their
superior discipline and efficiency; all of which
goes to show that it is not blood but circumstances and conditions that count for political
dominance. Negro domination is an absurd
and impossible issue which has served only
sinister political ends. The negro, with his traditional handicaps and political ineptitude, can
no more dominate any section of the nation
than the babies in the cradle. But conscience
makes political cowards who tremble at a
shadow. A timid statesmanship is dominated
by a fancied dread which sober judgment
shows to be impossible of realization.

The question of government of a heterogeneous population is always one of great diffi-

culty and complexity. The racial situation in the United States leads to an endless tangle. The negro is promiscuously scattered throughout the entire white population. The unequal density of distribution complicates the political question. If there were territorial compactness of this racial element, or if it were equally diffused throughout the whole area, the problem in its political aspect would be greatly simplified. It is a much simpler problem to formulate a satisfactory plan of political privilege for the Philippine Islands than it is for South Carolina or Alabama. The Filipino has territorial and racial solidarity, whereas in the South two dissimilar classes cover the same area. It is always easier to govern one race than two. On the other hand, if the negro were equally distributed among the States he would not constitute more than one-eighth of the strength of any community, and there would scarcely be any necessity for special political plans or policies to cover his case. As a political factor he would be absorbed in the general equation. The very complexity of the racial situation will ultimately compel political and civil uniformity. In this country political, social and economic conditions gravitate toward equality. We may continue to expect thunderstorms in the political firmament so long as

there exists inequality of political temperature in the atmosphere of the two regions.
Neither Massachusetts nor Mississippi will rest
satisfied until there is an equality of political
condition in both States. We are just beginning to appreciate the full significance of
Abraham Lincoln's philosophy when he said
that this country cannot exist "half slave and
half free." Democratic institutions can no
more tolerate a double political status than two
standards of ethics or discrepant units of
weight and measure.

All patriotic citizens must be interested in
any honest effort to purify and elevate the suffrage. Honest effort to eliminate ignorance
and corruption, in order to promote good government for all the people, must be appreciated as a political exigency, if not approved
as a political principle. But no plan, not based
on racial grounds and operated by tricky and
fraudulent manipulation, can be devised which
will shut in all white men and shut out all negroes. No such racial separatrix can be found.
The clear purpose of the revised constitution,
as is shown by ancestor clauses as well as by
unfair manipulation of these laws between the
races, is to eliminate the negro wholly from all
governmental control. The negro is willing to
take any test which the white race is willing to

impose upon itself. He is willing to drink of the political cup of which the white man drinks, and to be baptized with the baptism with which he is baptized withal.

There are in the United States ten millions of negroes, a large proportion of whom possess the requisite intelligence and general qualification for the exercise of the high function of citizenship, and yet they are without a voice in the government. There is no negro in either House of the National Congress, scarcely one in any State Legislature, to make the laws by which the race is to be governed, nor yet a judge on the bench to interpret these laws, nor an administrative officer to enforce them. If the nation desires the negro to develop into an effective factor of the American people he must be given the same consideration, both before the law and behind the law, as enjoyed by his white fellow-citizens. He merely asks for equality of rights; no more, no less, no other.

The contention that in a heterogeneous racial situation one race alone must govern is without sanction either in ethics or experience. No man is good enough to govern another without his consent. The rich are not good enough to govern the poor; the Protestant is not good enough to govern the Catholic; the white man is not good enough to govern the negro. The class that is shut out from all participation in government will soon be shut out from participation in everything else that is worth while and that the controlling class covets. The privilege to work, to acquire an education, and to accumulate property is indeed of great value, but it cannot atone for the loss of the right to vote, which under our scheme of government is the right preservative of all other rights and privileges.

Experience shows that schemes of disfranchisement are always accompanied by vehement onslaught on the negro, and proscriptive legislation restricting his general welfare. It is noticeable that, in sections of cities where disfranchised negroes reside, there are few public improvements, because the residents have no voice directly or indirectly in the choice of the city councilmen. The black resident has no say as to who shall be alderman from his ward, and consequently this prudent official, exercising ordinary political sagacity, gives first consideration to the insistent claims of his white constituents, who can influence his continuation in office. It is a law of human nature that where we are intent on our own interests we abate our zeal for the welfare of others who may not be insistent upon their own claims. If the Protestants had exclusive control of government, the Catholics would have little show of a "square deal" where their interests seemed divergent from or in conflict with the welfare of the dominant creed. It is precisely for this reason that all elements in a heterogeneous population should have some say in the common government. This country is making a mistake by depriving the negro of all participation in government, locally and nationally. The negro should be taught the beneficent purpose and principles of law and order. He should be led to have implicit faith in the righteousness and integrity of the law. Good citizenship cannot be secured by holding up the harsh, the cruel and repressive features of government. The policeman's club is oftentimes the only governmental instrument with which the negro comes in contact. No other enlightened nation on earth adopts this method of dealing with a backward or retarded people. England, France and Germany always make such a people see and appreciate the beneficent ends of government by making them a participant factor in it. There is no enlightened government on earth, with a prudent regard for its own best interests, that ruthlessly overrides the sensibilities of the governed.

The political status of the negro will probably culminate under the administration of

President Taft.[1] If by tacit acquiescence he lends implied encouragement to the retrograde tendencies of the times, the repeal of the Fourteenth and Fifteenth Amendments, which is now merely a matter of academic discussion, may become a practical issue. If on the other hand the last two amendments of the Constitution are regarded as a vital part of that instrument whose enforcement is regarded in the obligation of his high office, then an affirmative attitude will do much to check the growing sentiment which makes the last addition to the highest law of the land void and of no effect. President Taft comes of the highest patriotic and philanthropic ideals and traditions; but the tangle of the race problem will not yield to a generous disposition and personal goodwill, of which the President has an unlimited endowment. To the negro the danger seems that he may allow the rights of the race to be sacrificed on the altar of other pressing national problems. His ardent desire to establish peace and goodwill between the North and the white South must meet with sympathetic response in the heart of every true and loyal American; but a sacrifice of the Fourteenth and Fifteenth Amendments is too great price

[1] This essay was written during the early part of President Taft's administration.

to be paid even for a consummation so devoutly to be wished. Mr. Taft is the first American President to come to the office with a colonial experience and policy whose very foundation rests upon the inferior political status of the subject race. It is easy to transfer the habit of mind and bias of feeling from the Filipino in the islands to the negro in the States. In his letter of acceptance Candidate Taft said that he stood unequivocally by the Fourteenth and Fifteenth Amendments of the Constitution, both in letter and spirit. His advisory, though unofficial, attitude in the recent campaign in Maryland was to the same effect. But these utterances were more than offset by the statement in his inaugural address to the effect that he would not appoint colored men to office where local opposition was gathered. This suggestion is sufficient to invite the fiercest antagonism to the appointment of a negro to a Federal office in any community in the United States. It seems somewhat anomalous that in some places, where the majority of the population are negroes who belong to the President's political party, no one of this race can be appointed to any Federal office if the minority, who opposed his election, should enter protest. From the present appearance of things, under the operation of the announced policy of the

President, there will probably not be a negro officeholder in the South by the close of his administration. The elimination of the negro from office in the South means his eventual elimination in the nation. Elimination from office means elimination from politics.

The fact that a Cabinet officer, in open public utterances, boldly advocates the elimination of the negro from politics gives the whole race much anxiety. Usually a Cabinet Minister voices the policy and purpose of the administration of which he forms a part. President Taft has finished the first year of his administration. His policies are not yet distinctive and definitely set. It does not yet clearly appear what they shall be. Every patriotic and loyal citizen should be patient with an administration charged with such heavy duties and responsibilities, even though it may not be able at once to stress the issues in which he is especially, even vitally, concerned. The negro is watching the administration of President Taft with hopes and fears. May his hopes be triumphant over his fears.

FIFTY YEARS OF NEGRO EDUCATION

Experience is the rational outcome of experiment. Where there are neither fixed principles nor established precedent, the practical worker must feel after the right way, if haply he might find it. But he must have an open mind, ready to accept proved and tested results, and to discard discredited processes undertaken as an experimental necessity with equal acquiescence and cheerfulness of spirit.

Previous to the Civil War scattered schools for the instruction of persons of color existed in the North, and, to some extent, in a few Southern cities as well. Here and there a pious master or kindly mistress would teach a favorite slave the rudiments of knowledge, with connivance, evasion, or defiance of forbidding laws. Now and then an ambitious minded slave would snatch furtive bits of knowledge, with the traditional relish of stolen waters.

But, broadly speaking, it might be said that fifty years ago the systematic education of the negro race began near the absolute zero point of ignorance. The real intellectual awakening of the race began with the overthrow of slavery. When the smoke of war had blown away, when the cessation of strife proclaimed the end of the great American conflict, when the "war drum throbbed no longer, and the battle flags were furled," there emerged from the wreck and ruin of war 4,000,000 of human chattels, who were transformed, as if by magic, in a moment, in the twinkling of an eye, from slavery to freedom, from bondage to liberty, from death unto life. These people were absolutely ignorant and destitute. They had not tasted of the tree of knowledge which is the tree of good and evil. This tree was guarded by the flaming swords of wrath, kept keen and bright by the avarice and cupidity of the master class. No enlightened tongue had explained to them the deep and moral purpose of the Ten Commandments and the Sermon on the Mount. They were blind alike as to the intellectual and moral principles of life. Ignorance, poverty, and vice, the trinity of human wretchedness, brooded over this degraded mass and made it pregnant. The world looked and wondered. What is to be the destiny of this people? Happily, at this tragic juncture of affairs, they were touched with the magic wand of education. The formless mass assumed symmetry and shape. Nowhere in the whole sweep of history has the transforming effect of intelligence had a higher test of its power.

The circumstances amid which this work had its inception read like the swift-changing scenes of a mighty drama. The armies of the North are in sight of victory. Lincoln issues his immortal Emancipation Proclamation; Sherman, with consummate military skill, destroys the Confederate base of supplies, and marches through Georgia, triumphant to the sea; Grant is on his road to Richmond; the Confederate capital has fallen; Lee has surrendered; the whole North joins in one concerted chorus: "Mine eyes have seen the glory of the coming of the Lord." These thrilling episodes will stir our patriotic emotions to the latest generations. But in the track of the Northern army there followed a band of heroes to do battle in a worthier cause. Theirs was no carnal warfare. They did not battle against flesh and blood, but against the powers of darkness intrenched in the minds of an ignorant and degraded people. A worthier band has never furnished theme or song for sage or bard. These noble women—for these people were mostly of the female sex—left homes, their friends, their social ties, and all that they held dear, to go to the far South to labor among the recently emancipated slaves. Their courage, their self-sacrificing devotion, sincerity of purpose and purity of motive, and their unshaken faith in God were passkeys to the hearts of those for whom they came to labor. They were sustained by an unbounded enthusiasm and zeal amounting almost to fanaticism. No mercenary or sordid motive attaches to their fair names. They gave the highest proof that the nineteenth century, at least, has afforded that Christianity has not yet degenerated to a dead formula and barren intellectualism, but that it is a living, vital power. Their works do follow them. What colored man is there in all this land who has not felt the uplifting effect of their labors? Their monument is builded in the hopes of a race struggling upward from ignorance to enlightenment, from corruption to purity of life. These are they who sowed the seeds of intelligence in the soil of ignorance and planted the rose of virtue in the garden of dishonor and shame. They had no foregoers; they have no successors. It is said that gratitude is the fairest flower that sheds its perfume in the human heart. As long as the human heart beats in grateful response to benefits received, these women shall not want a monument of living ebony and bronze.

Those who enlisted in this cause had neither the lamp of experience to guide their feet, nor yet the assurance of hoped for results to strengthen their faith. At that time not only the policy, but the possibility, of educating the negro was in the bonds of dialectic doubt and denial. It was the generally accepted dogma of that day that the negro was not amenable to the intellectual and moral régime applicable to the white child. The institution of slavery made requisition upon the negro physical faculties alone, and therefore the higher susceptibilities of his nature were ingeniously denied and prudently suppressed. Ordained intellectual and moral inferiority is the only valid justification of political and social subordination. Hence, this became the ultimate dogma of the pro-slavery propaganda. Those who profess to doubt the possibilities of human nature are never quite sure of the foundation of their belief. Although the loud boast is ever on their lip, their conduct reveals the secret suspicion of the heart for fear it might be so. Thus we see that those who most confidently proclaim that the negro, by nature, is incapable of comprehending the intellectual basis of the Aryan culture and civilization are ever on the alert to prevent him from attempting the impossible. If the negro's skull was too thick to learn, as the dogma ran, why pass laws forbidding him to try? But after all it must be said that the slave régime possessed the wisdom of its policy and practiced the cunning necessary to carrying it out. It was deemed dangerous to communicate to the despised negro the mystic symbols of knowledge which reveal all the hidden secrets of civilization. This policy was based upon the well-founded fear of primitive jealousy: "Lest he should stretch forth his hand, and partake of the tree of knowledge, and become as one of us." But the flaming sword of jealousy and wrath can not for long guard the tree of knowledge against the quest of those who would partake of the fruit thereof. No one who sniffs the ozone of an atmosphere surcharged with the doctrine of equality, and to whom has been vouchsafed the talisman of knowledge, will ever be satisfied with a status that assigns him to a rank below the level of his faculties. Under the ancient régime of acknowledged and accepted political and social subordination, masters took pride in educating their apt and capable slaves. Indeed several names of this class attained the rank of respectable philosophers whose fame reaches down to our own day. But the doctrine of freedom and equality is a sure and swift contagion, without respect of race or color.

The missionaries who first came down from the North were not generally educators according to the requirements of the modern education. They brought the technical terms of knowledge in their left hand. In their right hand they brought religion, culture, civilization. They quickened the spirit, aroused the energies, and awakened the consciousness of a suppressed race that had been so long despised and rejected. As the traditional treatment had rested upon professed disbelief in the negro's capabilities, the method of the missionaries was based upon the belief in higher human possibilities. The colder calculating spirit of this later day may, with supercilious disdain, call it fanatacism, but none can deny its uplifting and sustaining power.

The missionary and religious organizations vied with one another in planting institutions of higher pretensions for the recently emancipated class. The establishment of institutions on the higher level of European culture for a people who had hitherto been denied the alphabet was a most daring experiment. It was a severe test of the faith of the founders. But fifty years of experience has abundantly justified the experiment. If we should subtract from the development of the negro life the influence contributed by and attributable to these much berated negro colleges and universities, the remainder would be niggardly indeed.

Of late we have heard much criticism to the effect that education of the race began on top instead of at the bottom. Naturally enough, these schools were patterned after the traditional academic type then prevailing in New England. Indeed, the education of people should begin at the top, if we are to look to historical development of the human race for the proper method. In education, as in religion, the good things proceed from above, and trickle downward, carrying their beneficence to the masses below. Just as Yale and Harvard are the foster mothers of New England educational progress, so these negro universities and colleges produced the teachers, ministers, physicians, lawyers, editors and enlightened leaders who are guiding and directing the race life to-day along better ways.

The Freedmen's Bureau coöperated with the missionary and religious societies in promoting the education of the recently emancipated slaves. These coöperating agencies, governmental and private, were conducted by men of like mind and spirit as regards the needs of the field in which they were engaged. On the dissolution of the Bureau, many of its agents took leadership in the recently founded colleges and universities. Its chief officer, General O. O. Howard, became president of the principal school which the bureau had founded or fostered. When the reconstruction governments were organized in the Southern States they made provision for the public education of all children, black and white, as part of the organic law. These governments have been and are still held up to public obloquy and scorn by those whose ambition has been promoted by their overthrow. But they have to their everlasting credit this one unchallenged measure of statesmanship, which is not equaled in the legislative annals of either the old South or the new.

At the time of the founding of these schools industrial training was, nowhere in America, considered a stated part of the educational program. Indeed specific scholastic preparation for life's work was limited to the learned professions. A knowledge of the three R's was considered adequate preparation for the ordinary duties of life. Fifty years ago General C. S. Armstrong stood almost alone as the earnest advocate of industrial training as an agency for fitting the freedmen for their new function. To-day, the necessity for this manual training, not only for black boys, but for all of the sons and daughters of toil who must shortly join the ranks of the world's workers, is universally acknowledged and extolled. Occupational training will demand a larger and larger place in the educational program of the future.

With the rise of industrial schools there sprang up a fierce and bitter controversy between the promotion of the two contrasted types of education. The one-eyed advocates aligned themselves in battle array, and would not so much as heed a flag of truce. Indeed the race problem seems to afflict the mind as a virulent intoxicant. Men of sane and sober judgment on ordinary issues seem to lose all logical balance and composure on this problem. Where passion enters, reason takes flight. The war between the hand and the head went merrily on. The situation was full of risible and grotesque possibilities. The Greek grammar and rosewood piano in a dingy cabin even now provoke mirth. The industrial advocates by adroit acquiescence in the political subjugation of the race gained the sympathy and assistance of those whose invariable policy is to reduce the negro to the lowest possible terms. Industrial education became a byword. In the mind of one man it meant that the negro should be

taught only to know the relative distance between two rows of cotton or corn, and how to
deport himself with becoming behavior behind
the chair while his white lord and master sits
at meat; while, in the mind of another, it stood
for the awakening of the best powers and possibilities. To the white man of the South it may
have meant that the negro was to be made more
serviceable to him and more easily amenable to
his imperious will. To the white man of the
North it may have meant that the black man
was to be made a competent worker, equipped
with intelligence and skill such as are demanded
of Northern workmen. However variant may
have been the interpretations of the meaning
of industrial education, there was a general
agreement to discredit the higher culture of the
race. The industrial advocates made the more
effective popular appeal. Philanthropic contributions were turned into their coffers. The
college and university seemed doomed to star-
vation. But fortunately a more sober and rational spirit now prevails. The erstwhile partisan zealots are beginning to see what a dis-
passionate judgment has always made plain.
A population of people ten million strong, with
all the varied capacities, aptitudes, opportunities and inclinations of human nature, stands in
need of every form and variety of education

that counts for progress. Industrial and higher education are complementary factors of the same product. They are both essential parts of the educational program, each in its proper place and proportion. Howard and Hampton, Fisk and Tuskegee are in no sense antithetic institutions, but supplementary co-workers in the same field. It is perfectly evident that no one school, nor any single type of schools, is adequate to the wide circle of racial needs.

There are some good people who are generally well disposed to the race, but who think that every negro, whatever his future calling is to be, should be taught a hand trade; that every negro school, whatever its grade and pretension, should have industrial work as a part of its curriculum. They are always looking for the apron as the traditional racial badge. It is true that the great bulk of the race must for all time that we can foresee earn their living by some form of manual work. Therefore the industrial training should have a large place in the educational program. Its importance cannot be overemphasized. But there is a higher field of service, on the plane of directive intelligence and professional skill. The negro teacher needs to know as much respecting the needs and necessities of the growing mind as does the white pedagog. The negro physician meets with every form of sickness and disease that human flesh is heir to. The negro preacher certainly confronts as grave moral and spiritual problems as ever devolved upon the sacerdotal office. The best welfare of any people will not be long safeguarded unless they raise up from their own ranks men who have power and preparation to state their case and defend their cause before the just judgment of mankind. The blind must be led; the leaders must have vision. Those who must stand in the high places of leadership and authority need all of the strengthening and sustaining power that the highest discipline and culture of the school can afford.

These warring factions are now beginning to open both eyes and to appreciate the value of binocular vision. Dr. Booker T. Washington, the chief apostle of industrial training, has accepted a place on the governing board of Howard University, the leading school for higher culture. Neither has surrendered, but both have struck hands on the high ground of mutuality and good will.

Among the most interesting features of negro education may be mentioned the rise of State colleges. The Federal Government appropriates, through the land grant and the

Morrill fund, a given amount for the encouragement of agricultural and mechanical training in each state. In those states whose constitutions provide for a scholastic separation of the races these funds are divided pro rata to the racial population. As a result every Southern state has an agricultural and mechanical college for the negro race. These schools are placed under negro faculties, and the federal allowance is supplemented by state appropriations, as a partial offset to larger sums devoted to state colleges for the white youth.

Another class of schools which deserve special notice are those institutions which fall wholly under negro support and control. Each of the leading negro denominations has a chain of schools and colleges fostered along the lines of its denominational policy. These schools furnish a most hopeful and interesting indication; for, in education as in physics, no body can for long maintain its stable equilibrium whose center of gravity falls outside of the basis of support. Many of the most forceful leaders of the race, especially in religious work, are the product of these schools. They are usually characterized by a marvelous optimism and virility of spirit.

The negro race is generally referred to as a unit, and its needs and circumstances as requiring a uniform mode of treatment. On the other hand, there is no other class of our population that is subject to so wide a diversity of conditions. Unlike the Indian, he lacks territorial solidarity and homogeneous environment. There are about three-quarters of a million negroes in the Northern and Western States, in which there is no scholastic separation of races. The colored children attend school along with their white fellow-pupils, and distribute themselves among the several grades and departments of instruction according to circumstances, aptitude and opportunity. They have open to them all of the educational facilities and privileges of the most favored portions of the nation. They do not, however, as a rule, take advantage of these opportunities, especially in the higher reaches of knowledge, because they do not feel the keen incentive of remunerative opportunity. It is only the boy of exceptional ambition who will take the pains to acquire an education which is not likely to be called into requisition in the vocation which he expects to follow. The occupational proscription of the North chills the ambition of the negro youth, despite the allurements of fine educational facilities. Several hundred negro students are pursuing higher academic and professional courses in Northern colleges and universities. But, for the most part, they are from the South with the fresh inspiration of the masses upon them. The best schools in the country, both as regards public systems and chartered institutions, are open to all applicants who are able to meet the intellectual, moral and financial requirements. The scholastic separation of the races is only a local provision for states where the negroes are relatively numerous. Through the broad policy of the North and West, where our educational systems have the highest perfection, the negro is brought in touch with the best scholastic opportunities that the teaching world affords.

Again the educational needs of the city negro must be carefully differentiated from those of the rural masses. The general environment and practical conditions are so diverse that we must separate the two in any scheme of profitable discussion. There are about one and a half million negroes in Southern cities of 2,500 or more inhabitants. Adding these to the Northern fragment it leaves something like three-fourths of the race in the rural parts of the South.

In the cities school funds are quite sufficient to maintain the graded schools for the average length of term with the requisite facilities and appliances of instruction. The duplication of

schools for the two races works less economic
disadvantage in cities where the number of
both races is sufficient to supply adequate
school constituencies than in the country, where
the population is sparsely scattered. The education of the city negro makes little or no
claims on outside philanthropy. The cities are
well able to educate their own children, and
there is no more reason why they should seek
outside aid for this purpose than for any other
branch of municipal government. School teaching furnishes about the only avenue of remunerative employment for colored women
above the grade of domestic service, and hence
the best equipped members of the race rush
into this field of work. Negro school teachers,
male and female, are often the best paid wage-
earners in the several communities, and are
looked up to as leaders in social life and general
activities. This gives the negro schools a relative advantage which the whites do not enjoy.
The best equipped members of the white race
are usually engaged in more remunerative and
attractive pursuits. Such cities as Washington, Baltimore, St. Louis, Louisville and Little
Rock maintain high schools for colored youth
which do respectable secondary work, even
when measured by New England standards.
Even where the municipality does not make

provision for high schools, philanthropic and denominational institutions have made some provision, so that there is scarcely a city in the South of considerable negro population that has not a school of secondary pretensions, maintained at either public or private cost. Broadly speaking, educational facilities are open to urban negroes, which among white youth have been accounted sufficient to prepare for the ordinary duties of life. The pressing educational problem of the city negro is rather one of adaptation than enlargement. Education on its practical side should be shaped to the obtainable pursuits of the pupil. The peculiar situation and circumstances of the negro race adds new emphasis to several educational principles. The negro race furnishes the richest possible field for educational experiment. There is the broadest scope for originality, or at least the interpretation of general principles in terms of new conditions. The perfection of the urban schools is of higher importance to the welfare of the race at large, for it is in the city centers that the torch must be kindled that is to give light to the remotest rural ramifications.

The education of the country negro is of itself a thing apart. The means are so meager and the provisions are so inadequate that what little schooling he gets can be called education only by courtesy of speech. His life preparation is woefully inadequate to the requirements of intelligent citizenship. The demand is imperative that the Federal Government should bring the light of knowledge to the shady places of the South. Statesmanship and philanthropy might well unite upon this patriotic task.

The Peabody, Slater, Hand, Rockefeller and Jeanes Foundations have been devoted wholly or in part to the education of the Southern negro. But only the last named fund is aimed directly at the spot where the need is greatest.

Fifty years of negro education has accomplished certain definite results, and suggests certain definite needs.

In the first place, it has settled for all time the negro's capacity to comprehend the rudiments, as well as the higher reaches, of knowledge and apply them to the tasks of life. The race which was once denied the possession of an educationable mind is thus proved to be responsive to the same intellectual stimulus as the great Aryan race. Those who affect to doubt this proposition need themselves to be pitied for their evident incapacity to grasp demonstrated truth.

In the second place, the colleges and universities have furnished the teachers, preachers, doctors, lawyers, editors, and general leaders who are now directing the activities of the negro people, and stimulating them to higher and nobler modes of life. This professional class, like the priest Melchizedek, sprang at once to places of authority and leadership, without antecedents or beginning of days. The instrumentality which in some measure helped to fit them to their high function performed a service rarely, if ever, equaled in the history of human betterment.

In the third place, the illiteracy of the race has been cut down to forty-five per cent., which marks the most marvelous advance in the technical elements of knowledge in the annals of human progress. It is true that the vast majority of those classed as literate have a technical rather than a practical grasp of the principles of knowledge. Of those who *can* read and write, comparatively few *do* read and write effectively, and bring their acquisition to bear upon the common tasks of life. They do not generally pass constitutional tests in Alabama, as the knowing registration officers assure us. While it is true that a mere technical knowledge of letters may have little immediate bearing upon practical tasks, yet its potential value is beyond calculation. It is a possession that is not destroyed, but is carried forward. Literate parents transmit their acquisition to their children, so that the current of acquired knowledge flows on in an ever-deepening and widening channel. This mystic key with twenty-six notches unlocks all of the hidden secrets of the universe. It opens up newness of life. Transition of a people from illiteracy to literacy is like changing the temperature of a region from several degrees below to a few degrees above the freezing point. The actual change may seem to be small, yet it effects a marvelous transformation in the surrounding flora and fauna. And so with a race, the transmission of the symbols of knowledge acquired by a few years' schooling thaws out the faculties frozen by centuries of ignorance, which will shortly begin to yield a new flower and fruitage.

The cost of negro education for these fifty years has been a vast sum in the aggregate, but is utterly inadequate when counted against the task to which it has been applied. Northern philanthropy has contributed a princely sum, unequaled in any other domain of vicarious service. The Southern States have appropriated to this use a part of the public tax which the negro's industrial activities and economic position make possible. The assertion that the Southern white man imposes a gratuitous tax upon himself for the benefit of the black man's education rests upon an economic fallacy and a total misapprehension of the responsibility of the State to promote intelligent citizenship. The claim for equal educational facilities for the negro child is not based upon civic charity, but upon justice and equity and enlightened policy.

It is blatantly and bitterly asserted that the education of the negro has not solved the race problem. It was but a shallow philosophy that prophesied this outcome in the first place. Indeed much of the reversion of feeling against the higher education was due to the fact that after twenty-five years of effort the race problem had become rather intensified than abated in acuteness. The industrial advocates shrewdly enough promised the American people that their program would result in the desired solution. The prophet always puts the fulfilment as remote as possible from the prophecy and relies upon popular forgetfulness to escape his just condemnation. When the day of reckoning comes, as it surely must, those who promised to solve the problem through industrial training will be declared to have been false prophets. Education must not be condemned as a failure because it has not accomplished results that lie outside of the sphere of its function. All of our complex national problems are intensifying and growing apace with increase of education. Rapacity and greed, the tangle of labor and capital, the wrangle of rich and poor, municipal corruption, and crime against property and persons seem to proceed *pari passu* with increasing popular enlightenment. Shall we condemn the education of the American people because it does not settle these grave problems? In the North where the negro has educational advantages equal to those offered the most favored class of children anywhere on earth, and in the cities where fairly satisfactory provisions prevail, the race problem persists in its manifold forms and phases. Education enables the individual to grapple with his environment; it makes the race a component coöperating factor instead of a negative force in the general equations of progress. Without it the negro must hang as a millstone upon the neck of the nation's advance. For, in the nature of things, ignorance is a menace to knowledge, vice to virtue, and degradation to the decencies of life. But we misinterpret its function if we expect a few years' schooling to settle the problems growing out of the contact, attrition, and frictional relations of the races. These far-reaching questions depend upon a

larger policy, and must be left to statesmanship, philanthropy, and religion, and, most of
all, to the propitiation of time.

Fifty years' experience has also taught certain clear lessons as to method which should not
go unheeded.

Early educational effort in this field was devoted largely to building up religious adherents
within denominational lines. The negro race
has become attached to two leading denominations, from which there is not likely to be much
serious proselytism. As the Irishman is a
Catholic, the Scotchman a Presbyterian, so the
negro is a Baptist or a Methodist. It seems to
be a practical waste of time to attempt to wean
him from this adherence by educational induce-
ment. Up to a few years ago, Northern philanthropy was promoted largely by the religious
motive. But the denominational institutions
are becoming a diminishing factor in our general educational equation. They are not generally able to compete with those institutions
which appeal to all of the people without religious restriction. Since the organization of
the general Board of Education, this philanthropy seems to be prompted more and more
by a sense of civic and social service rather
than to promote any particular religious polity.
A wise coördination would obviate the waste

of needless duplication. There should be called
a conference of representatives of the various
religious organizations and other agencies, to
advise upon some comprehensive plan of artic-
ulation and coördination of work. There have
been founded more colleges and universities
than can be adequately maintained. The high
sounding pretensions of an institution above
the level of its grade and facilities tend to discredit the whole scheme in the minds of serious
and sensible men, and to give the negro youth
a false notion of what education really means.
This conference might well consider the advis-
ability of reducing the number of colleges to
five or six, distributed with reference to the
needs of the population, and of providing faculties and facilities that would enable them to
live up to the name assumed. The others might
well be limited to the secondary grade, as feed-
ers for the higher institutions or as finishing
schools of a lower order of pretension. The
proper distribution of industrial schools might
also claim the attention of this conference. Institutions maintained by private philanthropy
were at first compelled to assume the lowest
grades of instruction. But as the public
schools have developed this is no longer a
necessity. These institutions should relegate
to the public schools all work which falls within

their sphere, and confine their energies to those lines which fall beyond or at least outside of the scope of public instruction. It is needless to say that there should be the heartiest coöperation with Southern school authorities for the betterment of the public school system. Each Southern state should maintain a normal school, with facilities and equipment equal to the best requirements of the teaching world. The teacher is an agent of the state. It is as much a disgrace for a sovereign state to employ incompetent teachers to enlighten its future citizens as it would be to engage incompetent persons to conduct any other feature of its affairs.

If the experience of the past fifty years has done nothing but enable us to follow the right method in the future, the means and effort will not have been spent wholly in vain.

NEGROES IN PROFESSIONAL PURSUITS

The world's workers may be divided into two well-defined classes: (1) Those who are concerned in the production and distribution of wealth, and (2) those whose function is to regulate the physical, intellectual, moral, spiritual and social life of the people. The sustaining element includes workers in the field of agriculture, domestic and personal service, trade and transportation, and in manufacturing and mechanical pursuits. The governing class comprises government officials, ministers, teachers, physicians, lawyers, editors and authors. The great bulk of the population representing the toiling masses is found under the first head, while a comparatively small number is required for the so-called learned professions. In the United States the two elements are divided in the approximate ratio of twenty to one. Traditionally these two classes have been separated by a wide and deep social gulf. All honor and glory have attached to the higher professional pursuits, while those who recruited the ranks of the toiling world have been accorded a distinctively lower order of consideration and esteem. The youth who were most highly gifted by nature or favored by fortune naturally sought careers in the genteel professions, leaving those of lesser gifts and limited opportunity to recruit the ranks of the lower order of service. The present tendency, however, is against this hard and fast demarcation. Distinction is made to depend upon success, and success upon efficiency, regardless of the nature of the pursuit or vocation. Honor and shame no longer attach to stated occupations or callings, but depend upon achievement in work rather than in choice of task.

The negro was introduced into this country for the purpose of performing manual and menial labor. It was thought that for all time to come he would be a satisfied hewer of wood and drawer of water and tiller of the soil. He was supposed to represent a lower order of creation, a little more than animal and a little less than human. The dominant dogma of that day denied him capacity or aspiration to rise above the lowest level of menial service. He was deemed destined to everlasting servility by divine decree. His place was fixed and his sphere defined in the cosmic scheme of things.

There was no more thought that he would or could ever aspire to the ranks of the learned professions than that a like ambition would actuate the lower animals. Much of this traditional bias is brought forward and reappears in the present-day attitude on the race problem. There still linger a rapidly diminishing element of infallible philosophers who assume intimate acquaintance with the decrees of the Almighty and loudly asseverate that the negro is God-ordained to everlasting inferiority. But those who assume foreknowledge with such self-satisfied assurance prudently enough fail to tell us of their secret means of familiarity with the divine plans and purposes. They do not represent the caliber of mind or quality of spirit through which such revelation is usually vouchsafed to man. From this school of opinion the negro's aspiration to enter the learned professions is met with ridicule and contempt. The time, money and effort spent upon the production and preparation of this class have been worse than wasted because they tend to subvert the ordained plan. Higher education is decried; industrial education, or rather the training of the hand, is advised, as the hand is considered the only instrument through which the black can fulfill his appointed mission.

But social forces, like natural laws, pay little

heed to the noisome declaration of precon-
ceived opinion. The inherent capacities of
human nature will assert themselves despite
the denial of the doctrinaire. The advancement of the negro during the last fifty years
has belied every prediction propounded by this
doleful school of philosophy. Affirmed impos-
sibilities have come to pass. The ''never'' of
yesterday has become the actuality of to-day.

In a homogeneous society, where there is no
racial cleavage, only the select members of the
most favored class of society occupy the professional stations. The element representing
the social status of the negro would furnish few
members of the coveted callings. The element
of race, however, complicates every feature of
the social equation. In India we are told that
the population is divided horizontally by caste
and vertically by religion. But in America the
race spirit serves as both a horizontal and ver-
tical separation. The negro is segregated and
shut in to himself in all social and semi-social
relations of life. This isolation necessitates
separate ministrative agencies from the lowest
to the highest rungs of the ladder of service.
During the days of slavery the interest of the
master demanded that he should direct the general social and moral life of the slave. The
sudden severance of this tie left the negro

wholly without intimate guidance and direction. The ignorant must be enlightened, the sick must be healed, the poor must have the gospel preached to them, the wayward must be directed, the lowly must be uplifted, and the sorrowing must be solaced. The situation and circumstances under which the race found itself demanded that its ministers, teachers, physicians, lawyers, and editors should, for the most part, be men of their own blood and sympathies. The demands for a professional class were imperative. The needed service could not be effectively performed by those who assume and assert racial arrogance and hand down their benefactions as the cold crumbs that fall from the master's table. The help that is to be helpful to the lowly and the humble must come from the horizontal hand stretched out in fraternal good will, and not from the one that is pointed superciliously downward. The professional class who are to uplift and direct the lowly and humble must not say "So far shalt thou come but no farther," but rather "Where I am there ye shall be also."

There is no more pathetic chapter in the history of human struggle than the smothered and suppressed ambition of this race in its daring endeavor to meet the greatest social exigency to supply the professional demand of the masses. There was the suddenness, the swiftness of leap as when a quantity in mathematics changes signs, passing through zero or infinity. In an instant, in a twinkling of an eye, the plow-hand was transformed into the priest, the barber into the bishop, the house-maid into the school mistress, the porter into the physician, and the day-laborer into the lawyer. These high places of intellectual and moral authority into which they found themselves thrust by stress of social necessity had to be operated with at least some semblance of conformity with the standards which had been established by the European through the traditions of the ages. The high places in society occupied by the choicest members of the white race after years of preliminary preparation had to be assumed by men without personal or formal fitness. The stronger and more aggressive natures pushed themselves to the higher callings by sheer force of untutored energy and uncontrolled ambition. That there would be much grotesqueness, mal-adjustment, and failure goes without saying. But, after making full allowance for human imperfections, the fifty thousand negroes who now fill the professional places among their race represent a remarkable body of men and indicate the potency and promise of the race.

The Federal census of 1900 furnishes the latest available data of the number of negroes engaged in the several pursuits. Allowance, of course, must be made for growth in the several departments during the intervening thirteen years.

Negroes engaged in productive and distributive pursuits, 1900:

Agriculture	2,143,254
Domestic and Personal Service	1,317,859
Trade and Transportation	208,989
Manufacturing and Mechanical Pursuits	275,116
Total	3,945,118

Negroes engaged in professional service 1900:

Clergymen	15,528
Physicians and Surgeons	1,734
Dentists	212
Lawyers	728
Teachers	21,267
Musicians and Teachers of Music	3,915
Architects, Designers, Draughtsmen	52
Actors, Professional Showmen, etc	2,020
Artists and Teachers of Art	236
Electricians	185
Engineers and Surveyors	120
Journalists	210
Literary and Scientific Persons	99
Government Officials	645
Others in Professional Service	268
Total	47,219

From these tables it will be seen that only one negro worker in eighty-four is engaged in professional pursuits. Whereas, one white person in twenty is found in this class. According to this standard the negro has less than one-fourth of his professional quota.

The negro ministry was the first professional body to assume full control and direction of the moral and spiritual life of the masses. As soon as the black worshiper gained a conscious sense of self-respect, which the Christian religion is sure to impart, he became dissatisfied with the assigned seats in the Synagogue. The back pews and upper galleries did not seem compatible with the dignity of those who had been baptized into the fellowship and communion of the saints. With the encouragement of the whites the negroes soon set up their own separate houses of worship. There arose a priesthood, after the manner of Melchizedek, without antecedent or preparation. But notwithstanding all of their disabilities, these comparatively ignorant and untrained men have succeeded in organizing the entire negro race into definite religious bodies and denominational affiliations. The Baptist and Methodist denominations, which operate on the basis of ecclesiastical independence, have practically brought the entire race under their spiritual dominion. This is the one conspicuous achievement placed to the credit of the race by way of handling large interests. Passing over the inevitable imperfections in the development of the religious life of the race, the great outstanding fact remains that this vast religious estate comprising 30,000 church organizations, with a membership of over three and a half million communicants upon a property basis of $56,000,000, has been organized and handed down as its most priceless inheritance. The negro church is not merely a religious institution, but comprises all of the complex features of the life of the people. It furnishes the only field in which the negro has shown initiative and executive energy on a large scale. There is no other way to reach the masses of the race with any beneficent ministrations except through the organizations that these churches have established. The statesmanship and philanthropy of the nation would do well to recognize this fact. The negro masses must be reached and uplifted through the instrumentality of the great Baptist and Methodist denominations, which alone can lay hold upon every man and woman of the race. Indeed, it is seriously to be questioned if any belated people, in the present status of the negro, can be wisely governed without the element of priestcraft. Broadly speaking, the negro is hardly governed at all by the State, but merely coerced and beaten into obedience. He is not encouraged to have any comprehensive understanding of or participating hand in the beneficent aims and objects of government. The sheriff and the trial judge are the only government officials with whom he is familiar; and he meets with these only when his life or his property is in jeopardy. If it were not for the church, especially the great Baptist and Methodist denominations, the great mass of the negro race would be wholly shut off from any organized influence touching them with any sympathetic intent. As imperfect as the negro church must be in many of its features, it is the most potential uplifting agency at work among the people. Eliminate the church and the masses of the people would speedily lapse into a state of moral and social degeneration worse than that from which they are slowly evolving. The great problem in the uplift of the race must be approached through the pulpit. The negro preacher is the spokesman and leader of the people. He derives his support from them and speaks, or ought to speak, with the power and authority of the masses. He will be the daysman and peacemaker between the races, and in his hands is the keeping of the destiny of the race. If these thirty thousand pulpits could be filled in this generation by the best intelligence, character and consecration within the race, all of its complex problems would be on a fair way to solution. The ignorance of the ministry of the passing generation was the kind of ignorance that God utilizes and winks at; but he will not excuse or wink at its continuance. It is a sad day for any race when the best they breed do not aspire to the highest and holiest as well as the most influential callings; but it will be sadder still for a retarded race if its ministry remains in the hands of those who are illy prepared to exercise its high functions.

The rise of the colored teacher is due to the outcome of the Civil War. The South soon hit upon the plan of the scholastic separation of the races and assigned colored teachers to colored schools as the best means of carrying out this policy. Hence, a large professional or semi-professional class was injected into the arena. There were at first a great many white teachers mainly from the North, but in time the task of enlightening the millions of negro children has devolved upon teachers of their own race. It was inevitable that many of the teachers for whom there was such a sudden demand should be poorly prepared for their work. It was and still is a travesty upon terms to speak of such work as many of them are able to render as professional service.

Among the white race the teacher has not gained the fullness of stature as a member of the learned professions. They do not constitute a self-directing body; both are controlled as a collateral branch of the State or city government, of which they constitute a subordinate part. The ranks are recruited mainly from the female sex. In case of the negro teacher these limitations are severely emphasized. The orders and directions come from the white superintendent, but there is some latitude of judgment and discretion in a wise and sensible adaptation. The great function of the negro teacher is found in the fact that she has committed to her the training of the mind, manners and method of the young, who are soon to take their place in the ranks of the citizenship of the nation. While there is wanting the independent scope which the preacher exercises in the domain of moral and spiritual control, nevertheless, the teacher exercises a most important function in the immediate matters committed to her. The negro teacher has the hardest and heaviest burden of any other element of the teaching profession. Education means more to the negro than it does to the white children, who from inheritance and environment gain a certain coefficiency of power aside from the technical acquisition of the schoolroom. The teacher of the negro child, on the other hand, must impart not only the letter, but also the fundamental meaning of the ways and methods of civilized life. She should have a preparation for work and a fixed consecration to duty commensurate with the imposed task.

The colored doctor has more recently entered the arena. At first the negro patient refused to put confidence in the physicians of his own race, notwithstanding the closer intimacy of social contact. It was only after he had demonstrated his competency to treat disease as skilfully as the white practitioner that he was able to win recognition among his own people. The colored physician is still in open competition with the white physican, who never refuses to treat the negro patient if allowed to assume the disdainful attitude of racial superiority. If the negro doctor did not secure practically as good results in treating disease as the white practitioner, he would soon find himself without patients. He must be subject to the same preliminary test of fitness for the profession and must maintain the same standard of efficiency and success. The negro physicians represent the only body of colored men who, in adequate numbers, measure up to the full scientific requirements of a learned profession.

By reason of the stratum which the negro occupies in our social scheme the race is an easy prey to diseases that affect the health of the whole nation. The germs of disease have no race prejudice. They do not even draw the line at social equality. The germ that afflicts the negro to-day will attack the white man to-morrow. One touch of disease makes the whole world kin, and also kind. The negro physician comes into immediate contact with the masses of the race. He is a sanitary missionary. His ministration is not only to his own race but to the community and nation as a whole. The dreaded white plague which the nation desires to stamp out by concerted action seems to prefer the black victim. The negro physician is one of the most efficient agencies in helping to stamp out this dread enemy of mankind.

The success of the physician has been little less than marvelous. In all parts of the country he is rendering efficient service and is achieving both financial and professional success. Educated negro men are crowding into this profession and will, of course, continue to do so until the demand has been fully supplied. The race can easily support twice the number of physicians now qualified to practice.

The negro lawyer has not been so fortunate as his medical confrère. The relation between attorney and client is not necessarily close and confidential as that of physician and patient, but is more businesslike and formal. The client's interests are also dependent upon the judge and jury with whom the white attorney is sometimes supposed to have greater weight and influence. For such reasons there are fewer negroes in the profession of law than in the other so-called learned professions. The negro lawyer is rapidly winning his way over the prejudice of both races just as the doctor has had to do. There are to be found in every community examples of the negro lawyer who has won recognition from both races, and who maintains a high standard of personal and professional success. A colored lawyer was appointed by President Taft as Assistant Attorney-General of the United States, and by universal testimony conducted the affairs of his office with the requisite efficiency and dignity.

As negro enterprises multiply and develop, such as banks, building associations and insurance companies, and the general prosperity of the people increases, the negro lawyer will find an increasing sphere of usefulness and influence.

Negroes are also found in all the list of pro-

fessional pursuits and furnish a small quota to
the list of editors, engineers, electricians, authors and artists. Merchants, bankers and
business men are rapidly increasing in all parts
of the country. Apprehension is sometimes felt
that colored men will rush to the leading professions to the neglect of the humbler lines of
service. The facts show that the race has not
more than a fourth of its quota in the professional pursuits. The demand will always regulate the supply. When the demand has been
supplied in any profession the overflow will
seek outlet in unoccupied fields.

The uplift and quickening of the life of the
race depend upon the professional classes.
The early philanthropist in the Southern field
acted wisely in developing leaders among the
people. Philanthropy at best can only furnish
the first aid and qualify leaders—they must do
the rest. Any race is hopeless unless it de-
velops its own leadership and direction. It is
impossible to apply philanthropy to the masses
except through the professional classes.

The higher education of the negro is justified
in the requirements of the leaders of the people. It is a grave mistake to suppose that because he is relatively backward as compared
to the white man, his leaders need not have
the broadest and best education that our civil-

ization affords. The more backward and ignorant the led, the more skilled and sagacious
the leader should be. It requires more skill to
lead the helpless than to guide those who need
no direction. If the blind lead the blind, they
will both fall into the ditch. The professional
class constitutes the light of the race. The
negro needs headlight to guide him safely and
wisely amid the dangers and vicissitudes of an
environing civilization. But if the light in that
race be darkness, how great will be that darkness!

The negro teacher meets with every form of
ignorance and pedagogical obtuseness that be-
falls the white teacher; the negro preacher has
to do with every conceivable form of original
and acquired sin; the doctor meets with all of
the forms of disease that human flesh is heir to;
the lawyer's sphere covers the whole gamut involving the rights of property and person. The
problems involved in the contact, attrition and
adjustment of the races involve issues which
are intricate as any that have ever taxed human wisdom for solution. If, then, the white
man who stands in the high places of authority
and leadership among his race, fortified as he
is by a superior social environment, needs to
qualify for his high calling by thorough and

sound educational training, surely the negro needs a no less thorough general education to qualify him to serve as philosopher, guide and friend to ten million unfortunate human beings.

"THE NEGRO IN THE NEW WORLD" *
AND "THE CONFLICT OF COLOR"†

These volumes represent bold and comprehensive attempts to grapple with the worldwide problems of race adjustment. The contact relation and final relations of the various races of mankind constitute the one all-embracing problem of modern civilization. The two volumes are devoted to the same general object, although the one is worldwide while the other is hemispheric in scope. Mr. Weale deals, in separate chapters, with the yellow, the brown and the black races in their relation to the European, while Sir Harry is concerned only with the African and the Caucasian in the New World. There are many points of agreement as well as striking divergencies. "The Negro in the New World" is the production of a scholar, with broad historical knowledge, long tropical residence and experience, wide observation, scientific spirit

* "The Negro in the New World," by Sir Harry H. Johnston.

† "The Conflict of Color," by B. R. Putnam Weale.

and philosophic turn of mind. On the other hand, ''The Conflict of Color'' is the attempt of an impatient publicist to promote a program with reliance upon race antipathy as the chief dynamic. The authors are alike unmitigated materialists and place as full and final reliance upon the concrete and practical factors of power in the final settlement of things as if they were dealing with the parallelogram of forces. They waive wide, as it were with the left hand, all restraint of conscience and higher sanctions of religion. Sir Harry ventures the judgment that the negro may in time rise to a position of ''all around equality with the white man''; while Mr. Weale passionately espouses the age-worn dogma ''that he cannot rise in the scale above a certain point.'' Both books lack the cohesiveness of consecutive and integral treatment due to the fact that the collected articles first appeared in scattered magazine form.

The ''Negro in the New World'' narrowly misses being a monumental treatise in the field traversed. In the wide range of historical, scientific and social knowledge, in firmness of grasp upon every essential feature of race relations during the last four centuries, it easily ranks among the first of books on the subject. The faults of the book are incident to the manner of its making. ''The rolling stone gathers no moss'' because its perpetual rolling does not give the spores the requisite time to take lodgment and reach structural maturity. And so the globe-trotting sociologist is not very apt to formulate a seasoned philosophy. Successive impressions are not given time to ripen into positive opinion or settled knowledge before others are superimposed, making a composite rather than a positive photograph. The sociological sojourner is always prone to hasty preachments, and is not willing to let his impressions convey their own lesson. The value of an impression is proportional to the object impressed; it may be made on mud or on marble. But the value and convincing power of a seasoned philosophy is independent of the medium by which it is conveyed. This book is a conglomerate of facts, historical and actual, impressions and preachments. The author also reaches general conclusions from insufficient induction. Single impressive incidents are magnified out of proportion to their inherent importance. For example, the author was so profoundly impressed with the work of Hampton and Tuskegee, involving some twenty-five hundred pupils, that he confined his treatment of negro education almost to these two foundations, with barely a word concerning the other negro universities and colleges with ten times as large a number or the great system of public schools with an enrollment of over a million.

The plan of the book is most excellent. The general conclusions are set forth in the preface, which are underpinned by subsequent chapters devoted to a detailed recital and analysis of history and actuality. There are several good maps and numerous excellent photographic illustrations. The first chapter is devoted to a labored effort to show that the negro belongs to a sub-species of the Genus Homo. The general reader will glance at the pictures as he flits the pages, but will pay little attention to finely and profoundly drawn ethnological analogies. However fascinating the discussion of the ''os calcaneum'' and the ''plica semilunaris'' may be to the scientific student, it makes the general reader somnolent.

The body and bulk of the book is devoted to a historical and present account of slavery under the several European powers, and the present position of the descendants of the African captives and their European captors in the West Indian archipelago, and in the two continents of the Western world. These chapters give the book its permanent importance and value. Indeed, if these chapters were disengaged from what precedes and follows and bound in a separate volume, the weight of its authority would be greatly enhanced.

His observations, impressions and conclusions concerning the present-day negro in the United States cannot be said to be in any marked way superior to those of several other writers, except that he shows throughout an inveterate hatred of cruelty and oppression, a genuine sympathy for the weak and overborne, and a fine sense of fair-play.

In "The Conflict of Color" Mr. Weale approaches the subject from the standpoint of an advocate defending a passionate dogma rather than a philosopher in quest of the truth. His general proposition is that the white race has been vouchsafed eternal dominion over the lesser breeds of men, yellow, black and brown, and that this dominion must be maintained though the heavens fall. With picturesque and characteristic portrayal he proclaims the imminent worldwide revolution, unless his program is followed. He holds a brief for the white race in general and for England in particular. In this threatened struggle between white men and non-white men "it is flesh and blood which form the true barrier." The dominant forces of the world are physiological and psychological. Of course, the innate everlasting superiority of the white man is assumed—

a superiority which, it is declared, exists even
after death. We read: "The vigorous white
man even after death possesses a certain
majesty of form—a certain resolution—which
is totally lacking in the rice-fed Asiatics."
Shakespeare tells us that "Julius Cæsar dead
and turned to clay might stop a crack to turn
the wind away." Mr. Weale thinks that the
dust of the European is of finer quality than
that of other men. Separate chapters are devoted to the yellow, the brown and the black
factors of the problem. The final conclusion is
reached that the peace of the world depends
upon a nicely calculated balance of power
among the elements, the white man holding the
scales and England taking heed that the balance is true. Of course, the negro is accorded
the lowest position on the scale from which "he
shall be lifted nevermore," according to Mr.
Weale's dismal philosophy. On this point the
author is wholly without originality. He
adopts the same hoary dogmas that have been
bandied about the world ever since the oldest
son of Noah took risible advantage of the bibu-
lous proclivities of that ancient patriarch.
"The black man is something apart—something untouchable." Along with received doc-
trines and animosities the author falls into the
traditional inconsistencies on this subject. The

anxiety to preserve race purity is a natural and commendable one. "It is one of nature's most zealously guarded laws"; this we read on page 230; five pages further on we note: "How to keep races pure with his contact with them certainly is an acute problem; for, as he scatters far and wide, he will leave—in spite of all precautions—some traces of his blood." The writer must have forgotten his premises before reaching his conclusion within the space of four pages. What need is there of precaution to enforce nature's "most zealously guarded laws"? How is it that nature allows her laws to be set aside even with the assistance, even in spite of the vicarious assistance of precautionary human prudence? A casual visit to Rio de Janeiro, Brazil, or to Richmond, Virginia, would surely convince Mr. Weale that for some centuries nature has been a great laggard in enforcing her own zealously guarded laws, and stands sorely in need of such assistance as his brand of statesmanship can afford.

Mr. Weale has also imbibed the traditional intolerance of spirit. Such expressions as "pulpit orators," "arm-chair philosophers," "ardent evangelists," and "individuals who refuse to see things as they appear to the mass of their countrymen and who simply argue academically on all so-called color questions—

are not worthy of being read" sound quite familiar to the student of anti-slavery and pro-slavery literature. The real value of the book, from a sociological point of view, consists in the display and the interpretation of the statistics of the various races, the potentiality of physical population, and the keen observation that the momentum of racial flesh and blood will probably fix the future bounds of habitation.

Taking these books together, which portray this great drama of which the world is the stage, and the various races but players thereon, one must feel that the vital weakness is that they both, purposely and in set terms, ruled out of account the motives which have exercised the highest influence on human conduct throughout all history. It is indeed rather fashionable in present-day philosophy to ignore religion as a practicable sociological factor.

Sir Harry avows that religious traditions are not of the slightest practical utility in the negro world of to-day. Mr. Weale declares that religion has little to do with the standard of living; religion has still less to do with the balance of power; and it is these things alone to-day which have a paramount racial importance. Again, avers Sir Harry: "Given the same temptation and the same opportunities, there is sufficient of the devil left in the white man for the three hundred years of cruelty of negro (or other) slavery to be repeated, were it worth the white man's while.'' This is the severest indictment drawn against the claim of the Christian religion to assuage the inherent deviltry of man. The Christian conscience of this continent cannot allow this indictment to stand unchallenged. We need not be surprised, then, at Sir Harry's final statement: ''Money solves all human difficulties. The one undoubted solution of the negro's difficulties throughout the world is for him to turn his strong arms, his sturdy legs, his fine sight, deft fingers, and rapidly developed brain to making money.'' The doctrine is of the earth earthy. The gospel, which is based upon the dollar as the highest common factor of values, cannot salve the deepest human feelings and passions. The dollar is mighty but not almighty. ''The love of money is the root of all evil,'' says St. Paul, and subsequent history confirms the verdict. It is certainly the cause of the conflict of color throughout the world today. It was this ''cursed love of gold'' which brought the African to the Western World to exploit his physical capacities and which has carried Europeans to the ends of the earth seeking what lands and peoples they might devour.

Until there is developed a higher sanction, which transcends the physiological basis of flesh and blood, and the desideratum of the market place, there can never be peace and good will among the rival nations and races of men. To bring the world under the controlling sanction of science and religion, which ignores the prejudices and pretensions of the haughtier sections of the human race is ''the one far-off divine event to which the whole creation moves.''

THE MINISTRY

The Field for the Talented Tenth

Is it not folly to encourage the "talented tenth" of the negro race when there is no outlet for its talent? The dollar is the highest common divisor of values, therefore all acquisition is useless which is not measured in terms of this standard. Of what avail is all of this vaporous effusion about knowledge and culture or the refinement of the higher faculties and finer feelings, if it cannot be reduced to a hard metallic basis according to the requirements of the market place? Why waste time in developing, on part of this despised race, susceptibilities which transcend things concrete and material? Can there be a more risible spectacle under heaven than a negro, whose income is less than that of a Pullman porter, reading Sophocles or descanting about Kant? If it be rejoined that Socrates in rags proclaimed the gospel of inner moral freedom; that Jesus redeemed the world without a bank account, and

that Robert Burns, in honest poverty, contributed an unrivaled share to the glory of his
beloved Scotia, such rejoinder is waived aside,
with the left hand, as being impertinent, or
sacrilegious. What has that sort of thing to
do with the benighted negro in Alabama? And
besides what does Wall Street care about such
impractical doctrinaires as Jesus, or Socrates,
or that scalawag of a songster, Robert Burns?
They are quoted by neither Bulls nor Bears,
and have no rating in Bradstreet's. We live
in a practical age, whose chief concern as respects the negro is to make of him a more valuable material asset. Every able-bodied negro
ought to earn a dollar and a half a day—merely
this and nothing more. A higher compensa-
tion is likely to make him bumptious and for-
getful of his place. Away with your impotent
moralizers and dreaming doctrinaires. We
want something that is tangible, concrete and
constructive. We have a million dollars for a
workshop, but not one cent to encourage your
talented tenth who produce nothing but vac-
uous mouthings, inculcating false notions
among their people by holding out hopes impossible of realization. They are a plague to
both races.

Such is an interrogative or declarative interpretation of the prevalent attitude toward the

higher side of negro development. This attitude is in full consonance with the current philosophy of the times, which has little patience with ideals not quickly convertible into a cash equivalent. If Homer's Iliad were now originally appearing, it would doubtless be listed as the leading serial in one of the uplift magazines, and the public would be astounded to learn from red headlines that the author was offered a larger *per verba* honorarium than a noted explorer received for a description of his discovery of the North Pole, or the Intrepid One for an account of shooting wild beasts in the Jungle. What fabulous sum would not some enterprising journal offer for the exclusive copyright privileges on "The Sermon on the Mount," were it now proclaimed for the first time?

What more, then, need we expect from the conventionalized attitude toward a new people, just peeping above the horizon of the world's consideration, in such a time as this?

AMBITION FOR RULERSHIP

But, despite it all, the talented tenth of any people has an irrepressible ambition to assert and exert itself. The natural outlet for the energies of the upper ten is always in the higher domain of government, regulation and control of the lower ninety. What we shall eat or drink, or wherewithal we shall be clothed has never engaged the highest energies of the human mind. The functions of the talented tenth have always been devoted to the exercise of political, intellectual or spiritual leadership and authority over the masses. The regulative activities of society have always been conducted by a higher order of talent than the alimentary pursuits. Even where economic affairs seem to absorb a large proportion of the higher powers of the people, a closer scrutiny will disclose that the superior minds are devoted to leadership, guidance and control within the economic and industrial domain. This is the law of human evolution to which the negro forms no exception. A capable and enlightened leadership is the first prerequisite.

"For just experience proves in every soil
That those who think will govern those who toil."

The Controlling Agency

Political government is the controlling agency in society. The regulation of the religious and more intimate life of the people is relegated to the church whose sacred sanction is supreme within its sphere of operation. The secular and sacred phases of government are so nearly equal and parallel in their influence and power that we frequently observe that statecraft and priestcraft are united in a common control. The boast of America is that Church and State are separate and distinct institutions, each dominant within its own domain. But when we consider segregated elements of our population, like the Jew, the Catholic, and the negro, the sacred sanction is intensified in proportion as it is felt that the obligations and responsibilities of secular control are usurped or assumed by the large embracing body.

SELF-GOVERNMENT

All peoples, or segregated parts of peoples, desire self-direction and leadership. That governments derive their just powers from the consent of the governed passes, or used to pass, as a political axiom. That no people or class ever gives their unconstrained consent to have others rule over them is equally axiomatic. Whenever such a people are shut out from the general equation of the political government, they inevitably fall back upon the inalienable right of control over their own more intimate and social affairs. No wise ruler of a subject people ever attempts to interfere in the sacred sphere of such matters, so long as they keep within the established bounds of law and order. The negro is a subject class in the American body politic, and is practically excluded from the political equation. Let us pass by, for the present, all ethical, or even prudential, considerations involved in this condition, and confine ourselves to the plain facts which are known and acknowledged of all men. This state of things is likely to continue as far into the immediate future as our powers of prevision can penetrate. In order that any class may form an effective part in governmental control it must not only possess the right of franchise, but must contribute to the personnel of the governing body. The right of suffrage is only political power in the passive voice; the active voice of government is vested in the officiary corps. No class of people may consider themselves an effective political factor unless a goodly number of the talented tenth may reasonably aspire to the pursuit of the Science and Art of government as a career. For the negro this is practically impossible. In the State of Georgia, where there are over one million negroes, constituting almost one-half of the population, there are 1,527 government officials; of this number only 54 are colored. It is well known that these are mostly in minor clerical positions under the federal authority, and that the number is likely to diminish rather than to increase. There is probably not a single negro in governmental place under state, county or municipal control. Out of 1,500 careers required for the government of this commonwealth, not a single one is open to the ambitious negro youth. It may be safely assumed that only those who find a livelihood in any pursuit are likely to follow that calling as a career. Elimination from office means elimination from politics. No negro can hopefully aspire to be a Senator, Congressman, legislator, judge, diplomat, an officer in the Army or Navy, or even to hold important appointive administrative positions. He is almost as completely blocked from the game of politics as the female sex. Rash indeed would be considered that counsellor who should advise an ambitious negro youth to engage in politics as a vocation.

THE FIELD

Assuming then his inherent desire for self-leadership, and that the more highly endowed youth of this blood seek to exploit their powers in the direction, regulation and control of their fellowmen, where is the field to be found? Evi-

dently within the circle of racial life and interests. The Church furnishes the widest arena.
It is seriously to be questioned whether any
people in the present stage of the negro race
can be efficiently governed without the elements
of priestcraft. The negro, broadly speaking,
is hardly governed at all by the State, but
merely coerced and beaten into obedience. He
is not encouraged to have a sympathetic understanding of or a consenting part in the beneficent aims and objects of government. The
sheriff and the trial judge are the only officers
of the government with whom he is familiar,
and he meets with these only when his property
or his liberty is in jeopardy. If it were not
for the Church, the great masses of the negro
race would be wholly shut off from any organized influence touching them with sympathetic
intent. As imperfect as is the negro church in
many of its features, it is the most valuable
ally of the government. Eliminate the Church
and the task of governing this people on part
of the State would be more than doubled in
difficulty.

Within the Church the opportunity for the
talented tenth is almost unlimited. The negro
preacher has a larger influence and function
than his white confrère. He is not only the
spiritual adviser of his flock, but also their

guide, philosopher and friend. Almost every feature of leadership and authority comes within his prerogative.

Those who stand in the high places of moral and spiritual authority among the people ought to represent the highest intelligence, character and manly powers. In this arena the talented tenth may exploit its talent without let or hindrance. Here is the one unlimited field already white unto the harvest. Let none imagine that, because people are ignorant and lowly, their moral and spiritual leaders do not require all discipline, learning, culture and practical wisdom that the completest education can afford. The more ignorant the led, the more skilful and sagacious should the leader be. If the blind lead the blind, will not both fall into the ditch? To partake of the things of God and show them to this simple-souled folk requires the deepest insight into things scientific, social and spiritual. No one can be too learned or too profound to whose direction has been committed the temporal and eternal destiny of a human being.

THREE RELATIONS

The negro in his Church affiliations sustains three more or less distinct relations to the

great ecclesiastical organizations with reference to control.

(1) In the Presbyterian, Congregational and
Episcopal churches he sustains a dependent or
missionary relationship. The parent organizations in large measure supply the means for
supporting the churches and furnish general
direction and control. The negro minister has
complete charge over the immediate matters of
his individual congregation, but in the larger
matters of general plans and policies he has
little or nothing to say. His numbers are so
small that he is regarded as a negligible quantity in the general equation.

(2) The colored membership of the Methodist Episcopal Church constitute a sufficiently
large element to impress considerable influence
on the general life of the connection. They
enjoy all but complete local independence in
their quarterly and annual conferences. The
white bishop does little more than register the
decision of his colored cabinet, and serves as a
guarantee that the procedure shall be in harmony with the connectional discipline. The
colored churches are self-supporting and have
a proportional voice in all of the deliberations
of the General Conference. They are numerous
enough to be reckoned with in all important
plans and policies for the general life of the

Church. In the missionary and educational work the two races are brought into friendly and helpful relations. The negro element has the opportunity to study at first hand the intimate workings of one of the greatest organizations of the world.

(3) The great bulk of negro church members belong to those denominations which have cut loose wholly from all white control. These organizations are managed and manned from top to bottom by negro officials.

Each of these modes of relationship has its advantages and its disadvantages. But the logical and inevitable tendency is toward negro ecclesiastic autonomy, and must continue so, as long as the evil spirit of prejudice seeks and finds lodgment in the Christian Church.

Ecclesiastical Independence

There are 30,000 negro religious organizations reporting over 3,600,000 communicants. The value of the property involved amounts to $56,000,000. This wonderful religious development is found mainly in the Baptist and Methodist denominations, which from the start assumed ecclesiastical independence. The Presbyterian, Congregational and Episcopal denominations, which have enjoyed the greatest measure of white contact and control, have thriven but feebly, at the expense of much watering, as a root out of dry ground. While there is a certain orderliness and decorum of procedure, the spirit and puissance which spring from the conscious power of self-propulsion are wanting.

They fail to arouse the people and inspire them with spiritual enterprise and aggression. The more thoughtful leaders of these denominations are beginning to appreciate the heavy handicap of their subordinate positions. Annual conferences are being held of the colored segments of these several bodies in which the sprouting spirit of ecclesiastic self-control is beginning to assert itself. There are nearly 200,000 negro members of the Methodist Episcopal Church who, up to the present time, have maintained loyal vassalic relations to the parent body. But the more ambitious and aggressive spirits among them are becoming restive, even under such a complaisant subordination, and are already formulating a declaration of ecclesiastical independence.

The negro church is the most effective expression of the desire for self-government. It has been abundantly demonstrated that the church life of the race will not thrive on any other basis.

Business Talent Required

The negro minister in the conduct of his church often transacts a greater volume of business than any other member of the race in his community. He should be a business man as well as a spiritual adviser. Because of the general business inexperience of his membership, it is necessary for him to understand business principles and methods in church management. The most striking indication of worldly success among negroes is not seen in the business places which they conduct, but in the magnificent churches which they control. Whatever claims may be made for the ministry on its sacred side, in its financial feature it is as much a business as any other material interest. By virtue of his confidential relation to his membership the minister often becomes their financial adviser. He inculcates the spirit of economy and thrift—advises the inexperienced men of his congregation to start bank accounts and directs them in the purchase of property. The ministry affords a splendid field for the educated negro to exercise business as well as spiritual talent.

This immense religious estate requires 20,000 ministers and managers to conduct its affairs. In the larger cities there are costly edifices ranging from $50,000 to $100,000 in value, with an annual fiscal budget of from $5,000 to $20,000.

THE BAPTISTS

Even in the smaller cities and towns, especially among the Baptists, it is easy to find churches counting from 500 to 2,000 members over whom the pastor exercises as complete and as effective control as many a king on his first-class throne. When we consider that a colonel in the army has under him only a thousand men, the influence and power of the negro Baptist preacher begins to loom upon us. According to the policy of the church, the local pastor is supreme in his jurisdiction, and the larger opportunities for connectional activities afforded by the more highly organized bodies are counterbalanced by the intensity of his local sway. Although his principality is small, there is no authority higher than that of the prince.

THE METHODISTS

The Methodist churches have a smaller membership, but a more perfect scheme of organ-

ization. There are twenty-six bishoprics in
these several bodies. A bishop controls more
persons and exercises greater authority than
a general in the army. These positions carry
with them more authority, dignity and power
than any other openings to which the negro
youth can reasonably aspire under our civilization. These 30,000 pulpits and twenty-six
bishoprics, together with numerous collateral
and connectional offices, must be filled in this
generation; and they ought to be filled by the
most highly endowed and gifted of the race.
Every man of them should be a worthy workman that maketh not ashamed.

The Unlettered Negro Minister

The vast estate has been built up by comparatively unlettered and untrained men. This
is indeed the one miracle of the age. Here was
a set of men without preparation or announce-
ment, like Melchizedek of old, stepping at one
bound from the cotton patch into the pulpit,
and from the barber's chair to the bishop's
bench,—from the humblest to the highest human pursuits; and, with all of their disabilities,
they have succeeded in organizing and holding
together so great a body in Christian fellowship. That there have been imperfections,

grossness and grotesqueness goes without saying. But the great, outstanding, concrete fact remains that this religious estate has been developed and handed down to the rising generation as its most valuable inheritance.

When the Church history of the past fifty years shall have been written these humble unlettered priests of God will be accorded a high meed of praise which is their just due. All of the money and effort that have been expended for missionary purposes throughout the world for the past two generations have not brought as many souls into the folds of Christian churches as these ignorant black preachers, who are too often held up to ridicule by the more haughty Christian co-workers who are disposed to hide even as it were their very faces from them.

RIGHTEOUSNESS OF DOCTRINE

I have listened to negro preachers of every degree of ignorance and ungainliness. I have heard them indulge in many utterances that seemed to me to be crude, grotesque and absurd. But I have never in a single instance heard the pronouncement of a doctrine that did not point in the right direction. It is doubtless true that in many instances the life of the preacher did not square with his preachments. Even the Apostle Paul appreciates the possibility that he might himself be a cast out while being the means of saving many.

The ignorance of the negro ministry of the generation just past and now passing is the kind of ignorance that God Himself winks at; but He will not wink at this ignorance if it is allowed to continue in the generations to come. Great indeed will be the condemnation of this generation if it allows this sacred office to be conducted by ignorant and incompetent men. Their forbears, whose prayers, in the darker days, went up to the throne of God from the low grounds of sorrow, will rise up and condemn such spiritual degeneration. But, great as will be the condemnation of this generation, it will be excelled by its folly, if it neglect so great an opportunity.

Let me repeat here what I said in another place. "The Church is not merely a religious institution, but embraces all of the complex functions of negro life. It furnishes the broadest field for the exercise of talent, and is the only sphere in which initiative and executive ability can abound. Frederick Douglass began his public life as a local preacher in the A. M. E. Church, and, if a wider career had not providentially opened up to him, he doubtless would

purposes to aid the race efficiently. Philanthropy can only furnish the first aid. It encourages the leaders; they must do the rest.
The only help that is helpful in the long run is
that help which helps the helped to help themselves.

Slighting the Ministry

Educated negroes are not entering the ministry in such numbers as might be expected
when we consider the opportunities afforded by
this high calling. There is, on the other hand,
a tendency away from the ministry on the part
of the negro youth with splendid educational
equipment. During the past twenty-five years
the colored public schools of Washington, D.
C., have not furnished a half a dozen candidates for the ministry out of the several thou-
sands who have completed the High School
courses within that time. I do not now recall
a negro graduate from a Northern college
within the past ten years who has entered upon
the sacred office. A very small proportion of
the graduates of the negro colleges are turning
in that direction. The educated men have not
yet in considerable numbers turned their attention to the larger opportunities of the Baptist and Methodist churches. This indifference
or neglect is due to the natural feeling which

the educated man has against too close affilia-
tion with the more ignorant body of clergy now
filling these stations. It is also in part due to
the prevailing tendency of the times, which
seems to be away from the Church. The white
race is complaining that it is almost impossible
to induce the ablest young men to enter the
theological seminaries preparatory to the sacred office.

ATTRACTIVE SECULAR PURSUITS

Among the whites, however, there are various other lines of opportunity which prove
equally or even more enticing to the aspirations of ambitious youth. Politics, business,
law, medicine, journalism, literary and leisurely
pursuits conspire to rob the ministry of its
former claim as an exclusive field for the high
powers and talents. In the earlier years the
graduates of Harvard, Yale, and Princeton
mainly were recruited to the ranks of the ministry, not so much because they were more pious
and consecrated than they are now as because
the ministry at that time afforded the one great
field for educated men. The negro race to-day
is in the same relative position which the white
race occupied a hundred or more years ago.
The ministry requires and can maintain a

larger number of educated youth than all of the other so-called learned professions combined.

When the talented tenth awakens to a realizing sense of the demands and opportunities of the situation then will the tide turn toward the ministry as to a harvest field ready for the reaper.

THE HIGHER AIMS OF THE MINISTRY

I have so far avoided dealing with the mystic side of religion or of the sacerdotal office. The negro has a high religious and emotional endowment. Those who are endowed or endued with a double portion of this power will feel the "cosmic urge" impelling them to consecrate themselves to the work of moral and spiritual awakening. Without a conscious sense of this enduement, the pursuit of the ministry as mere enterprise is unworthy the contemplation of an honest mind.

It has been my purpose to point out in concrete terms the opportunities which the ministry affords the talented tenth, which will, of course, be doubly enhanced by the higher claims of the sacred office, which always render the devoted priest "more skilled to raise the wretched than to rise."

THE ULTIMATE RACE PROBLEM

The adjustment of the forward and backward races of mankind is, without doubt, the most urgent problem that presses upon the twentieth century for solution. The range of this problem is not limited to any country or continent or hemisphere; its area is as wide as the inhabitable globe. The factors involved are as intricate in their relations, and as far-reaching in their consequences, as any that have ever taxed human wisdom for solution. A problem as wide as human interest, and as deep as human passion, will not yield to hasty nostrums or passionate dogma, but calls for statesmanlike breadth of view, philanthropic tolerance of spirit, and exact social knowledge.

The local phase of this question in the United States has become so aggravated and acute that our solicitous philosophers are prone to treat it as an isolated phenomenon, separate and apart from the worldwide problem of which it forms a fragment. But the slow processes of social forces pay little heed to our fitful solicitude. Indeed, the bane of sociological endeavor is the feverish eagerness of the extemporaneous reformer to apply his premature program of relief to every local symptom, without adequate knowledge of social law and cause. We get a broader and better grasp on the race problem in America, when we view it in the light of the larger whole. As the astronomer cannot divine the course and career of a particular planet without a broad knowledge of the underlying laws that govern the solar system, nor the naturalist gain any adequate notion of a single animal or plant unless his observation and study are based upon a general conception of the species to which it belongs, so the student of social problems will not wisely draw conclusions from a single contributory factor, to the neglect of the general product. In the great social scheme of things, the adjustment of man to man is a unitary problem, and the various modes of manifestation, growing out of place and condition, are but parts of "one stupendous whole."

In attempting the solution of any problem of a social nature, we should first seek to separate those factors that are universal and unchanging in their operation from those that are of a special and peculiar nature. The primary principle, which runs like a thread through all human history, is the communicability of the processes of civilization among the various branches of the human family. This is, indeed, the determining factor in the solution of the universal race problem that confronts the world to-day.

It so happens, in the process of human development, that the whiter races at present represent the forward and progressive section of the human family, while the darker varieties are relatively backward and belated. That the relative concrete superiority of the European is due to the advantage of historical environment rather than to innate ethnic endowment a careful study of the trend of social forces leaves little room to doubt. Temporary superiority of this or that breed of men is only a transient phase of human development. In the history of civilization the various races and nations rise and fall like the waves of the sea, each imparting an impulse to its successor, which pushes the process further and further forward.

Civilization is not an original process with any race or nation known to history, but the torch is passed from age to age, and gains in brilliancy as it goes. Those who for the time being stand at the apex of prestige and power are ever prone to indulge in "Such boasting as the Gentiles use," and claim everlasting superiority over the "lesser breeds." Nothing less can be expected of human vanity and pride. But history plays havoc with the vainglorious boasting of national and racial conceit. Where are the Babylonians, the Assyrians and the Egyptians, who once lorded it over the earth? In the historical recessional of races they are "one with Nineveh and Tyre." Expeditions must be sent from some distant continent to unearth the glorious monuments of their ancestors from beneath the very feet of their degenerate descendants. The lordly Greeks who ruled the world through the achievements of the mind, who gave the world Homer and Socrates and Phidias in the heyday of their glory, have so sunken in the scale of excellence that, to use the language of Macaulay, "their people have degenerated into timid slaves and their language into a barbarous jargon." On the other hand, the barbarians who, Aristotle tells us, could not count beyond ten fingers in his day subsequently produced Kant and Shakespeare and Newton. The Arab and the Moor for a season led the van of the world's civilization.

Because any particular race or class has not yet been caught up by the current of the world movement is no adequate reason to conclude that it must forever fall without the reach of its onward flow. If history teaches any clear lesson, it is that civilization is communicable to the tougher and hardier breeds of men, whose physical stamina can endure the awful stress of transmission. To damn a people to everlasting inferiority because of deficiency in historical distinction shows the same faultiness of logic as the assumption that what never has been never can be. The application of this test a thousand years ago would have placed under the ban of reproach all of the vigorous and virile nations of modern times.

In present-day discussion concerning the advanced and backward races of men much stress is laid on what is called the white man's civilization, as if this color possessed exclusive proprietorship in the process. We might as well speak of the white man's multiplication table. It is impossible to conceal the secret and method of civilization as a quack conceals the formula of his patent nostrum. The lighted candle is not placed under a bushel, but on a candlestick, and gives light unto all who come within range of its radiant influence. We reward with a patent right the originator of a new process, guaranteeing him the benefit of the first fruit of the creation of his genius; but its value to the inventor is always proportional to the diffusion of benefits among his fellow men. And so the race or nation that first contrives a process or introduces an idea may indeed enjoy its exclusive benefit for a season, but it will inevitably be handed down to the rest of the world, which is prepared to appropriate and apply its principles. When a thought or a thing is once given to the world, it can no more be claimed as the exclusive property of the person or people who first gave it vogue than gold when it has once been put in circulation can be claimed as the exclusive possession of the miner who first dug it from its hiding place in the bowels of the earth. The invention of letters has banished all mystery from civilization. Nothing is there hidden that shall not be revealed. There can be no lost arts in the modern world. England to-day can utilize no process of art or invention that is not equally available to Japan. The most benighted people of the earth, when touched by the world-current, become at once "the heirs of all the ages, in the foremost files of time."

There is in every potential cult the pent-up spirit to multiply and expand itself. The impulse to disseminate as widely as possible that which stirs our own feelings or moves our own imagination is a law of social, as well as of individual, psychology. It becomes the gospel of glad tidings which we are constrained to proclaim to all the people. "Go ye into all the world, and preach the gospel to every creature" is a vital mandate that applies to every

type of civilization as well as to the religion of
Jesus. While it is true that it is only in religious propagandism that the missionary motive is conscious and purposive, yet the principles of secular civilization are no less effectively imparted because the altruistic motive
may not be a conscious part of the policy of
those promoting them. The blessings of a
higher civilization have always been vouchsafed
to overridden peoples by their ambitious ex-
ploiters, and its secret and method proclaimed
to "every creature" within the expanding circle of its influence. The self-seeking aggressor
becomes the unconscious missionary of the language, laws, institutions, customs, manners and
method of the higher form of development
which he represents; the soldier in quest of
dominion brings system and discipline; the
merchant's greed for gain introduces the comforts, conveniences and refinements of the
higher life; the pedagog looking for a livelihood spreads a knowledge of literature and
the subtler influences that minister to the
higher needs of the mind.

The European races are now overrunning
the world in quest of new resources to exploit,
and are thus coming into close and intimate
contact with the various weaker breeds of men.
The commercial spirit is the ruling passion of

the dominant world to-day. The whole surface of the habitable globe is practically parceled out among the stronger nations within defined spheres of influence. It is easy to predict the continuance of this process until ''every creature'' has been touched by modern civilization. The wonderful growth of exact knowledge and its application to the forces of nature is rendering this contact easy and inevitable. Steam and electricity have annihilated distance and banished the terrors of the deep; preventive and remedial medicine has neutralized the baneful influence of climate, and checked the ravage of disease; the hardship of pioneer life is lessened by the easy transportation of material comforts, and the loneliness of isolation is relieved by the transmission of intelligence which is flashed around the world swifter than the wings of morning. We may naturally expect that less and less heed will be paid to the fixity of the bounds of habitation of the various races and nations that dwell upon the face of the earth. The outcome of this contact constitutes the race problem of the world. As water when unrestrained flows from a higher to a lower level till equilibrium is established, so we may expect this stream to flow down and out from the higher fount until the various races and tribes of men reach an equilibrium of civilization and culture.

The place of education in human development is a principle whose importance is just beginning to dawn upon the world. Knowledge is the great equalizing factor in modern civilization. At one time it was thought that divine favor made one man lord over another. It was but a short step from the divine right of the ruler to the divine right of the race. But we are gaining a clearer and clearer conviction that racial, like individual, superiority depends upon knowledge, discipline and efficiency, which may be imparted largely by education. A people may gain or lose its place according as it holds aloof from or keeps in touch with the highest attained efficiency of the world. The powers and forces of nature are not enchanted by any sorcery of race, but yield their secret and mystery to the application of knowledge. Steam and electricity, wind and wave and sunlight, will work as willingly for a backward as for a forward race. The only advantage that the latter possesses is a predisposition to a better discipline and a higher social efficiency. It does not appear that it possesses a better grasp upon the recondite principles of knowledge. Education can be relied upon to discount if not to liquidate the disadvantage under which the

backward races labor. Nor is it necessary for
such races to repeat the slow steps and stages
by which present greatness has been attained.
He who comes at the eleventh hour is placed
on equal terms with him who has borne the
heat and burden of the day in the vineyard of
civilization. It takes the child of the most
favored race twenty-five years to absorb the
civilization of the world. The child of the
backward race can accomplish the same feat in
the same space of time. Japan is teaching the
world that she can appropriate and apply the
agencies of civilization as readily, and wield
them as effectively, as the most favored nations
of Europe. What Japan has done can be repeated by China or India, or Africa, or by any
hardy people with territorial and national integrity who will assimilate the principles of
modern progress through education and helpful contact with those nations which are now
in the forefront of things.

There are three distinct modes of race-contact: (1) where the European takes up permanent residence among the weaker race, as in
Australia, South Africa, and Hawaii; (2)
where the white man has no expectation of permanent residence, but aims merely at political
and commercial domination, as in India, North
and Central Africa, and the Polynesian Isles;

and (3) where the weaker race has been introduced into the land of the stronger for the sake of industrial exploitation, as in the United States, South America, and the West Indian archipelago. The several phases of the race problem growing out of these different modes of contact are too often overlooked in current discussion.

The conceivable lines of outcome of race-contact are: the enslavement of the weaker, or, what amounts to the same thing, its subordination into an inferior caste; the extermination of the weaker or of the stronger; amalgamation or absorption; and amicable adjustment and continuance of distinct ethnic types. All of these processes will doubtless contribute in part to the solution of this problem. The outcome will not be uniform and invariable, but will depend upon the nature and complexity of underlying conditions.

In the United States this problem presents many interesting and unique phases which cause the student of social subjects to bestow upon it a degree of attention beyond that accorded any other point of race-contact throughout the world. Its workings are watched with the keenest interest, and much reliance is placed upon its indications, because it presents the widest types of ethnic divergence in the closest intimacy of contact.

(1) In this terrible process of race-attrition, millions of the weaker races will be utterly destroyed. Whole tribes and groups and sub-races will perish from the face of the earth. Civilization is a savor of life unto life and of death unto death, and its beneficence is reserved only for those who are endowed with power to endure. The red and brown races have faded before the march of civilization as a flower before the chilling breath of autumn. The Australian has gone; the red Indian has been dispatched to his happy hunting ground in the sky; many of the scattered fragments of the isles of the sea have vanished away, while others are waiting gloomily in the valley of the shadow of death. These people have perished and are perishing, not so much by force and violence, as because they were not able to adjust themselves to the swift and sudden changes which an encroaching civilization imposed. In Hawaii they have faded under the mild and kindly dispensation of the missionary of the Cross, quite as inevitably as if swept away by shot and shell. Even the American Indian has not succumbed so much as the victim of violence as the prey of the easily communicable vices of civilization. The frontier

of civilization will always be infested with socal renegades and outcasts, who flee from the light to hide their evil deeds. They carry with them the seeds of degenerative evil which destroy both mind and body. These become the consorts of the weaker race among whom they sow the seeds of death.

It seems that, where the backward race is thinly scattered over a wide area or thickly settled upon a limited territory, the white race is inclined to take up permanent settlement, which in the end is apt to lead to the destruction of the feebler element. After the disappearance of the eliminable elements the fittest, or, at least the toughest, elements will survive. The yellow and black races, through sheer physical toughness, have demonstrated their ability to look the white man in the face and live. They not only decline to vanish before his onward march, but actually multiply and replenish the earth in face of his most strenuous exactions. In India, in South Africa, in America, and in the West Indian Islands these races are increasing at a rate that plainly forbids the prophecy of extermination. Wherever the European establishes his high standard of governmental efficiency, checks the ravages of disease, and puts an end to internal tribal strife, these races have increased their strength

at an accelerated ratio. Three-quarters of a
million slaves in the United States in 1790, under the rigors of a slave régime, had swollen
to four and a half million in 1860. While fresh
importations from Africa contributed somewhat to this remarkable expansion, yet it was
due mainly to the reproductivity of the original
stock. From 1860 to 1900, during a transitory
interval as trying as any people ever passed
through, this four and a half million had
doubled itself without outside reënforcement.
The white, the yellow and the black races will
doubtless constitute the residuary factors in
the world's ultimate race problem.

(2) In the nomadic state of society, where
population was only slightly attached to the
soil, and roamed at will, without fixity of abode
or permanence of abiding place, the expulsion
of the feebler element was not an unusual outcome of race-contact. But under modern conditions, where the whole surface of the earth
is preëmpted, and population irremovably
rooted in the soil, the hegira of a numerous
race from one land to another is the most absurd of all possible solutions. This method has
been suggested as a possible outcome of the
negro problem in America, but the proposition
has always been regarded as an idle specula-
tion. No publicist, who has regard for the san-

ity of his social judgment, would entertain it
for a moment as a serious, practicable policy.

The temporary shifting of small groups of
native peoples from one locality to another has
been, and doubtless will continue to be, a minor
process in the scheme of race adjustment. The
American Indian is confined to reservations of
diminishing boundaries, the Australian will be
pushed to the outer verge of the island continent, the moribund remnants here and there
will flee to the hills to hide them from the wrath
of the approaching pale-face. But this is
merely the preliminary stage of extermination
which is the evident doom of these flying fragments. Where the weaker race constitutes the
numerical majority, and thrives in multiplying
numbers, the European is apt to withdraw under the sheer force of racial momentum. The
white race has been expelled from most of the
West Indian Islands, because the black race
proved too prolific in such a congenial habitat. In the United States the whites are
gradually growing relatively fewer in the black
belts, and the bedarkened regions are steadily
growing in intensity. Wherever any one of
the hardier races is thickly settled it is not
likely to be interfered with by competing numbers of any other race. Where the stronger
race sends out only a handful of representa-

tives to command the superior governmental and commercial positions, ultimate expulsion of the stronger is the only predictable result.

(3) Wherever the white man has touched the weaker races he has never scrupled to mingle his blood with theirs. The sons of the gods are ever prone to look lustfully upon the daughters of men. There arises a composite progeny which enters as an important factor into race-adjustment. In this regard it is necessary to make a sharp distinction between the Teutonic and Catholic races of Europe. The Latin or Catholic nations give the mongrel offspring the status of the father, while the Teutonic or Protestant races relegate them to the status of the mother race. In one case the white race becomes mongrelized while the feebler element remains comparatively pure; whereas, in the other, the white race remains pure while the lower race becomes mixed. In Cuba, where the Latin dispensation prevails, the mixed element is returned as white; but in the United States it is classed with the negroes. In Cuba, Porto Rico and South America the mongrelization of the races is either an accomplished or an assured result.

The Mohammedan religion and the Catholic branch of the Christian faith are, without dispute, superior to the Protestant type in allaying the rancor of race-passion. The amity of race feeling in Constantinople and Rio de Janeiro is in marked contrast with that at Richmond and Baltimore. If the Mohammedan and Catholic races were in the ascendency in the world's affairs, the mongrelization of races would assume a different aspect from what may be predicted under the dominance of the Teuton. But as these more tolerant races seem to have spent their forces as world-ruling factors, we may as well place the stress of attention upon what is likely to take place under the dominance of the more intolerant races of northern Europe. An increasing mixed breed will be the outcome of illicit intercourse between the white male and the darker female, and will be thrown back upon the status of the mother. Where the number of the weaker race is small in proportion, this will form an important factor in the final solution, but where the number is relatively large it may be regarded as a negligible quantity.

A continuous infusion of white blood would bring about a closer and closer approachment between the two types, until all social restrictions would be removed upon the disappearance of the ethnic difference upon which it rests. If the negro element in our American cities was not constantly reënforced by black invasion from the rural districts it would be easy to predict its final disappearance through extinction and amalgamation. But in South Africa, portions of the West Indies, and the heavy negro states of America, race fusion will have but little determining effect upon the general equation.

According to the United States census of 1890, there were 956,689 mulattoes, 105,135 quadroons, and 69,936 octoroons. The proportion of negro blood in this admixture would represent about 500,000 negroes of pure blooded type. It must also be remembered that illicit intercourse between the races is largely limited to the mixed element, and there is likely to be very little fresh absorption of undiluted blacks. On the other hand the degree and grades of admixture returnable in the census represent but a small proportion of persons actually affected by admixture of blood. It is estimated that fully three-fourths of the colored race are affected by some slight strain of white blood. The octoroon and the quadroon class will be apt to pass over clandestinely to the white race, in order to escape the inferior status of their mother blood. Such transition tends to widen the breach between the races. The white race will take in only such homeopathic dashes of negro blood as to remain sub-

stantially pure. The white blood already in-
fused in the negro race will be more equably
diffused and the colored American will represent a more solid ethnic entity, being brown
rather than black in color.

We are forbidden to prophesy any general
fusion of races by the sure knowledge that,
when the white race becomes conscious of what
it deems the evil of miscegenation, it bars the
process both by law and public sentiment. In
all the heavy negro states the laws forbid intermarriage between the races, and, even where
there is no law, public sentiment is pronounced
and unmistakable.

(4) There will be an attempt to relegate the
backward race to an inferior status wherever
the white race takes up permanent residence.
When slavery was an accepted system throughout the civilized world, the process was simple
and easy. But, in the absence of the fixed
status of servitude, the same result is sought
to be accomplished through connivance and
cunning. This policy is most clearly noticeable
in the United States. Although the negro enjoys theoretically all the rights and prerogatives of an American citizen, yet in public sentiment and in actual practice he is fixed to an
inferior social, civil, political, and industrial

status. But this scheme of subordination can only be local and temporary.

A caste system must be like a pyramid, each layer representing a broader area than the one resting upon it. It is impossible to form a lasting system of caste with a superincumbence of ten white men upon the substratum of one negro. If the negroes were everywhere relatively as numerous as they are in some parts of the Southern states, and if the whites were not smothered out by numerical predominance, the permanence of caste might be counted on as a calculable factor. The slave system in America was doomed to destruction because the slave element was not sufficiently numerous to support the entire white population. Even in the South there were only five hundred thousand slaveholders, who controlled four million slaves, leaving six million free whites practically on the level with negro bondmen, a condition which could exist only until the non-slaveholding class became conscious of their condition. The free laborer of the North was the first to awake to consciousness of the fact that he was made the competitor of slave labor, a condition which he resented and resisted to the bitter end. The overthrow of slavery was due to economic as well as to moral and philanthropic causes. It is impossible to relegate the negro to any status without at the same time affecting a sufficient number of white men to make up the full quota of that status. Any degradation placed upon the negro laborer must react upon the white workman of the same grade.

The caste system in America is bound to fail, not so much from humanitarian considerations as because it lacks a sufficient physical basis upon which to rest. Abraham Lincoln possessed an illumined understanding. His motto that a country cannot exist half slave and half free is just beginning to be appreciated by those who are devoted to the study of our complex national problems. New England does not make a fixed status for the negro, because, as President Eliot informs us, she does not deem it worth while. The country at large will ultimately be brought to the view that it is not worth while to establish a separate and distinct status for a diminishing fraction of the total population.

(5) After the red and brown races shall have perished from the face of the earth; after the fragmentary peoples have been exterminated, expelled or absorbed; after the diffusion of knowledge has established a world equilibrium, there will be left the white, the yellow and the black as the residuary races, each prac-

tically distinct in its ethnic identity, and occupying its own habitat. We can only prophesy peace, amity and good will among these types, who will more fully appreciate than we do now that God has made of one blood all nations to dwell upon the face of the earth, within assignable bounds of habitation. Whether this will be but a stage in the ultimate blending of all races in a common world type transcends all of our present calculable data, and must be left to the play of the imagination.

I SEE AND AM SATISFIED

The vision of a scion of a despised and rejected race, the span of whose life is measured by the years of its Golden Jubilee, and whose fancy, like the vine that girdles the tree-trunk, runneth both forward and back.

I see the African savage as he drinks his palmy wine, and basks in the sunshine of his native bliss, and is happy.

I see the man-catcher, impelled by thirst of gold, as he entraps his simple-souled victim in the snares of bondage and death, by use of force or guile.

I see the ocean basin whitened with his bones, and the ocean current running red with his blood, amidst the hellish horrors of the middle passage.

I see him laboring for two centuries and a half in unrequited toil, making the hillsides of our southland to glow with the snow-white fleece of cotton, and the valleys to glisten with the golden sheaves of grain.

I see him silently enduring cruelty and torture indescribable, with flesh flinching beneath the sizz of angry whip, or quivering under the gnaw of the sharp-toothed bloodhound.

I see a chivalric civilization instinct with dignity, comity and grace rising upon pillars supported by his strength and brawny arm.

I see the swarthy matron lavishing her soul in altruistic devotion upon the offspring of her alabaster mistress.

I see the haughty sons of a haughty race pouring out their lustful passion upon black womanhood, filling our land with a bronzed and tawny brood.

I see also the patriarchal solicitude of the kindly hearted owners of men, in whose breast not even iniquitous system could sour the milk of human kindness.

I hear the groans, the sorrows, the sighings, the soul striving of these benighted creatures of God, rising up from the low grounds of sorrow and reaching the ear of Him Who regardeth man of the lowliest estate.

I strain my ear to supernal sound, and I hear in the secret chambers of the Almighty the order to the Captain of Host to break his bond and set him free.

I see Abraham Lincoln, himself a man of sorrows and acquainted with grief, arise to execute the high decree.

I see two hundred thousand black boys in blue baring their breasts to the bayonets of the enemy, that their race might have some slight part in its own deliverance.

I see the great Proclamation delivered in the year of my birth of which I became the first fruit and beneficiary.

I see the assassin striking down the great Emancipator; and the house of mirth is transformed into the Golgotha of the nation.

I watch the Congress as it adds to the Constitution new words, which make the document a charter of liberty indeed.

I see the new-made citizen running to and fro in the first fruit of his new-found freedom.

I see him rioting in the flush of privilege which the nation had vouchsafed, but destined, alas, not long to last.

I see him thrust down from the high seat of political

power, by fraud and force, while the nation looks on in sinister silence and acquiescent guilt.

I see the tide of public feeling run cold and chilly, as the vial of racial wrath is wreaked upon his bowed and defenceless head.

I see his body writhing in the agony of death as his groans issue from the crackling flames, while the funeral pyre lights the midnight sky with its dismal glare. My heart sinks with heaviness within me.

I see that the path of progress has never taken a straight line, but has always been a zigzag course amid the conflicting forces of right and wrong, truth and error, justice and injustice, cruelty and mercy.

I see that the great generous American Heart, despite the temporary flutter, will finally beat true to the higher human impulse, and my soul abounds with reassurance and hope.

I see his marvelous advance in the rapid acquisition of knowledge and acquirement of things material, and attainment in the higher pursuits of life, with his face fixed upon that light which shineth brighter and brighter unto the perfect day.

I see him who was once deemed stricken, smitten of God and afflicted, now entering with universal welcome into the patrimony of mankind, and I look calmly upon the centuries of blood and tears and travail of soul, and am satisfied.

The
SKATER'S
HANDBOOK

The
SKATER'S
HANDBOOK

John Misha Petkevich

CHARLES SCRIBNER'S SONS · NEW YORK

401915

Library of Congress Cataloging in Publication Data
Petkevich, John Misha.
    The skater's handbook.

    Bibliography: p.
    Includes index.
      1. Skating—Handbooks, manuals, etc. 2. Skating—
Societies, etc.—Directories. 3. Skating—United
States—Equipment and supplies—Directories. I. Title.
GV849.P387 1984   796.91'025'73   83-16514
ISBN 0-684-18016-2

Opposite title page: *Peggy Fleming (1968 Olympic Champion) and Robin Cousins (1980 Olympic Champion) in a beautiful moment during* Ice *at New York
City's Radio City Music Hall in 1983. Margaret S. Williamson*

To my mother and father,
who did everything right

CONTENTS

ACKNOWLEDGMENTS

This book could not have been completed without the help of many gracious individuals. In particular, I would like to thank the following, with whom I was in constant contact during the preparation of the manuscript:

Helen (Pat) Cataldi, the curator of the United States Figure Skating Association Hall of Fame and Museum, was an indispensable source of information and assistance, particularly in obtaining photographs and verifying facts.

Jean C. Winder, Ritter F. Shumway, Benjamin T. Wright, and Frederick C. LeFevre of the USFSA freely provided me with specific information about the workings of their organization, about the International Skating Union, and about the course of skating history.

Justine Smith of the Ice Skating Institute of America cordially shared much useful information about recreational skating in the United States.

I must also thank the equipment manufacturers and distributors who responded to my letters and forwarded the necessary details about their products.

Several members of the Canadian Figure Skating Association also helped in every way possible: David M. Dore, Barbara Graham, and Petra Burka (1965 World Champion).

A very special thanks to Mary, Michelle, and Lisa for their support and patience, particularly during the final phases of preparing the manuscript.

FOREWORD

I have known John Petkevich for some time, but even before we were formally introduced I was a great admirer of him as a champion as well as one of the finest representatives figure skating has ever had. Not only was he the 1971 United States Men's Champion but he was also a student at Harvard University—soon to become a Rhodes scholar. Now he has become an author. It is exciting for me to know someone with the amount of talent and intellect that John possesses, and enjoyable to see him apply these attributes to the common good.

This book *is* for the common good of all figure skaters. It is not the kind that describes the struggle of a child who starts with nothing and, against all odds, becomes an Olympic gold medalist. Rather, it is a book that will help you avoid some of the costly mistakes that are inevitable, particularly if you are a person unfamiliar with this sport.

Skating is costly and complex. Choosing the right equipment, instructor, and facility can be difficult, if not impossible, without some sort of guidance. How, without any assistance, can someone begin skating and correctly choose an instructor right for his or her level? Or buy the right quality of skates, or decide how much time should be spent on the ice to match their desire for improvement? Needs vary, and it isn't always necessary to use the highest quality skates, or take lessons from a coach of champions to reach the peak of your individual talent level. This book

can help you determine your specific needs. It introduces the beginner to all of the complexities of figure skating. It also helps the novice and accomplished skater make decisions or adjustments needed after certain plateaus of improvement.

As a veteran (although I'm not that old) of many years of competitive figure skating, I have learned many things. I have also made many costly mistakes. I have observed the neophyte become an instant expert following the decision to pursue competition seriously. But there is no way you can walk into a highly specialized and technical field without some sort of education. *The Skater's Handbook* can give you that education and competitive direction. That is why this book is so important and timely. I hope you will learn from it and refer to it whenever necessary. Enjoy!!

—SCOTT HAMILTON
World Figure Skating Champion
for 1981, 1982, and 1983

The
SKATER'S
HANDBOOK

THE STORY OF SKATING

HOW IT ALL STARTED

No one knows when the very first pair of skates was donned, heralding the birth of skating. The first literary reference to skating occurs in the *Elder Edda,* a collection of Norse mythical and heroic poems. Although this manuscript was transcribed in the thirteenth century, most of the poems date from the tenth century and before. And William Fitz-Stephen, an Englishman, mentions skating in a manuscript written in Latin and dated 1189. The earliest dated skates, which transported people some time between A.D. 700 and 900, are made of bone and were found in Bjorka, Sweden.

The impetus to skate was probably at first a practical one, with skaters taking to the ice for transportation and for hunting. They could travel far greater distances in the same amount of time using skates on frozen rivers and lakes than they could using snowshoes or sleds on snow-covered ground. On the heels of these practical considerations surely came pure pleasure. The joy of gliding across the ice, however awkward on bone skates, must have enticed more than one merry Scandinavian onto its glassy surface.

Wooden skates with iron facings appeared in the fourteenth century,

Axel Paulsen, best known for inventing the Axel jump, was an expert in "creative figures," which were designs of the skater's choosing and invention. He won the special figures contest at the International Competition in St. Petersburg in 1882. Courtesy USFSA

and they are depicted in a fifteenth-century woodcut of St. Lidwina, the patron saint of skating. They had a graceful curve in front and terminated under the heel of the foot. These were more than likely the skates worn by the Dutch in 1572 when they massacred a squad of Spanish soldiers who were attacking the Dutch fleet in Amsterdam's IJesselmeer. In war, their use had been proven.

From the sixteenth century to the present, skating has appeared in etchings, paintings, posters, and sculptures. The Dutch masters of the sixteenth and seventeenth centuries were particularly fond of skating scenes: the works of Brueghel, Van der Neer, de Hooch, and even Rembrandt show how important skating was in the daily lives of the people.

Everyone from peasants to royalty took to the ice. Many a royal personage enjoyed a good skate—King Harold of Saxony (eleventh century), Marie Antoinette of France (in the 1770s), Queen Victoria and Prince Albert of England, and even Napoleon Bonaparte. Goethe found skating a healthy pastime, one whose tranquillity aided poetic reflection, as did Henry David Thoreau during his sojourn at Walden Pond.

It wasn't so easy for everyone! Courtesy USFSA

In the early 1800s, the steel blade made its appearance and prepared the way for different types of skating. Greater precision was possible with steel blades, and skaters were better equipped to carry their particular skills further. This opened the way for the development of two kinds of skates: one for speed skating and one for figure skating. From this time on, the two distinct sporting activities developed rapidly in different directions. The invention of artificial ice and the construction of indoor ice rinks in the nineteenth century provided additional impetus for the two sports to go their own ways.

A group venture. Courtesy USFSA

THE RISE OF CLUBS AND COMPETITIONS

The rapid development of skating was helped along by the formation of
skating clubs and associations. In 1742, the Edinburgh Skating Club was
founded; London followed suit about a hundred years later. The first U.S.
skating club was the Philadelphia Skating Club, founded in 1849. The
New York Skating Club followed in 1863, and the Cambridge Skating
Club in 1898. Although the Cambridge Skating Club no longer has the
prestige it once did, it is one of the few clubs that has remained in its
original setting since its inception. Furthermore, its founder, George H.
Brown, was very influential in bringing the "international style" (see
below) to the United States. The Cambridge Skating Club sponsored the
first exhibition of the international style on February 22, 1908.

During the latter part of the nineteenth century, skating clubs blos-
somed all over the world, including the Vienna Skating Club (1867), the
Nouvelle Société (Paris, 1872), the English National Skating Association
(1879), the National Amateur Skating Association (U.S.A., 1886), and the

International Skating Union, the oldest winter-sport international governing body (1892).

As skating organizations proliferated, so did competitions. The first international competition, held in Vienna in 1882, was called the International Skating Tournament. The first World Championships took place in St. Petersburg in 1896, and the International Skating Union sponsored the first Pair Skating Championships in 1908. Skating was first included in the Olympics in the 1908 Summer Olympic Games (there were no Winter Olympic Games until 1924). The first United States National Championships, in the international style, were held in 1914.

Although only a few countries participated in the first international competitions and even fewer had national championships of their own, the numbers have increased dramatically over the last three decades. There are now twenty-nine national competitions sanctioned by the national governing bodies of the International Skating Union. At the 1982 World Championships, twenty-four countries were represented.

THE EVOLUTION OF SKATING

In the nineteenth century, formal recreational and competitive skating (competitive being understood to apply to any contest of skills) was of two types: creating geometric designs on the ice, and dancing in pairs with a formal and stylized posture. It was all very restrained and proper.

Jackson Haines

In the 1860s, the American Jackson Haines (who may have been a ballet master, a ballroom dancer, or an actor—his exact background is not known) created a revolutionary style of skating that became known as the international style. The principal difference between Haines and other skaters of his generation was that he treated skating as an art form. He skated to music and brought a number of balletic moves to the ice, and he also created new moves based on the many possibilities inherent in skating. This became the foundation of what has evolved into "free skating"—jumps, spins, footwork, and positional moves skated to music.

Haines was not accepted in the conservative skating circles of the United States, so he crossed the Atlantic in the hope of finding recognition for this new art form. All did not go well at first. In England, the skaters were practiced in the English style: they skated with a rigid torso,

Dancing on ice to a live band, in what may have been the English style, stiff and regulated and somewhat akin to square dancing. Courtesy USFSA

concentrated on creating patterns on the ice, and used restrained movements when skating as couples. They were not about to relinquish their style for something that seemed vulgar and plebian. Haines moved on to Vienna. It was there, skating to the music of Johann Strauss, Schubert, and Mozart, that he found success and notoriety. The international style of skating was born, forming the basis for the evolution of modern figure skating as we know it.

Jackson Haines died in 1875, and the world of skating was very slow to adopt the new style. There were some, however, who had been touched by its fluidity and grace, and they carried the tradition on.

At the 1890 International Competition in St. Petersburg, the international style received its first official stamp. The mere fact that there were

Jackson Haines is considered by most people to be the father of modern figure skating. To a large extent, he opened the doors for the development of free skating. Courtesy USFSA

Ulrich Salchow won ten World Championships, more than anyone else in the history of figure skating. He invented the Salchow jump. Courtesy USFSA

Emphasizing style and artistry, Gillis Grafstrom was the only man in the history of the sport to have captured the Olympic gold three times. Courtesy USFSA

entrants from important skating countries competing in the style gave it a great boost. Eighteen years later, the skaters George H. Brown and Irving Brokaw introduced the style to the United States.

Other Early Developments

Ulrich Salchow of Sweden was not the first World Champion, but he was certainly one of the first skaters after Haines to leave a mark on the sport. A very strong skater, Salchow emphasized athleticism and executed more difficult technical maneuvers than had previously been attempted. His technical expertise brought him ten world championship gold medals (he missed out on only one in the years from 1901 through 1911). He invented the Salchow jump, now a standard part of any free skater's repertoire.

The next big step was taken by Gillis Grafstrom, also of Sweden. In everyday life, Grafstrom was an architect. He brought something a bit different to the world of skating. Taking Salchow's contributions as a foundation, Grafstrom went on to emphasize the art of skating. He too was a strong athletic skater, but he coupled this with a sophisticated style that suited the music he skated to. At that time, all skating programs were improvised, and Grafstrom was able to improvise a skating program that meshed remarkably well with the music played. Grafstrom won three Olympic titles (1920, 1924, and 1928) and three World titles (1922, 1924, and 1929).

The Middle Era

In the late 1920s there was a rather unexpected development—skating suddenly became widely popular. The first international skating star appeared. After winning ten World championships and three Olympic gold medals, Norway's Sonja Henie went on to become a movie star and the star and producer of many musical ice extravaganzas. Henie was an excellent spinner and a vibrant personality, and it was she who brought skating to the public for the first time.

Karl Schaefer of Austria was at the same time pushing forward the technical boundaries of the sport by adding a second revolution to single jumps. Although double jumps were rare even in a Schaefer program, he did set the stage for the cataclysmic changes that were to occur after World War II. He won seven World championships and two Olympic gold medals.

The decade of the thirties saw two new developments. In the 1936 European Championships, Cecilia Colledge of Great Britain performed the first double jump in the ladies' event. In addition, she may have been the first skater to enter a competition with a program choreographed in advance.

Athleticism and Art

Shortly after World War II the international skating world was revolutionized again when Dick Button burst upon the scene doing double jumps that sent everyone back to the drawing board. To every single jump that was performed during that period, he added another turn. And as if that were not enough, he executed the first triple jump, now one of the most important technical moves in a skater's program. Button has

Although Cecilia Colledge won the World Championships only once, in 1937, she contributed far more to both the artistic and technical sides of the sport than her record might indicate. Courtesy USFSA

been the only American ever to win two Olympic gold medals and five World gold medals.

There were a number of tremendous skaters who followed Dick Button's lead while at the same time continuing to refine the stylistic aspects of skating. Some of these were Hayes Alan Jenkins (1956 Olympic Champion), Tenley Albright (1956 Olympic Champion), David Jenkins (1960 Olympic Champion), Carol Heiss (1960 Olympic Champion), and Don Jackson (1962 World Champion).

Skating began to become a true art form under the influence of Ludmila and Oleg Protopopov, who won the pairs event in the 1964 and 1968 Olympic Games. They brought a classical line to skating that had never before been quite so developed and sophisticated, and they paid meticulous attention to every detail of artistic impression.

Dick Button, 1948 and 1952 Olympic Gold Medalist, is considered one of the all-time greats. While skating, he maintained his interest in educa-tion and subsequently became a successful businessman in the world of sports television. Courtesy Dick Button

Tenley Albright overcame polio and won the 1956 Olympic Gold Medal. She then pursued her education and became an eminent surgeon and sports medicine consultant. Courtesy USFSA

Among the skaters who followed in this tradition were Peggy Fleming, Melissa and Mark Militano, Janet Lynn, Toller Cranston, and John Curry. Each of these great skaters brought something artistically special to figure skating. Fleming brought exquisite grace; the Militanos introduced a line that was both dramatic and elegant; Lynn brought the reality of the total skater, excellence in both technique and artistry; Cranston created dramatic and innovative forms and moves; Curry drew inspiration from classical ballet. In my own skating, I strove for musical expressiveness coupled with unusually high jumps that created a dramatic moment. Of all the skaters mentioned above, only two—Peggy Fleming and John Curry—captured the Olympic gold. Perhaps it was the Jackson Haines story all over again; the skating world was simply not ready for the innovations and did not know how to react to them.

World and Olympic Champion Hayes Alan Jenkins displays some of his elegant, athletic style. His brother, David, was also an Olympic Champion. Courtesy USFSA

Carol Heiss, 1960 Olympic Champion, a vibrant and very athletic skater with charm both on and off the ice. Courtesy USFSA

Ludmila and Oleg Protopopov, 1964 and 1968 Olympic Gold Medalists, had supreme artistic refinement. They, more than any of the other great skaters of that era, are responsible for the present emphasis on artistry and style. Courtesy of Ludmila and Oleg Protopopov

In the amateur world of competitive skating, the focus ultimately centers on athleticism. This is understandable, particularly when there is a sudden step forward in technical achievement, as we are seeing in the difficult feats executed by skaters such as Dorothy Hamill (who, along with Sonja Henie and Peggy Fleming, has helped bring skating to the public), Linda Fratianne, Jan Hoffman, Scott Hamilton, Robin Cousins, and Elaine Zayak.

Yet even now, the ice dancing teams of Jayne Torvill and Christopher Dean (Great Britain) and Judy Blumberg and Michael Seibert (United States) are striving to create new artistic directions. There is no doubt that as time passes, there will once again be a change in emphasis to the artistic aspects of skating. We can see this happening already at some of the lower levels of competition.

A daringly innovative pair team with impeccable line, Melissa and Mark Militano, 1973 United States Pair Champions. Courtesy of Melissa and Mark Militano

ICE DANCING

Ice dancing is quite distinct from pair skating, which consists of pair lifts, spins, throws, death spirals, and other positional moves, as well as singles spins, jumps, footwork, and positional moves. The focus in ice dancing is on sequences of intricate and elaborate steps and partnering positions that complement the music and express its rhythm and mood. Ice dancing did not become a world championship event until 1952, and was allowed in the Olympic Games only as recently as 1976.

For the first eight years of its inclusion in the World Championships,

Ludmila Pakhomova and Aleksandr Gorshkov, the great Soviet ice danc-ing team, captured the World dance title six times; they also won the 1976 Olympic Gold Medal. Courtesy Dick Button

the event was dominated by the British. They made a clear distinction between dance and pairs, priding themselves on precise, difficult footwork done in perfect unison. The teams of Westwood and Demmy and Denny and Jones excelled.

British domination of ice dancing was broken by the Romanovs of Czechoslovakia in 1962. For four years they held the title, until the British team of Towler and Ford reclaimed it.

In 1970, the Russians rose to dominate the event for the next decade. Ludmila Pakhomova and Aleksandr Gorshkov won the Worlds for six years. Their dancing was exciting and theatrical. Instead of concentrating only on the feet, the Russians thought about all parts of the body as they pertained to the dance in progress. This kept them at the top until the British once again got a firm hold. Jayne Torvill and Christopher Dean could do the same thing better, and with far greater versatility, and they claimed the World Championship in 1981 and 1982.

PROFESSIONAL SHOWS

The first professional show, aside from those that Jackson Haines created for himself while touring Europe, took place in 1913 in Berlin. Its star was Charlotte Oelschlagel (known simply as Charlotte), and she brought the same production to New York's Hippodrome in 1915, where it was renamed *Flirting in St. Moritz*. It was a great hit and so was she.

At about the same time, skating began to be seen in hotels, restaurants, and theaters. In New York City the Biltmore, the St. Regis, and Hammerstein's Roof Hotel hosted skating shows. Other hotels with ice spectacles were New York's Hotel New Yorker in the 1940s, the Morrison and the Stevenson hotels in Chicago, the Winton Hotel in Cleveland (1914–16), the Ben Franklin in Philadelphia, the Waldorf in New York, and the Beverly Hilton in Los Angeles. These and other prominent hotels across the country iced the way for many important skating stars. Healey's Golden Glades and Schubert's Forty-fourth Street Theater (New York City) and the Cafe Bristol (Los Angeles) coupled a skating show with dining in the second decade of the twentieth century. Most of these shows were done on relatively small ice surfaces. Nonetheless, they hosted stars such as Norval Baptie, Gladys Lamb, Dorothy Lewis, Everett McGowan, Ruth Mack, and Arthur Godfrey, who staged his television show on ice in 1952.

In 1936, Oscar Johnson and Eddie and Roy Shipstad debuted their

Charlotte in her "Dying Swan" routine. She starred in the first motion picture featuring ice skating, the 1916 Frozen Warning. Courtesy Dick Button

ice-skating road show, *Ice Follies. Ice Capades* hit the road in 1940 under the direction of John H. Harris, and five years later *Holiday on Ice* was born. These are no longer the little road shows they were then. Shortly after their inception, they started growing extravagantly, and many stars' names have graced their marquees. No cost is spared to make the presentation spectacular—costumes, lighting, and sets all glitter.

Although even now there is plenty of glamour and vibrancy, the trend is toward shows that appeal to children. *Ice Follies* and *Holiday on Ice* have merged to become *Walt Disney's World on Ice* and *Disney's Great Ice Odyssey. Ice Capades* has adopted the Smurf theme (Smurfs are gnome-like T.V. cartoon characters, each having a distinct, singular character trait).

At the same time that Johnson and the Shipstads were organizing *Ice Follies,* Sonja Henie brought her own ice show to Madison Square Garden, breaking attendance and receipt records. The show toured and

Katherine Healey, figure skater, ballet dancer, and movie star (Six Weeks, 1982). This teenage phenomenon is a familiar performer to those who attend Superskates, *the benefit for the Olympic fund held at Madison Square Garden every year, and she has managed to pursue three very rigorous endeavors with great success.* Margaret S. Williamson

eventually evolved into the *Hollywood Ice Revue*. In the 1940s, along with Arthur Wirtz, Henie produced *It Happens on Ice* at the Center Theater in New York City. These two shows (the *Hollywood Ice Revue* ran for twenty-one years, thirteen of which featured Henie), along with eleven starring roles in motion pictures, made Henie one of the most famous skaters in history.

An unsuccessful show blending ballet and skating was staged in 1930 at Covent Garden, London. Belita, a skater turned movie star, and the pair team of Pierre Brunet and Andree Joly (1928 and 1932 Olympic Pair Champions) starred in the production, but it was panned by the critics.

Musicals hit the ice in London in the 1950s and were greeted with some enthusiasm. *Sleeping Beauty, Jack and the Beanstalk, Sinbad the Sailor,* and *Babes in the Woods* were among the shows iced at that time.

Since then, there have been two productions that are particularly notable for their attempts to make show skating a legitimate art: Toller Cranston's *The Ice Show* and John Curry's *Ice Dancing*. Both drew from the heritage of Jackson Haines, Charlotte, Sonja Henie, and the musicals. Cranston and Curry added their own personal comments to theatrical ice presentations. Although their companies are no longer together, temporary companies have formed to present new versions of theatrical ice skating. In February 1983, *Ice,* starring Peggy Fleming, Toller Cranston, and Robin Cousins, played for three weeks at Radio City Music Hall in New York. It is only a matter of time before a formula is found that will make ice skating a legitimate theatrical art form.

2

THE
REWARDS OF SKATING

In our time, skating is rarely used as a means of transportation. Pleasure, athletic and artistic achievement, and, for some, a way of life—these are the reasons people skate. The sensations of speed, of gliding, of spinning and jumping are seductive. Once we experience them, most of us want more. I can remember what it felt like to see ten thousand people as if in slow motion from the middle of a jump at the 1968 National Championships in Philadelphia. It is unforgettable.

Almost anyone can skate; only a serious handicap can prevent a person from enjoying this sport. One of skating's greatest assets is that it can be pursued throughout a lifetime. Almost as soon as you can walk, you can skate; and you need not stop until you can no longer walk. It can be taken up at any age, although it does get harder to learn as you grow older. You can start skating at two years old, as I did, or you can start at a ripe old age—with care, of course.

THE BEST AGE TO START

When to start skating depends on what you wish to achieve. For most, circumstance brings them to the ice; the goals are then established. And

1982 World Champion Elaine Zayak, showing a spark of exuberance during the exhibitions following the 1981 World Championships in Hartford, Connecticut, where she was a Silver Medalist. Margaret S. Williamson

more often than not, goals are dictated by starting age rather than starting age by goals.

The recreational skater can start at any age. The more serious competitive skater, on the other hand, faces a special set of considerations. As figure skating is an Olympic sport, there are many who skate to reach the top. Most of these skaters start relatively young. Generally this is a prerequisite to attaining effortless motion and natural fluidity on the ice. Starting young makes it easier to acquire and maintain the unusual movements and unique balance needed for skating. When these skills seem to be second nature, the skater is referred to as a "natural." Natural skaters are most often drawn from the group of children who started

between the ages of six and ten. They have the best chance of achieving Olympic status.

This does not mean that those who start between the ages of eleven and fifteen should throw in the towel and go home. I would never discourage a talented skater who has an intense desire to be great and an intelligent plan for attaining that goal. Physical maturity is not reached until the late twenties and mid-thirties. There is plenty of time for a fifteen-year-old beginner to achieve excellence.

Short competitive careers are often cited to support the notion that only the young can reach the top. However, it is usually psychological disposition and weak technique, rather than age, that clip short a competitive career. The psychological pressures of present-day life can be very distracting. Educational interests, social desires, and long-term goals can sway a young skater away from his or her singular athletic pursuit. A weak technical foundation can have serious consequences in late adolescence. With a positive disposition and sound technique, a skater can continue to develop and achieve in skating well into the late thirties.

If you are only moderately serious about skating competitively, starting at any age before twenty-one makes sense.

THE QUESTION OF TALENT

Talent is a very difficult quality to define; there are as many expressions of talent as there are people who have it. Once it has been developed, of course, it is easy to identify. It is not difficult to single out a skater with high jumps, fast spins, agile footwork, smooth stroking, interesting choreography, dramatic expression, and a coherent program. Eighteen thousand people attending the 1981 World Professional Championships in Landover, Maryland, did this en masse in response to each skater. What *is* difficult is spotting talent in the beginner, talent that has yet to be brought out.

There are a number of traits people look for when trying to assess talent. There are also a number of qualifying factors that must be kept in mind. In brief, these are:

1. Learning ability—the ability to learn quickly. With youngsters, apparent lack of learning ability may have little to do with lack of talent and a lot to do with lack of concentration and interest. Both of these could easily be developed as the child matures.
2. Coordination—the ability to manage physical feats easily. A

skater's particular growth stage or a lack of confidence can mask coordination. With time, increased confidence could well bring coordination to the surface.

3. Speed—the capability for rapid motion. To a certain extent, this physical ability can be trained. In a beginner, lack of confidence or little previous experience with activities requiring quick movement can obscure speed potential.

4. Strength and flexibility—the capability for power over the full range of movement. If these are not naturally present, they can be acquired.

5. Grace—the appearance of being one with the ice, of moving smoothly across the ice, of perfect balance. As mentioned before, grace comes easily with an early start; with a later start, it comes only with time and hard work.

6. Desire—the deep-rooted wish to attain goals. This is not usually the first trait to surface. I, for one, demonstrated only moderate interest during the first seven years of my skating career.

These are the qualities that help make a successful skating career. If all or many of them are apparent in a beginning skater, that skater has natural talent for the sport. The absence of any one of them, however, does not mean a skater is not talented. It often means simply that the circumstances are not right. Only time and the right opportunities can determine unequivocally the presence or absence of talent. Dick Button, for example, started slowly in his career. During his early years, he was told by his coach that he did not have an ideal body for the sport and lacked the necessary athletic ability to make it to the top. Then, of course, he went on to become one of the greatest athletes and figure skaters of all time.

THE JOY AND THE CHALLENGE

Skating was a very special experience for me, an activity that provided much enjoyment and good fortune. Not only was I able to develop my athletic abilities—engage in constant exercise, develop speed, stamina, agility, and strength, and acquire precise body control—but skating also

The author practicing. Ruth Silverman

gave me a medium for artistic expression. Perhaps it was this last that I found most attractive. Combining physical and technical expertise, artistry, and the drama of music is a unique and exhilarating experience.

Of course, there are other, secondary aspects of figure skating that make it a rewarding and fulfilling career. It is a sport of both solitude and sociability. For the top skaters and the enthusiastic fans who attend competitions and travel the circuit, there is the chance to visit many different countries, talk with the people, and participate in their culture. There is also the discipline, the rigors of training, and the chance to pit your skills against those of another skater. On the other side, there is a fraternity among skaters that lasts a lifetime and nurtures many profound relationships.

But by far the best reason in the world to take to the ice is for the sheer joy of it. If you love to skate, the thrill, the satisfaction, and the fun of it can all be yours. In my experience, nothing can equal the total fulfillment skating brings—if you love it!

3

EQUIPMENT

Before taking that first step onto the ice, you need equipment—one of the most important elements of figure skating. Complaints about weak ankles, pulling edges, excessive rocking, lack of flow, and discomfort can frequently be attributed to problems with equipment. To avoid unfounded discouragement and to obtain the best edge for maximum achievement, you must begin with the right gear.

GENERAL CONSIDERATIONS

It is unfortunate in a way that the most high-priced and sophisticated equipment is not necessarily right for a given skater. This would make the choice easy, but expensive. Since this is not the case, you will have to spend some time finding equipment that's right for you while possibly saving money in the process.

Skates are the major piece of equipment you will need, and most of the following discussion pertains to selecting them. There are three general considerations that enter into your choice.

Stage of Growth

What is your growth prospectus: are you presently growing, are you about to enter a growth spurt, or have you stopped growing? If you are

presently growing or about to enter a spurt, it obviously makes sense to reduce the financial outlay as much as possible without sacrificing important quality concerns. We'll discuss how this can be done later in the chapter. If you have stopped growing, your choice of skates will be subject to other criteria.

Level of Skating Expertise

Your level of expertise further narrows the available choice of skates. Different levels demand different technical feats, and frequently a specific skate can help you master certain complicated moves. On the other hand, it makes no sense for a beginner to get stiff boots, suitable for an advanced skater, since he or she will probably spend an inordinate amount of time just trying to break them in. This time could be better spent learning how to skate.

Type of Skating

Each category of skating has its own technical demands and seeks a different end result, and manufacturers have designed skates with these ends in mind. Beginners who are learning the basics of skating will more than likely not have decided what type of skating they most want to pursue; they will find the considerations of growth stage and level of skating more helpful in making equipment choices. For the more advanced skater, this final consideration is the most important.

SHOULD YOU RENT OR BUY?

If you are a beginning skater, renting is probably the best way to find out if you like the sport before investing heavily in equipment. Several companies manufacture skates suitable for rental. These can usually be rented at your local rink. These skates are made to be durable; comfort, support, and precision workmanship are not the issue. For these reasons, you should never buy a pair of rental skates for personal use, and you should buy your own skates after no more than two or three rentals.

BOOTS

Skating boots differ in design and in support. The former is partially a matter of aesthetics, while the latter is entirely a question of function. In

certain circumstances, both aesthetics and function are critically important; but in most cases function is all you must concern yourself with, as designs vary only slightly.

Design aesthetics enter the picture when the level of artistry is so refined and sophisticated that the shape and fashion of the boot can radically alter the artistic end or the overall artistic impression. This happens only at the pinnacle of skating and does not warrant further discussion here.

Other aspects of design are functional rather than simply aesthetic, and these are important to consider at all levels of skating.

- *Height of boot.* Boots are usually between 4½ and 7 inches high. If they are too low, they will not provide adequate support around the ankle. If they are too high, the top of the boot can interfere with the muscular action of the calf.
- *Tongue thickness.* The tongue should be sufficiently thick to prevent discomfort from the laces but not so thick that the boot cannot be tightened properly at the critical areas.
- *Internal padding.* Padding increases comfort. It is also used to provide comfort zones around the ankle bones.
- *Lace-hole construction.* Ideally, lace holes should be metal-ringed. This reduces the risk of leather tear due to lace tension.
- *Outer sole.* The important thing to look for here is that the sole is level and even with the bottom of the heel. Without a level sole, blades cannot be mounted evenly onto the bottom of the boot. Improperly mounted boots can lead to improper balance.
- *Height of heel.* Heels on adult skates are about 2 inches in height. The high heel tips the body weight forward to the center of the skate, enhancing balance. Since beginners frequently encounter difficulty with the toe picks at the front of their blades, heels on junior skates tend to be lower.

Support is a very important consideration. The degree of support needed depends on the weight of the skater, the type of skating, and how vigorous the skater is. Let it be said that boots with no support are unsuitable for skating, period. Stiff leather is located in four critical areas: toe, instep, heel, and ankle. A hard toe protects against spiking your toe with the other blade, particularly on jumps. Stiffness at the instep provides arch support and retards breakdown of the boot, as does stiffness at the heel. By far the most critical area of support is the ankle. Stiff leather there prevents the ankles from flopping from side to side—the proverbial

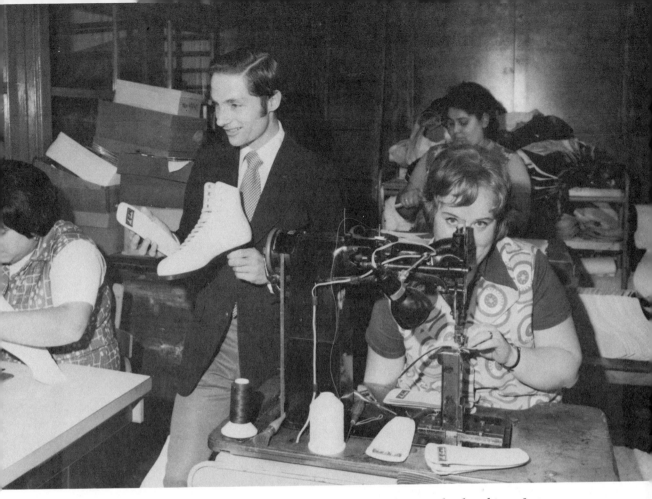

Don Jackson, 1962 World Champion, at the Czechoslovakian factory where his line of boots is manufactured. Courtesy Don Jackson

weak-ankle syndrome, which is nothing more than a weak boot condition.

The following are guidelines for the type of support required at each level and in each skating category.

Beginner

A person starting skating for the first time will need a boot of moderate or slightly less than moderate stiffness. Body weight of more than 170 pounds could make a stiffer boot necessary.

Preliminary

A person who has learned the basics of skating and is beginning to learn several specialized areas will definitely need a moderately stiff boot.

Intermediate

A person who has a solid foundation in several areas of skating and is beginning to move up the ranks in the different categories may require more than one pair of boots. From this point on, the important considerations are the area of skating and the individual's needs and idiosyncrasies, and not the skater's relative level.

Figures

A boot appropriate for compulsory school figures will be of moderate to slightly more than moderate stiffness. Since figures require the most exacting precision, the levelness of the sole is also an important feature.

Freestyle

This discipline requires a very stiff boot, possibly even the maximum stiffness. Jump landings in particular are made with substantial force, and support around the ankle is an absolute necessity.

Pairs

A boot similar to that used in freestyle is appropriate for pair skaters.

Dance

Boots of moderate to maximum stiffness are appropriate for ice dancing. Deep knee bending and rapid footwork are enhanced by a boot that has been well broken in, while the deep lean makes substantial support a necessity.

The Fit

Once the type of boot has been determined, you must find one that fits. In brief, a boot should fit like a glove. It should not be so tight that the circulation in the foot is reduced or that the boot is uncomfortable. Your toes should be able to move a little in the boot, while your heel should remain in place when your knee is bent. Generally, the skating boot will be a size smaller than your shoes, and should be worn with thin socks.

Although many areas of the foot can cause problems when fitting a pair of boots, there are four common trouble spots: the ankle bone, the arch, the outside bone of the foot (the tuberosity of the fifth metatarsal), and the top of the heel (the calcaneous bone). Spurs and large calluses can develop in the area of the ankle bone, on the fifth metatarsal, and on the calcaneous bone from ill-fitting boots. Incorrectly fitted arches can cause excessive pain and preclude all skating.

If your feet are peculiar in any way, you may need to buy custom boots, specially made to fit your feet. The comfort and long-term health of your feet are well worth the extra cost.

Breaking Them In

To break a pair of boots in properly, many coaches and boot manufacturers suggest that you wet a pair of thin socks and wear them in the skates while walking around the room for a half hour for three or four days. (Blades must be mounted on the boot before this is done—see page 42— and guards must be on the blades.) When lacing up the boots for this exercise, tie them snugly around the toes and tightly at the ankle, and stop lacing one or two hooks up from the ankle. This procedure should also be followed for the first three or four outings on the ice. Then gradually lace the boots all the way up in the following weeks. This helps break the boots in without damage to the heel support and enhances the molding of the boots to your feet, which should occur in all well-made boots.

Manufacturers

There are several major manufacturers and a few "cottage-industry" boot makers. Although differences in the quality, design, support, and life of boots do exist, most manufacturers market several models, covering the whole range of quality. Design, comfort, and satisfaction are the main reasons for choosing one manufacturer over another. Unfortunately, just about everyone has a different opinion about who best satisfies these three criteria.

Appendix B in the back of the book lists the addresses of boot manufacturers and individual boot makers.

Cost

The price of boots ranges from about $42 to about $300. Generally, the more expensive the boot, the greater its durability and the greater care taken in its production. Custom-made boots are more expensive than stock boots.

A final reminder: there are many excellent boots in the middle price range. Always examine boots carefully, discuss the purchase with someone knowledgeable in skating, and then buy.

BOOTS: MANUFACTURERS AND MODELS

Don Jackson's Skating Products
     Unit Sole Outfit (boot and blade)
     Junior Competitor Outfit (boot and blade)
     Junior Competitor Padded Outfit (boot and blade)
     Junior Competitive
     Junior Competitive Padded
     Competitor Outfit (boot and blade)
     Competitor II Padded Outfit (boot and blade)
     Competitior II Padded
     Competitior
     Super Competitor
     Super Competitor Padded

Prices for these boots and boot and blade combos range from $39 to $110.

Harlick & Co., Inc.
     Junior Ladies' or Men's Competitor
     Junior Ladies' or Men's High Tester/Gold Tester
     Junior Ladies' and Men's Elk
     Elk
     Elk, High Tester/Gold Tester
     Elk Competitor
     Pig Suede
     Custom Boots in calf and pig suede
     Continental Styling

Prices range from $120 to $350.

Micron Sports Products, Inc.
     Artistique (boots and blades)
     Caprice
     Allegro

Prices range from $45 to $75.

Oberhamer Shoe Co.
     Professional Pairs (boots and blades)
     Blue
     Red
     Bronze
     Silver

continued from page 35

Silver Professional
Gold
Supreme Custom

Prices range from $44 to $250.

Riedell Shoes Inc.
116 and 216
116 and 216 outfits (boots and blades)
101 and 220
101 and 220 outfits (boots and blades)
102 and 192
102 and 192 outfits (boots and blades)
Silver Star
Gold Star
Royal
Imperial Custom Boot

Prices range from $36 to $300.

S. P. Teri Inc.
Pro Teri
Super Teri
Super Deluxe
Customs

Prices range from $130 to $300.

John Knebli Ltd.
Stock Boots
Customs

Prices and models are constantly changing, but this list is an indication of the models available and the prices you might expect to pay.

BLADES

Blades are as various as boots in design and structure. There are three parts of a blade: the boot plate, upon which the boot sits; the stanchions, which connect the boot plate to the body of the blade; and the body of the blade itself, the bottom of which touches the ice. In general, it is the body of the blade that differs significantly from model to model and from

manufacturer to manufacturer. Of course, there are exceptions. The stock Gold Seal blade made by John Wilson, for example, has a solid front boot plate, while most other boot plates have a hole. Another exception is the higher stanchions available on the custom Pattern 99 blade, also made by John Wilson.

The differences I will outline here all pertain to the body of the blade. There are four distinct features to this part of the skate: the toe pick; the width; the lengthwise curvature, known as the radius, and the length. All are designed to satisfy a particular need of the skater.

The toe pick is never forgotten by anyone who has donned a pair of figure skates. It has been the downfall of many a great skater. The teeth on the bottom of the blade, closest to the ice, help prevent the skater from falling over the front of the skate during backward skating and spins, and assist in creating a pole-vaulting action on the takeoff of forward-edge jumps. The upper teeth are used for toe jumps, pivots, certain stops, and footwork performed on the toes. For figures, skaters use a blade with a very small bottom tooth that is set high. Pair and freestyle blades have larger teeth, the bottom one being set close to the ice. Toe picks for dancing are set significantly higher off the ice to prevent tripping.

The only type of blade that varies in width from the customary one-eighth inch is the dance blade; it is thinner, to allow for a better grip on the ice with less friction. The dance blade also has a different length compared to the norm. The heel of the blade is chopped at the back, primarily to reduce the risk of injury from spiking, which can easily occur when two skaters are executing rapid movements in close proximity to each other.

The final consideration in choosing a blade for a specific type of skating is its radius. The dance blade tends to be flatter than a singles blade. Dancers are looking for speed and flow, and the increased contact of the dance blade with the ice helps. The many turns in figures call for a blade that has a smaller radius, particularly at the ends. The middle of the figure blade is generally flatter than the other types. The freestyle blade for pairs and singles is flatter than the figure blade, but not quite so flat as the dance blade. Freestyle blades must have some rocker (smaller radius than that of a figure blade) for spins, yet they must be flat enough to enhance speed and to provide stability on jump landings.

There is one other consideration in the different types of skating blades—the hollow, or the depth between the parallel edges traversing the length of the blade. This issue will be taken up in the section on sharpening (page 42).

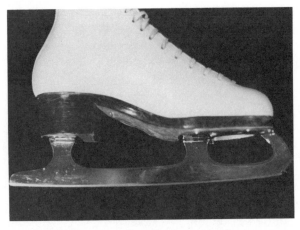

Figure blade. Note the absence of a bottom toe pick and the relative flatness of the blade. Courtesy John Misha Petkevich

Another freestyle blade. This blade is very similar to the first freestyle blade pictured, but it has a smaller radius along its length—that is, it has more curvature.

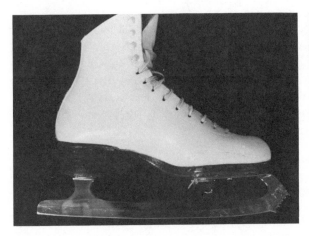

Freestyle blade. Note the large toe picks, particularly at the top (for toe jumps) and at the bottom (for forward edge jumps and stroking). Courtesy John Misha Petkevich

Dance blade. The toe picks are less pointed than those on freestyle blades, and the bottom toe pick is lifted higher off the ice due to the relatively great curvature of the blade toward the front; note the short heel on the blade.

In addition to the figure blade, the dance blade, and the freestyle blade, there is a fourth type that blends both figure and freestyle characteristics—the all-around blade. This is the best blade for beginners to use. It compromises a bit on all the elements, allowing the skater to have a single pair of skates that is adequate for all types of figure skating.

Manufacturers

Unlike the situation with boot manufacturers, there are only a few good blade manufacturers. All of them make a range of blades, which differ in quality and design. Every skater and coach has his own opinion about the superiority of one manufacturer over another. It is largely a matter of which blade works for you. As your skill improves, you will probably have to try a number of different blades. Assuming that you use blades appropriate to the area of skating you are specializing in, the differences will be subtle and will not wreak havoc on your skating during the trial periods.

Costs

Blades range in price from $12 to $300. The lower-priced models are generally all-around blades, while those designed for a particular purpose are the most expensive.

- *All-around blades.* These are suitable for the beginner, the preliminary skater, and the casual skater. For this type of blade you can pay as little as $12 and as much as $200. Blades under $25 tend to have a short life span and can be easily damaged during sharpening and through lack of care.
- *Figure blades.* Any skater who has passed the United States Figure Skating Association (USFSA) third figure test, or the equivalent, will surely need a separate blade for skating compulsory school figures (see page 41). These blades range from $80 to $300.
- *Freestyle blades.* If a skater has passed the USFSA juvenile free-skating test or the equivalent, he or she will more than likely have a pair of blades specifically for free skating. These cost anywhere from $80 to $280.

BLADES: MANUFACTURERS AND MODELS

Don Jackson's Skating Products
Mark I	all-around
Mark II	all-around
Mark III	all-around and freestyle

These are all medium-priced ($80 to $200).

MK (Mitchel and King) Skates Ltd.
Mr. Sheffield	all-around
Rink Master	all-around
Ice Time	all-around
Single Star	all-around
Professional	freestyle
Phantom	all-around and freestyle
Gold Star	freestyle
Dance Model	dance
Silver Test	figure
Gold Test	figure

Prices range from $17 to $274.

Perfecta Blades
RF 11	all-around
RF 44	all-around
RF 55	freestyle
RF 66	figure

Prices range from $12 to $105.

John Wilson Blades
Mecurio	all-around
Majestic	all-around
Coronation Ace	all-around
Coronation Ace Comet	freestyle
Four Aces	freestyle
Taylor's Special	figure, freestyle, dance
Hans Gershwiler	freestyle

Pattern 99	freestyle
Gold Seal	freestyle
Futurist	figure
Futurist T	figure
Coronation Dance	dance
IPSA Dance	dance
Pattern 88	figure
Comet	figure

Prices range from $30 to $300.

Prices and models are constantly changing, but this list is an indication of what is available at a certain price.

- *Dance blades.* These blades cost from $80 to $200. A skater in USFSA junior or senior dance competition events will generally opt for a blade designed specifically for ice dancing.

Remember, each type of blade requires a separate and distinct boot. A list of blade manufacturers, with addresses, is given in Appendix B.

SETS OF EQUIPMENT

Many companies market a boot-and-blade combination. For the beginner and the preliminary and recreational skater, the set is the most sensible skate to purchase. They are usually significantly less expensive than boots and blades purchased separately. In addition, the blades come already mounted to the skates, so you don't have to pay an expert to do this. Sets range from $40 to $150.

MICRONS

These new designs in skates also deserve mention. Microns are boots made not of the traditional leather but of nylon and polyurethane. They are feather-light, and are available with a Perfecta blade that is also different from the traditional blade. A plastic housing for the body of the

blade is riveted onto the boot. As yet very few skaters have been wearing these boots. Their lack of acceptance in skating circles may be due to their lesser support and their unnerving lightness. Time and further development will determine the value of the concept.

MOUNTING

Before mounting the blade on a boot, the sole and heel of the boot must be waterproofed. Shellac, mink oil, and boot and heel enamel are frequently used for waterproofing.

Once this is done, the blades are temporarily screwed onto the boots. They should be slightly to the inside of the boot's center line, which is determined by the overall mass distribution of the boot as assessed from its bottom. Since everyone's feet and body are different, no setting is right for any two people. If the skater walks on the temporarily set blades, an expert mounter can tell if the weight is properly distributed. Newly mounted blades should always be tried on the ice a few times before they are mounted permanently by filling all the screw holes.

After you have determined that the blades are set correctly, return the skates to a mounter to be permanently secured. If blades are improperly secured, there can be damage to the sole of the boot and possibly even a bent blade. To find an expert mounter, ask a skating equipment distributor in your area or approach one of the coaches at your local rink.

MAINTENANCE AND SHARPENING

To preserve the leather of skating boots, keep them polished and treated with boot cream. After skating, take them home to dry. Place them in a warm, dry spot, but away from any source of direct heat such as a radiator. Dampness from the humidity of the rink and from sweating feet is a common cause of boot deterioration.

Never walk in skates off the ice without using skate guards, rubber or plastic covers for the blades that reduce the chance that they will become nicked or dull. After each skating session, the blades should be wiped dry. Do not put wet guards on blades for storage. Blades need air to dry or, better yet, they should be covered with blade booties, terry-cloth covers. If blades are not dry when stored, rust will very quickly set in. For long periods of storage, blades should be treated with some kind of petroleum product, oil or jelly.

Sharpening blades is one of the most important aspects of skate care. How often they must be sharpened depends on the frequency of your skating and how well you care for your blades. If you skate once a week, a once-a-year sharpening is sufficient. At the competitive level, skates should be sharpened almost every month. Of course, if you walk around without blade guards, you will need to sharpen them more often no matter how much you skate. Nicks, which are irregular protrusions or indentations on the edges of the blade, are the death of flow and clean edges, and they seriously diminish the enjoyment of skating.

It can be difficult to find a good skate sharpener. The best way is to ask your skate dealer, and then check that recommendation against those of some coaches at your local rink. Untrained or inexperienced sharpeners can ruin a pair of blades in one go. Toe picks can be removed, edges made uneven, hollows done incorrectly, the radius of the blade changed, or a pair of blades made uneven. You can't be too careful when choosing a skate sharpener.

The purpose of sharpening is to thin the edges on each side of the hollow of the blade. Freestyle blades have a deep hollow, figure blades a shallow one. Dance blades tend to have a more shallow hollow than freestyle blades. A multipurpose blade should be somewhere between that of a freestyle and a figure blade. Within these general ranges, there are, naturally, individual preferences.

The cost of sharpening varies. The typical fee ranges from $3 to $10. Remember, it is vitally important to find someone who does quality work. It is much cheaper in the long run to pay $10 periodically than to replace a pair of blades that have been sharpened only once.

Sharpening Procedures

If you are interested in learning how to sharpen your own blades, there are two elements to keep in mind: the degree of concavity along the length of the blade, and the radius of the blade. The way in which a blade is approached for sharpening depends on what happens to these two elements.

Generally, a rough grinding stone is first taken to the blade to remove large nicks and gashes in the edges. Do not run it along the blade too many times; excessive grinding with a rough stone drastically reduces the life of the blade.

After the nicks are removed, a much finer-grained stone is taken to the blade. The camber of the stone—its degree of convexity—will determine the amount of hollow or concavity of the sharpening. A tool called a

diamond dresser is used to adjust the stone's camber. When the edge of the stone looks almost flat, the hollow will be shallow. When the edge of the stone is severely curved, the hollow will be deep.

During this part of the procedure, the blade must form a line parallel with the line of the stone, and it must be level and centered with the stone. If not, the edges will be uneven. In order to maintain the present radius of the blade, a constant pressure must be exerted on the stone with the blade.

Once the blades are sharp and smooth, they are polished. There are a couple of ways to do this. One is to "stone" the blades gently with a hand stone. While doing this, you must keep the stone centered in the hollow so that it does not hit the edges and curl them outward. Lasers have also been used by the experts to polish blades. This technique was developed by Jacques Hebert in Montreal, Quebec. Preliminary results suggest that it is an excellent way to polish and it results in increased flow.

Sharpening equipment is available for most general equipment distributors, and from the specialists listed in Appendix B.

REPAIR

With the rising cost of equipment, skaters are searching for ways to prolong the life of their skates. Unfortunately, blades do not lend themselves to repair. But a wise investment in blades can result in quite a long life for them—an occasional skater can use a pair of blades for almost a lifetime. For the active competitor, the life of a blade is one to two years.

Boots, on the other hand, can be repaired. Provided that the soles are in good shape, they can be rebuilt to a state approximating the original. Generally, you can do this only once because the soles will not last long enough for a second rebuilding. The recreational skater will find that boots last as long as ten to fifteen years. Competitive skaters wear theirs out in six to twelve months.

The names and addresses of two rebuilders can be found in Appendix B.

OTHER EQUIPMENT

There are several other pieces of equipment integral to the skater's stock, including the skate guards and blade booties already discussed. The

scribe is a tool that deserves special mention. For those wishing to learn the skills of compulsory school figures, a scribe is a must. It is simply a compass that is used to draw circles on the ice for reference during practice. Scribes generally cost about $50, and may be ordered from the companies listed in Appendix B.

CLOTHING AND FASHION

When skating was done outdoors, it was essential to bundle up. Now that most people skate indoors, warm clothing is still necessary, but the absence of wind chill makes thinner, more flexible material possible.

For practice and training sessions, several different types of clothing are appropriate: for women, skating dresses, leotards and tights, and warmup or sweat suits; for men, pants and sweaters and warmup or sweat suits. The important thing is to be warm yet not confined. Skating requires an extended range of movement, which your clothing should not restrict.

Jimmy Ayers, a middle-level test skater, checking his circles with a scribe.
Courtesy John Misha Petkevich

Michelle Noce, ten years old, pre-pares for a freestyle move; note her excellent form and the practice out-fit. Courtesy John Misha Petkevich

If you are taking a skating test, the style of dress should be more formal. Women can wear a skating dress and a sweater or trim jacket. White gloves are a nice touch. Men often wear stretch pants and a sweater. When choosing a particular outfit, remember that you are on the ice to skate, that you must be able to move easily, and that the judges must be able to see your movements.

In skating competitions, the same principles apply but the end result is often different. When skating compulsory school figures, follow the guidelines for test outfits. For compulsory dances, costumes can be a bit more innovative but should still be slightly conservative. When it comes to freestyle, the only considerations are freedom of movement and harmony of the costume with the music and the choreography in the program.

Scott Hamilton, 1981–83 World Champion, wearing a flashy competition costume. Scott overcame a potentially fatal childhood disease to become one of the most consistent skaters ever. Margaret S. Williamson

For the most part, the only outfits requiring custom tailoring are those for competitive freestyle events. A tailor or seamstress who knows anything about movement should be able to produce a perfectly suitable costume after being given some design recommendations. Such costumes can cost anywhere from a few dollars to several thousand dollars. Appendix B will guide you to a number of clothing and fashion suppliers.

4

RINKS
AND ORGANIZATIONS

If you have the necessary equipment and are ready to start skating, it may be that you can simply suit up and step out onto your neighborhood frozen pond. Most of us, however, don't have that luxury at our doorsteps. In any case it may not even be winter, and skating is a sport that is practiced all year round. Fortunately, since the turn of the century, there has been a blossoming in the construction of indoor rinks with artificially maintained ice. Many of these rinks are affiliated with skating organizations that you may want to join, depending on your goals and interests. They also offer a variety of programs for learning and developing skating skills.

FINDING THE RIGHT RINK

You will want to find a rink offering a program that satisfies your skating needs. There are fundamentally three types of skaters: the casual skater, the recreational skater, and the amateur skater. For the casual skater who is content with his or her skills and who simply enjoys getting out and skating, any rink offering general and public sessions will suit the purpose admirably.

A recreational skater may have one of several ends in mind: determining how enthusiastic he or she is about the sport before embarking on a more vigorous commitment; learning skills in preparation for a professional career; or improving skills for greater enjoyment and satisfaction. In the United States, a rink offering an Ice Skating Institute of America (ISIA) program would be appropriate for this type of skater. In other countries, the national governing body of the sport of figure skating generally offers similar programs. (More about these later in the chapter.)

The amateur skater is one who is interested in amateur competitions and amateur tests, and who does not receive direct remuneration for skating activities. The goal may be as modest as competing in a local interclub meet, or as grand as obtaining a place on the Olympic team. The United States Figure Skating Association (USFSA) is the national governing body responsible for operating amateur programs, and any rink affiliated with the USFSA is the right place to skate if these are your goals.

In Appendix C in the back of this book you will find a directory of skating rinks in the United States. Those associated with or run by a skating club and those that are members of one of the national skating organizations are identified. New rinks open from year to year and others close, so if you do not find a rink listed in your area, you should contact the USFSA or ISIA; they will be able to help you locate a suitable one. For information on Canadian rinks and skating clubs, contact one of the divisional heads of the Canadian Figure Skating Association, also listed in Appendix C.

JOINING A SKATING ORGANIZATION

If you belong to the ranks of the casual skater, there is no need to become a member of a skating organization. However, if you want to improve your skating skills for whatever reason, joining a national sports federation is essential.

National governing bodies (NGBs) are recognized by the International Skating Union in Switzerland as the official groups charged with the operation of the sport within their countries. NGBs are restricted to Olympic sports and, therefore, to the amateur side of the sport. The primary purpose of the NGB is to nurture the sport by giving it structure and organization at the local level. NGBs maintain amateur and athletic standards; develop learning programs; monitor tests, competitions, and amateur show events; and regulate all aspects of amateur skating.

In some countries, including the United States and Canada, the sport of figure skating has its own NGB. In other countries, a single NGB may govern more than one sport. The National Skating Association of Great Britain covers roller and speed skating as well as figure skating; in Germany, France, and Italy, all ice sports are governed by a single NGB.

Most NGBs have affiliated clubs throughout the country, representing official local branches of the NGB. Through these clubs, you can become a member of the NGB and will then be eligible to participate in any of its activities for which you are qualified.

As mentioned previously, the United States is peculiar in that it has two different national organizations for figure skating: one for the recreational skater, the ISIA (not an NGB), and one for the amateur skater, the USFSA (the NGB recognized by the International Skating Union). Although both organizations offer beginners' programs, the ISIA's is slightly broader-based. The main difference is in the skater's purpose and ultimate goal. The ISIA concentrates on developing programs suitable for recreational skating and for skaters who want to pursue a career in professional skating. The programs of the USFSA are dedicated to nurturing amateur skaters who may one day have a place on the Olympic team. This does not mean that the potential level of skating achievement in the ISIA programs is lower than that found in the ranks of the USFSA. Both organizations and programs are immensely valuable.

It is important to note that members of one organization can participate in events sponsored and run by the other, provided that USFSA members do not benefit financially from skating in ISIA events.

The number of people participating in organized skating programs in North America has grown substantially over the past ten years. At present, the numbers are staggering. The USFSA has nearly 40,000 members and about 450 member clubs. The ISIA has 20,000 members with another 20,000 participating in their programs; member rinks number more than 300. In Canada, there are 160,000 members of the Canadian Figure Skating Association (CFSA) skating at 1,200 member clubs.

The fees for membership in these organizations are very reasonable; the USFSA charges $10 per year, the ISIA $7.50, and the CFSA $5. The fees for the USFSA and the ISIA include a year's subscription to their official journals, *Skating* and *Recreational Ice Skating*, respectively.

The relationship among the different governing bodies around the world is fairly simple, although not as simple to describe. For every sport represented in the Olympic Games, the International Olympic Committee (IOC) charges a group called the International Federation to operate

that sport and run the events at the Games. The International Federation also makes the rules that govern international events. Traditionally, the IOC determined eligibility for participation in international competitions; but recently the trend has been for the International Federation to do so. In turn, the International Federation, which in the case of skating is the International Skating Union (ISU), directs the national governing bodies to run the sport in their various countries and to select the athletes who will compete in the Olympic Games. In the United States, as a result of the arbitration law passed by Congress, the U.S. Olympic Committee is charged with appointing an NGB independent of any recommendation or decision made by the ISU.

The names and addresses for NGBs throughout the world are listed in Appendix A, under the heading "Amateur and Recreational."

If you are interested in participating in the programs offered by the national skating organizations, the best contact is through your local or regional member club, which more than likely uses the facilities of a nearby rink. These local clubs provide detailed information about the programs offered. The next chapter deals more specifically with these programs and explains the nature and order of tests and competitions.

ALL ABOUT PROGRAMS, TESTS, AND COMPETITIONS

Nearly all figure skating programs, with the exception of special seminars and master classes, are designed to prepare a skater for a test, for entrance into competition, or for a career as a professional performer. Tests are a means of assessing your progress against a standard. In competitions, you can compare your abilities with those of other skaters. Tests and competitions are also exciting, and, when success is achieved, they bring an extraordinary sense of satisfaction.

The enthusiasm that skaters have for tests is borne out by the fact that from April 1981 through December 1982, there were nearly 100,000 USFSA tests taken. Competition evokes a similar response: at the 1982 ISIA National Team Competition in Chicago, 1,200 skaters ranging in age from four to sixty-six entered. Clearly, skaters involved in learning programs want to test their skills.

PROGRAMS

Most programs involving group instruction and a unified approach to learning concentrate on teaching the fundamentals of skating. In the

United States, as mentioned in the previous chapter, there are two such programs: one sponsored and designed by the ISIA, and one developed by the USFSA. Other countries have similar programs, usually sponsored and run by the national governing body of that country. Here we will restrict our discussion to the programs available in the United States.

Learning the Basics

In both the ISIA and the USFSA, learning the basics of skating is done within a test structure. As you improve your skills, you pass tests in increments. The ISIA has a nine-part basic skating test, while the USFSA basic skating tests number twelve. The test programs are similar—both consist of fundamental moves that are prerequisite to participating in any area of skating. At this level, skaters learn stroking, edges, turns, basic steps, positional moves, basic jumps, basic spins, and, last but not least, how to fall.

Each test in the program has only a few requirements, so the skater can make rapid progress. The standards are not so stringent as to discourage a skater from further efforts. And coaches generally do not test skaters until they are prepared to pass.

Specializing

When you have successfully completed the basic tests, you are ready to decide what area of figure skating you want to concentrate on. Whether your interests are purely recreational, professional, or amateur-oriented (perhaps with the Olympics in mind), you will probably want to specialize in one of the four different types of figure skating: singles, pairs, ice dancing, and chorus or precision skating. There are competition events in all these areas and tests for all but precision skaters.

- Singles skating is divided into two areas for testing purposes, the compulsory school figures and the freestyle program. In competition, both types of skating are included in each singles event—one men's event and one ladies' event.
- Pair skating involves only freestyle, a man and a woman performing together in a pas de deux. There are both pair tests and pair competition events. In addition, some competitions contain an event for two pair team programs, called Fours.
- Ice dancing is divided into two areas for both tests and competitions, compulsory dance and free dance. In higher competition

events, there is also another form of compulsory dance, the original set-pattern dance.

- Precision skating, in which a group of from ten to twenty-five skaters perform step sequences and positional moves in unison, is rapidly rising in popularity. Although there are no tests for this type of skating, the number of competitions is increasing due to the demand.

There are no set criteria for determining which type of skating you might best pursue—it is largely a matter of personal preference and interest. Of course, there may be circumstances that preclude specializing in a particular area. For example, you may not be able to find a suitable partner who is as interested in dance as you are. There are also a number of objective factors that may influence your choice. If you have the ability to jump well, singles might be the event for you. If you have a great deal of control in your skating, again singles might be the right direction because compulsory school figures, which demand precision, are a major part of singles skating. An exceptionally tall person might best steer toward dance, since both singles and pair skating require instantaneous response of the extremities, which is more difficult for those who are tall. These are minor factors, however, and none of them should preclude your pursuing a specific type of skating. The best way to choose an area of specialization is to consult with your coach and do a candid self-evaluation of your abilities and interests.

Once your decision is made, you can begin to think about the best equipment to buy and make a learning plan. Most likely, this will include taking tests and possibly entering competition.

TESTS

Tests at this level serve a number of purposes.

- They give the skater an opportunity to test his or her skills against a fairly objective standard.
- They provide the skater with concrete goals.
- They enable skating organizations to maintain a high standard of skating.
- They serve as qualifying steps for certain categories of events in competition.
- They give skaters a way to assess a coach's past skating experience (see Chapter 6).

In short, they are an asset to the sport of skating and provide valuable opportunities for skaters to improve and refine their skills.

Singles—Compulsory School Figures

In the USFSA program, there are nine figure tests, consisting of variations on the figure eight. As you progress through the tests, the difficulty of the figures increases and so does the standard of execution necessary for passing the test.

The first category of figures consists of two or three circles, which are generally about three times the height of the skater. At different points around the circles, the skater executes turns—a three-turn, a bracket, a counter, or a rocker. These turns must be executed on a single edge of the skate and they must have a specified, symmetrical shape. Their placement on the circle is of great importance. On some figures, the skater must execute three tracings without stopping, while on others, six tracings are required.

The second major category is loop figures, which are smaller circles, about the skater's height. Inside these circles, the skater must execute

Fifteen-year-old Connie Mezardash practicing figures in a "patch" session. During patch, each skater is given a portion of ice on which to lay out figures. Courtesy John Misha Petkevich

The author practicing a forward paragraph loop figure on an outdoor pond. Ruth Silverman

small ellipses. No matter what kind of figure you are skating, precision, balance, style, and flow are of prime importance. The way the figure is skated and the resulting tracing on the ice are the two main points taken into account when the tests are judged. A full rundown of the tests and the requirements for passing them are given in the USFSA *Rulebook,* which you can order from the USFSA (see page 141). Those who pass all nine tests are figure gold medalists.

The ISIA figure test program consists of ten tests, the figures being the same as those tested by the USFSA. Differences between the ISIA and the USFSA tests occur in emphasis, standards, and the source for the judges. The emphasis on what is most important at each test level changes regionally and is difficult to define. Since the primary purpose of the ISIA is to promote recreational skating, the test standards are necessarily not as high as those found in the Olympic-oriented USFSA, and rightly so. Judges for ISIA tests are drawn from the ranks of its instruc-

tors, whereas USFSA judges must disassociate themselves from participation in the instructional process and so remain amateurs in good standing (see page 72 for more about judging).

Singles—Free Skating

Free-skating tests consist of jumps, spins, jump and spin combinations, footwork, and positional moves such as arabesques and spread-eagles. There are six tests in the USFSA program, and ten in that offered by the ISIA. In all USFSA free-skating tests except the first (called the prelimi-

The author executing his famous death drop, perhaps one of the highest ever done. Roger Turner

A fast forward scratch spin performed by the author; the blurred effect is what skaters strive to achieve. Roger Turner

nary), the freestyle moves are done to music. The ISIA free-skating tests are divided into two parts: execution of certain freestyle elements individually, and the performance of freestyle moves to music. The duration of the freestyle program set to music increases as you get to each higher test level. A skater is free to choose his or her music and to choreograph the program in any way, provided that it is coherent and that it includes the required elements.

In evaluating a free-skating test, judges examine the sureness of execution of each required move; the skater's speed, style, originality, and musical expression; and the choreographic coherence. The final judgment is based on the two distinct aspects of free skating: technical merit and artistic impression.

Pair Skating

The elements executed by pairs are drawn from two categories, singles freestyle moves and pair moves. Any move performed by a single skater can also be done by a pair. Special pair moves are lifts, spins involving a hold or partnering position, pair throws, twists, death spirals, and a variety of pair positional moves and holds. In lifts, the man lifts the woman up into the air and holds her there in a hand-to-hand hold or in a

Sandra and Val Bezic, five-time Canadian Pair Champions, performing the spectacular death spiral. Courtesy Sandra and Val Bezic

hand-to-body hold. Pair spins are simply variations on singles spins, incorporating some kind of hold or partnering position. In a throw, the woman is "thrown" or lifted into the air into a singles jump, from which she lands on her own without the assistance of her partner. A twist is basically a throw in which the man catches the woman before she touches the ice. Death spirals entail a very deep edge, which the woman maintains while the man pulls her around in a circle; her body should be almost horizontal to the ice.

Like singles, pair skaters are free to choose their own free-skating music and to incorporate the required elements into the program in any way they find appropriate.

The USFSA sponsors four pair tests, while the ISIA offers five. As in singles free-skating tests, the ISIA pair tests are divided into a compulsory section, consisting of moves executed individually, and the program portion, consisting of the required elements set to music. They are judged in the same way that free-skating tests are judged.

Couples Skating

This category is technically a division of pair skating and is unique to the ISIA testing program. It is also called shadow skating, and has long been particularly popular in professional skating shows. Both mixed couples (a man and a woman) and similar couples (two men or two women) can take the ten tests offered. Unlike pair skating, the emphasis is on unison singles free skating and not on lifts and pair spins.

The couples tests are structured in the same way as the pair tests. Although a few basic lifts are included, the primary elements of the tests are drawn from singles free skating, with the emphasis on unison as well as on technical merit and artistic impression.

Compulsory Dances

Compulsory dances are set-pattern dances, in which all the aspects of the dance are meticulously prescribed. There are twenty compulsory dances in the USFSA dance test program, and twenty-one in that offered by the ISIA. Steps such as Mohawks, three-turns, and Choctaws are required, as are certain rhythms, partnering positions, and elements of musical expression. The patterns resulting from the steps, which must be placed at specific spots on the rink for each dance, are described in the USFSA *Rulebook*.

Judges assess two different elements of a compulsory dance perfor-

1981–83 U.S. Ice Dancing Champions, Judy Blumberg and Michael Seibert, in their famous rendition of Ginger Rogers and Fred Astaire.
Margaret S. Williamson

mance: dance rhythm and the excellence of execution. The former takes in the artistic aspects of the dance: musical interpretation, the skaters' expression of the mood and rhythm of the dance, whether it be a waltz or a tango; and the stylistic presentation. The second part of the total mark deals with the technical side: the precision of the steps, of the pattern, and of the partner positions, and the exactness of the movements in general.

Free Dance

Intricate steps, limited lifts, and some stylistic positional moves comprise free dance. There are elaborate rules regulating the type and nature of the moves permissible in free dance. The idea is that it should be a dance

above all else, and not a pair or free-skating routine. The skaters are free to choose their music and must choreograph their program. The program must have no more than three changes of music and must convey a sense of dance rhythm throughout.

The USFSA test program has two free-dance tests and the ISIA program has one. These are judged in much the same way as the compulsory dances, except that the artistic aspect receives greater emphasis. Such considerations as originality of choreography and dramatic coherence with rhythmic variety are given much weight.

Other Testing Programs

All national governing bodies offer test programs of their own. The one sponsored by the Canadian Figure Skating Association closely resembles that of the USFSA. The significant difference is that in the CFSA the standards on tests for skaters seeking to qualify for competitions are significantly higher than the standards on ordinary tests. In the United States, the standards are the same.

In the test structure of most other NGBs, there are generally fewer tests, although all the same elements are covered. The tests are judged in basically the same way, with only minor regional variations in standards.

The International Skating Union also designs and regulates tests, with regulations similar to those that govern the USFSA tests. Some NGBs have adopted the ISU test structure for their own.

COMPETITIONS

There are two types of figure skating competitions, non-qualifying and qualifying. While new non-qualifying competitions are continually being developed, qualifying competitions remain a relatively constant feature of the competitor's schedule. As before, we'll look primarily at U.S. and major international competitions.

Non-Qualifying Events

This type of competition does not lead to or serve as a heat or preliminary round for a later competition. They are one-time events. Both the ISIA and USFSA, as well as other national governing bodies and the International Skating Union, host non-qualifying competitions.

ISIA-Sponsored Competitions

The very purpose of the ISIA dictates that all its competitions are non-qualifying. And they are open to anyone who wishes to compete. The ISIA sponsors several different types of competitions and many different events in each category—singles, pairs, couples, and ice dancing. There are head-to-head and team events. Skaters are grouped according to skill, which is determined by test level, and according to age, and they compete against others of similar skill and age. There are also precision team and improvisational skating events.

The ISIA sponsors rink, inter-rink, and district championships (the United States is divided into fifteen districts for this purpose). There is also a National Team Championship.

USFSA-Sanctioned Competitions

The USFSA sanctions many non-qualifying competitions each year. Most of these are national in scope, although there are some that draw skaters from other countries. There are both open competitions, in which any skater can participate, and invitational competitions. Generally, these competitions parallel the four Olympic events, men's singles, ladies' singles, pairs, and ice dancing.

A CALENDAR OF NON-QUALIFYING
COMPETITIONS THROUGHOUT THE WORLD

TSK-Pirutten, Ladies and Men, in Trondheim, Norway; generally in January

The Trophy of the Polish Figure Skating Association, in Warsaw, Poland; January

International Basler Cup im Eistanzen, in Basel, Switzerland; January or February

Sofia Press Cup, in Sofia, Bulgaria; generally in February

Nordic Figure Skating Championships, in Gothenburg, Sweden; February

Merano Spring Trophy, in Merano, Italy; generally in March

International Senior and Junior Competitions for Ladies and Men, in Bucharest, Rumania; generally in March when held

Druzbha Cup, International Junior Competitions, in Leningrad, USSR; generally in March when held

Friendship Junior Competition, in Budapest, Hungary; April

R. J. Wilkie International Ice Dance Competition, in England; May

Grand Prix International de Patinage Artistique de Saint Gervais, in Saint Gervais, France; generally in August

Nebelhorn Trophy, in Oberstdorf, West Germany; generally in August

Pokal der Stadt Wien, Ladies, in Vienna, Austria; generally in September

St. Ivel Ice International, in London, England; generally in September

"Skate America," in Lake Placid, New York; generally in October

International Junior Figure Skating Competition, in Barcelona, Spain; October

Yantarnye Konki, International Junior, in Riga, USSR; generally in October

Merano Autumn Trophy, Junior Ice Dance Competition, in Merano, Italy; generally in October

Prize of USSR Trade Unions, in the USSR; generally in October

"Skate Canada," in Canada; generally in October

Prague Skate, Ladies, Men, and Pairs, in Prague, Czechoslovakia; generally in November

Golden Spin of Zagreb, in Zagreb, Yugoslavia; November

Grand Prize SNP, Junior, in Banska Bystrica, Czechoslovakia; generally in November

Pokal der Blauen Schwerter, in Karl-Marx-Stadt, East Germany; generally in November

Prize of Stroitelnaya Gazeta, Junior, in the USSR; November or December

November 17th Cup, Senior Ice Dance Competition, in Czechoslovakia; November

NHK Trophy, in Japan; generally in November

International Junior Competitions, Ladies, in Vienna, Austria; generally in December

Prize Nouvelles de Moscou, in Moscow, USSR; generally in December

A CALENDAR OF
INTERNATIONAL QUALIFYING COMPETITIONS

European Championships, generally in January or February
World Championships, generally in March
Winter Olympic Games, once every four years in February

The singles events have three phases: the compulsory school figures (30%), the short freestyle program (20%), and the long freestyle program (50%). Although the starting foot (left or right) for a figure is not known, the figures for qualifying and international competitions are announced in the spring of each year. The short freestyle program (two minutes or less) consists of required elements drawn from the freestyle tests that the skater has already passed in order to be eligible to compete in a particular division. These include a certain number of jumps and spins, and they generally draw from the positional moves and footwork sequences required in the tests. The program is skated to music of the skater's choosing and is choreographed by the skater. The long program has no specific requirements except its length, which can be from $1\frac{1}{2}$ to $4\frac{1}{2}$ minutes depending on the division or level. In the long program, any kinds of jumps, spins, footwork, positional moves, and combinations of these can be included. The more difficult the elements of the program are, the better the marks will be, provided they are skated well. The way the elements are woven choreographically into the context of the program is a decisive factor as well.

The pairs event consists of short and long freestyle programs that are essentially the same as those in the singles events. There are only two differences: pair moves must be included, and, in the long program in the higher events, there are restrictions on the number of technical maneuvers, both singles and pairs.

Ice dancing competition, like the singles events, has three phases. Skaters must first execute set-pattern dances. Then they devise an original set-pattern dance, consisting of dance steps set to a defined rhythm and performed expressively, in a way that is appropriate to the rhythm, music, and type of dance. The final phase of competition is a free dance that is either three or four minutes long.

Some competitions do not include certain aspects of an event, while others exclude some events altogether. Occasionally, the event is restructured. The great variety of non-qualifying competitions allows the skater to gain experience in his or her particular weak areas.

There is another type of non-qualifying competition that has only recently been developed, and which is rapidly gaining in popularity: the precision team competition. Generally, the routines done by precision teams consist of sequences of steps and turns that must be done in unison. Some basic singles moves are used infrequently. The crux of the competition is to perform the elements together, with the same kind and extent of movement. More and more skaters are enthusiastically pooling their talents for such events.

The national governing bodies in most other countries host non-qualifying competitions like those described above. Usually the structure and emphasis are similar. If you are interested in participating in such competitions, you should get the specifics of each event from the appropriate organization.

Club Competitions

Figure skating clubs often organize their own non-qualifying competitions. These need not be sanctioned by the USFSA, and they are organized strictly for the purpose of giving a greater number of skaters the chance to compete in their localities.

International Competitions

International non-qualifying competitions are restricted to top-level skaters—junior and senior events. For some, a country is permitted to send representatives by explicit or implicit invitation only. It is customary for the national governing body of each country to choose its representatives. Attempts are often but not always made to spread the opportunities around.

Qualifying Events

The most widely publicized and well-known figure-skating events are the qualifying competitions. In part, this is because the ultimate aim of qualifying competitions is to determine the national skating team. After all, it is the members of the national team who compete in the Olympic, World, and European championships.

To that end, there are a number of critical, one-shot contests in which a skater must excel. In many countries, such as the United States and Canada, there are many contestants working their way to those coveted places on the national team, so there is an elaborate series of competitions just leading to the national championships, the final contest that determines the team members. Countries such as Holland and Belgium that have smaller numbers of competitive skaters have only a national championship. In some cases, a country such as Korea has practically no need for a national championship, though it may conduct one to determine the standing of its few skaters.

The United States has two categories of competitions leading to the Nationals—regionals and sectionals. Canada has the same format but different names for the events—there they are called sectionals and divisionals.

The first step on the road to the Nationals is to enter a regional competition. However, in order to be eligible for a particular event, you must have passed the prerequisite test for that division of the event. The eligibility requirements are delineated in the USFSA *Rulebook.*

There are twelve events in the regional competitions: five men's and five ladies' singles events (preliminary, intermediate, novice, junior, and senior), three pairs events (novice, junior, and senior), and four dance events (preliminary, bronze, silver, and gold). The top three finalists in all the pairs divisions, in the three top dance divisions, and in the four top singles divisions qualify to compete in the sectional championships.

The sectional championships bring together the three best competitors in each division from each region of the country. This competition represents the final step before the Nationals. The top three skaters in the novice, junior, and senior singles divisions; in the junior and senior

The author during the freestyle phase of the 1968 Olympic Games in Grenoble, France.

Janet Lynn, one of the greatest all-around skaters, never won an amateur world title, although she outdistanced her contemporaries by miles.
Margaret S. Williamson

pairs divisions; and in the junior and senior dance divisions qualify to compete in the Nationals.

National Championships

Nearly all the national governing bodies conduct national championships. Only the winner of the top division in each event is guaranteed a place on the team. Those who make the team represent their country in the World Championships, and, every four years, in the Olympic Games. The second and third place finishers will go to the World Championships only if they placed sufficiently high in the Worlds the year before. The

Rosalyn Sumners, 1983 Ladies World Champion, exhibits grace and sweetness on the ice, making her one of the sweetheart skaters of the 80s. Christie Jenkins

QUALIFYING COMPETITIONS

USA	*Regionals*	*Sectionals*	
	New Englands		
	North Atlantics	Easterns	
	South Atlantics		
	Eastern Great Lakes		
	Upper Great Lakes	Midwesterns	NATIONALS (generally in January)
	Southwesterns		
	Northwest Pacific		
	Central Pacific	Pacific Coast	
	Southwest Pacific		
CANADA	*Sectionals*	*Divisionals*	
	British Columbia		
	Alberta	Western	
	Saskatchewan		
	Manitoba		
	Northern Ontario	Central	CANADIAN (generally in January)
	Western Ontario		
	Central Ontario		
	Eastern Ontario	Eastern	
	Quebec		
	New Brunswick		
	Nova Scotia	Atlantic	
	Prince Edward Island		
	Newfoundland		

number of team members depends on where that particular country's competitors placed in the previous year's World Championships. A team must have at least eight members, but cannot have more than eighteen. Every member country can enter at least one representative in each of the four events. All national team members from European countries and the Soviet Union also compete in the European Championships.

National competitors in the junior divisions may also be chosen to represent their country at the Junior World Championships. Again, this depends to a large extent on how well they place in the Nationals.

International Championships

The European and World Championships and the Olympic Games all have the same format. However, only national teams from European countries and the Soviet Union participate at Europeans; competitors at Worlds and the Olympics are drawn from all countries recognized as eligible by the International Skating Union. The Worlds is far more prestigious than the Europeans, because it is more all-encompassing. At the pinnacle of amateur competition, of course, are the Olympic Games.

RULES AND REGULATIONS

The rules governing tests and competitions vary from country to country. To ensure that you understand the many details in each event, you must consult the rulebook, available through the main office of that country's national governing body (see Appendix A).

JUDGING

Consider for a minute how difficult it must be to judge a skating performance. Human beings tend to be subjective by nature, and yet here they are asked to be unerringly objective in the interests of fair competition. There are many aspects of figure skating that call for aesthetic appraisals, not just calculated, quantified judgments. It is not surprising, then, that judges' decisions are sometimes colored by what seem to be irrelevant or unimportant considerations; occasionally a narrow-minded or tunnel-visioned judge will misuse his or her position. For the most part, however, the judges' efforts are directed toward the just outcome of a competition.

There is no shortcut to becoming a judge—it is by necessity a lengthy, involved process. In the United States, there are four steps leading to a judging appointment and three procedures required to maintain it. To be named a judge, a candidate must act as trial judge at a particular level of skating. And both to obtain and to maintain their appointments, they must attend judges' seminars, pass the annual Judge's Examination, and participate in a minimum number of judging engagements each year.

At a test session or a competition, a trial judge's results are compared with those of the official judges. When the results consistently concur over a significant number of judging engagements, the trial judge is appointed by the USFSA to judge officially at a particular level. The newly appointed judge, while judging at the level of the appointment, begins once again to trial-judge at the next level. This continues until the judge reaches the pinnacle, a World Championship judging appointment.

In an effort to educate judges further, the USFSA sponsors a number of seminars throughout the year. These provide an opportunity to keep abreast of new developments in the sport, to broaden understanding of the sport, to review previously acquired knowledge, and to discuss new ideas and controversies. Judges are advised to attend these seminars to maintain their appointments.

Recently, the USFSA has devised an annual Judge's Examination. This tests the judge's breadth of knowledge, telling both the judge and the organization where the weak areas lie.

Perhaps the most important part of maintaining a judging appointment is working in the field as much as possible. This means taking every opportunity to judge tests and competitions. Provided that a judge's scores concur most of the time with the majority, his or her appointment is likely to go unchallenged.

There are of course other less well-defined criteria used in selecting judges, including assessments of the individual's character and temperament. In addition, an applicant for appointment must be an amateur in good standing.

Judges for tests come from the USFSA's group of judges. These same judges, albeit of higher standing, judge the National Championships. At international competitions, nine of the highest level of judges from the participating national governing bodies are selected by a draw.

What makes judging so very difficult are the numerous variables that a judge must consider when making a judgment. As alluded to above, there are both quantitative and qualitative aspects to the assessment of a

performance. The judges work on a scale from 0.1 to 6.0, 6.0 representing perfection. In all events, there are specific quantitative deductions for certain errors. For example, when a single skater omits the required jump combination during the short freestyle program, 0.8 is deducted. Other quantitative deductions are less clear, such as in the case of a dance team that lacks rhythm, expression, and dance character during the free dance number. In this situation, the judge must deduct 0.5 to 1.0 from the score, depending on how severe the weakness is. This is a case in which a qualitative judgment precedes the final quantitative deduction.

In addition, there are many other factors that simply cannot be quantified: originality, dramatic coherence and movement, sureness of landing, and relative strength of jumps.

With all this uncertainty, there are many things a judge must do to assure finely tuned perception. To maintain standards of excellence, he or she must make every attempt to see as much good skating as possible, confer with coaches, trainers, and sports medicine physicians, and keep abreast of new technical developments, artistic trends, and formal regulations. This also helps broaden a judge's foundation for making fair and informed judgments.

INSTRUCTION

To improve your skating, you will want to take lessons. Your age, skating level, and goals are all factors determining the type of instruction that's best for you at any given point in your development. There are group lessons, semi-private lessons (alas, not as many of these opportunities as there might be), and private instruction. Choosing the right coach for private instruction is a difficult issue, to which you must devote some time, research, and analysis. As you get more and more serious about your skating, you will find yourself investing a good deal of time, money, and effort in training, and you will want to develop the best coach-pupil relationship possible. Above all, you want to *enjoy* your skating.

This chapter deals with the various types of instruction available, the costs involved, and the choice of a coach.

GROUP LESSONS

In group instruction, there can be as few as three or four skaters and as many as forty to fifty. The number of pupils on the ice will depend on the demand on a particular facility. Most classes have ten to twenty skaters on the average.

Regardless of a skater's age or goals, group instruction is one of the

Group instruction at the Hayden Recreation Center, Lexington, Massachusetts. Courtesy John Misha Petkevich

best ways for the beginner to learn the basics of skating. First of all, it teaches the general concepts of skating. Questions arising in a group context are varied and often help to elucidate the less easily understood principles. There is a psychological advantage in seeing that everyone has to confront the same difficulties in learning how to skate, while at the same time the underlying peer pressure can prompt you to try a little harder. You also become accustomed to a very important fact of life, one that arises in many areas besides skating: criticism in front of your colleagues. And last but certainly not least, group instruction does not severely strain the bank account at the outset. Most group lessons range from $1 to $5 per half hour.

Group instruction can be valuable for skaters other than beginners. More adept students may wish to attend a seminar given by a well-known skater; these are excellent opportunities to learn new techniques and tricks. Or large classes may be available on a more or less permanent

basis for the more advanced skater—possibly taught by a very prominent coach or choreographer.

Group lessons are generally given at rinks affiliated with the ISIA or the USFSA, or any other national governing body. The time to start this type of instruction is as soon as there is the desire to improve skills. Young children may have to be coaxed into taking lessons; their parents will have to make the decision for them based on an understanding of their desires and personalities. (See Chapter 10 for more about the parents' role in a skating career.)

SEMI-PRIVATE INSTRUCTION

At this writing, semi-private instruction is not readily available. It is, however, deserving of development. Semi-private lessons have all the advantages of group instruction and some of the advantages of private lessons. If four were the maximum number of students in a class, each student would receive more attention than is possible in a group lesson and yet derive all the benefits of skating with others and learning from everyone's triumphs and mistakes.

Any level of skater would benefit from this type of instruction. At the advanced level, semi-private lessons would ideally accompany private coaching. The cost is generally determined by the private hourly rate of the instructor in question, and it is shared equally by the students.

I would urge all coaches and skaters to assess the value of this type of instruction with their particular needs in mind.

PRIVATE INSTRUCTION

Once a skater has progressed beyond the level of a rank beginner, the private lesson is the most popular type of instruction and one that is invaluable. For many skaters, it is the only type of instruction they take.

The advantages of private lessons are many.

- A coach can attend to the specific problems of the skater being taught.
- The pace of the lesson is determined solely by the progress of the individual.
- Personal style grows unrestrained and is not subject to the unfounded criticisms of one's peers.

- Creativity flourishes.
- An individual style of choreography can be developed.
- The vital relationship between coach and protégé can develop freely and harmoniously.

Skating is very much an individual sport, and so the methods of teaching must ultimately cater to the individual.

Fees charged by coaches for private lessons vary from $6 to $30 per half hour of instruction. Generally, the more qualified the instructor, the higher the fee.

Every skater can benefit from private lessons. They are useful to the beginner as an adjunct to group instruction. For the middle-range skater, they provide an opportunity to get answers to the many questions that arise as individual skills develop. And the top rank of skaters cannot do without private instruction.

HOW MANY LESSONS SHOULD BE TAKEN?

This is a question I hear all the time. The bottom line is that it depends on the individual. Such factors as skating level, age, ability to concentrate, maturity, and goals are some of the important criteria entering into the decision. For example, younger skaters should have time to participate in other activities and to develop in areas other than skating. Furthermore, their powers of concentration are limited, as is their supply of disciplined energy. To encourage them and nurture their interest, it is important that skating not become drudgery. For adults and more advanced skaters, the considerations should be based on the minimum amount of skating time needed for growth and to avoid developing bad habits.

The following schedules are generally considered average for skaters at the various levels, and they may help you make the decision about how much time to spend on lessons.

- The young beginner: one half-hour group lesson and one half-hour private lesson per week, with an equal amount of time for practice.
- The older beginner (fifteen years and up): one half-hour group lesson and one half-hour private or semi-private lesson per week, with twice as much time for practice.
- The purely recreational skater: one group, semi-private, or private half-hour lesson per week, with as much time for practice.

Michelle Noce stepping into a double Salchow. Courtesy John Misha Petkevich

Oops! Well, you advance only if you are willing to attempt moves that are slightly beyond your present level. Courtesy John Misha Petkevich

- The young competitor or test skater: three private half-hour lessons and, if it is available, one semi-private lesson in each area of skating per week, with three to four times as much practice.
- The older competitor or test skater (twenty-five years and up): two private and, if possible, two semi-private half-hour lessons in each area of skating per week, with twice as much time for practice.
- The advanced competitor: three to four private and one semi-private half-hour lessons per week, or three to five private half-hour lessons, in each area of skating; three to five times as much practice.
- The top professional: a private lesson whenever an appraisal turns up the need, for whatever length of time is required; two to three hours of practice, five days per week.

These suggested schedules should be regarded as very general guidelines. Some individuals will need more instruction, others less. A candid

discussion with your coach will help you decide just how many lessons are right for you.

Note that it is recommended that you put in at least as much practice time as you do instruction time, and in some categories of skating you should be practicing up to five times as long. Skating is an individual sport, as has been pointed out before, and it is essential that you acquire self-discipline and self-motivation—qualities that come only from practice on your own. After all, in any performance situation, it is entirely up to the skater. The coach cannot give help at that point.

At the same time, long stretches without instruction only encourage bad habits. Perfecting bad habits is easy; displacing them with good ones is difficult and time consuming. Your aim should be both practice and adequate supervision.

HOW TO CHOOSE A COACH

When you are looking around for a coach, use three types of criteria: background information, on-the-spot analysis, and personal rapport. The importance of each of these depends, to a certain extent, on your reasons for wanting lessons in the first place. The first step is to collect the necessary data.

Background information can usually be obtained from the coach or from the rink at which the coach works. The facts of interest are:

Past skating experience. What is the coach's test, competition, and professional performing record? A coach who has passed all the tests, has competed in the highest division in national or international competition, and has performed professionally in some way rates highest. Certainly some competitive and professional experience is helpful; but the most vital piece of information is the coach's test record.

Past coaching experience. How well has the coach done with other pupils? Coaches who have taught competitors in sectional or national competitions rate well in this category; protégés who have gone on to international events give them an even higher mark.

Educational background. A coach who has had some education beyond secondary school may have slightly more to offer a pupil when decisions unrelated to skating but directly affecting the skater's development come up. Decisions about education, agents, and even music for programs are cases in point. However, this is perhaps the least important consideration, particularly at the outset.

The author with his coach, Arthur Bourque, during a 1970 figure lesson.
Thomas Parry

Professional rating. How high has the coach been rated by the Professional Skaters Guild of America (PSGA), or by the appropriate national professional union? This information is readily available at the rink or through the professional union.

Reputation. What do others in the skating world say about the coach?

Fee. How much does the coach charge?

Following. How many pupils does the coach have? Why so few? Or so many?

Personality. What do others say about the coach's personality, and how do they get along with him or her?

The answers to these questions are by no means an absolute way of determining how good a coach is. They merely provide a basis for comparison with the results of the following two tests.

To form your own opinion of the coach, you must head for the rink to watch him or her in action. Observe how the pupils are doing. If they are having problems, is it their fault or the coach's? This is surprisingly easy to discern with careful, extended observation. How do the pupils react to the coach, and he or she to them? What kind of instructional method and training program are used? If your observations are positive, then you are on the track of a good coach. If the coach also has a good background, excellence is almost confirmed.

The final test of a good coach requires a personal encounter. If, after a bit of conversation, you seem to have some common ground, to get along smoothly, you will probably be able to establish rapport. For the beginner, this is the number-one consideration, and it's high on the list even for advanced skaters. While most coaches are capable of communicating the basics, there are only a few who can take a skater to the top.

Generally, your list of criteria should be taken in the following priority: personal rapport—without a positive learning environment, nothing will be accomplished; on-the-spot analysis—the present performance of a coach has always been the most reliable indicator of excellence (this has been borne out by such great coaches as Gustav Lussi, Slavka Kohout, and Arthur Bourque); and, finally, background.

There are certain circumstances in which you would want to reorder these priorities. You might be looking for a coach who will satisfy a specific need—for example, improved technique on jumps. In this case, personal rapport would be of lesser importance than the insight one particular teacher could provide. Or you might want to engage several different coaches, each for a specific aspect of your skating; in this case, the head coach would be the only person you'd have to get along well with.

Finally, remember that you can always get another coach if you are not doing well with your present one.

7

TRAINING

There are nearly as many training procedures as there are coaches, and this diversity makes it difficult to single out even the common principles. Knowledge about what maximizes a skater's strength, speed, stamina, consistency, and grace is still debated, and the formulation of a unified approach is only in the initial stages. Fortunately, coaches the world over are seeking to learn from biomechanics, from the study of sports medicine, from trainers, and from athletes in other sports. To promote improved training procedures, the U.S. Olympic Committee has established training centers in Colorado Springs, Colorado, and Lake Placid, New York. With further research and continuing cooperation among coaches, improved training methods are inevitable.

THE TIME SPENT ON TRAINING

To a great extent, the time you should devote to training depends on your goals. If you simply want to learn to skate around the rink for pleasure and exercise, then skating an hour every week for a month or two will be more than adequate. If your goal is to obtain a place on the Olympic team, you may need to train as much as four to six hours, six

days per week, ten months out of the year. This includes both lessons and practice time.

Once your goals are established, other factors arise, influencing the amount of training time needed to achieve them. Talent, the ability to translate concepts and verbal instructions into physical movement, and powers of concentration are all involved. The better you are at these things, the less time you will need to spend training; you will be able to concentrate instead on conditioning. Every skater is different, and consultation with an expert, preferably your coach, is the best way to determine how much time you should devote to training.

The following is a rough estimate of the amount of training time skaters at different levels usually require. It gives some idea of the hours the average skater should expect to commit to the sport.

Casual skater	1 hour/week
Beginner—recreational	2 hours/week
Beginner—amateur	3–4 hours/week
Preliminary—recreational	2–3 hours/week
Preliminary—amateur	4–6 hours/week
Intermediate—recreational	4–5 hours/week
Intermediate—amateur	6–8 hours/week
Novice—recreational	5–6 hours/week
Novice—amateur	10–14 hours/week
Junior and Senior—recreational	6–10 hours/week
Junior and Senior—amateur	16–24 hours/week

STRUCTURING A TRAINING PROGRAM

The time of day that you skate depends less on an ideal plan than on the vagaries of rink, school, and job schedules. It is nearly always necessary to make compromises in scheduling. Although it's best to have a routine, if you have the discipline and adaptability, you can make almost any well-conceived schedule work.

More important than the time of day is what the time is devoted to. There are two parts to a training program: on-ice work (the actual skating), and off-ice work.

Tai Babilonia and Randy Gardner, 1979 World Pair Champions, were the first American pair to win the title since 1950. Tai and Randy achieved finesse, unison, and precision by following a regular and disciplined training schedule with on-ice and off-ice practices. Margaret S. Williamson

On-Ice

Since skating is governed by physical principles that are very different from those governing other sports and training activities, it is imperative that you train on the ice as much as possible. The less time spent on solid ground, the better. Of course, there are certain aspects of training that cannot be done on skates; these must be carried out during the off-ice phase of the training program.

For top-level skaters, skating for four to five hours per day is quite sufficient. The sample schedule provided is by no means the only way to organize on-ice training, but it does indicate the relative emphasis that should be placed on the various elements in each specialty. Some competitors may think that four to five hours of skating, six days a week, is a paltry amount of time. I must qualify the schedule by saying that it requires total concentration and complete use of time for determined, well-directed, hard work. Also, it is true that constantly improving training methods are enabling skaters to spend less time and get better results.

Off-Ice

Regardless of the area of skating you are specializing in, some off-ice training is essential. For top-level skaters, one hour per day, six days each week is suitable. The type of off-ice work done will depend on your individual needs. Generally, it should accomplish the following goals.

- Increased strength—you should be able to do the same amount of work (lift weight, move an object) at the extreme point of a stretched arm, leg, hip, or neck, or at your bent torso, as you can in the middle range of motion for that joint.
- Improved mental control—instantaneous, precise response of your body to mental commands.
- Versatility—being comfortable in a number of musical modes and dance styles.

Ideally, the first fifteen minutes of off-ice training should be spent warming up. Warm-up exercises that are suitable for this as well as on-ice work are the most efficient. The remaining forty-five minutes should be spent working in a particular dance medium or on a particular aspect of strength training. (Methods of training are discussed later in this chapter).

SAMPLE DAILY SCHEDULE FOR— TOP-LEVEL COMPETITORS

Singles

compulsory school figures	2 hours
free skating—technique	1½ hours
training for speed and stamina	½ hour
artistry and choreography	1 hour

Pairs

pair moves technique	1½ hours
singles free skating technique	1 hour
training for speed and stamina	½ hour
artistry and choreography	1 hour

Dance

compulsory dance	1½ hours
original set-pattern dance	½ hour
training for speed and stamina	½ hour
artistry and choreography	½ hour
free dance	1 hour

A sample week might be structured something like this:

Monday	15 min. warm-up, 45 min. classical ballet
Tuesday	15 min. warm-up, 45 min. jazz
Wednesday	15 min. warm-up, 45 min. strengthening exercises with particular emphasis on upper body development—especially important for dancers and pair skaters
Thursday	15 min. warm-up, 45 min. classical ballet
Friday	15 min. warm-up, 45 min. modern ballet
Saturday	15 min. warm-up, 45 min. strengthening exercises

Skaters face two difficulties in structuring an off-ice training program: designing one that absolutely fits their needs, and finding experts in dance and strengthening exercise who understand the needs of a skater. If the right people are not found, much time may be wasted following a program that at the very least is unproductive and, at worst, destructive.

There is as yet no simple, straightforward way to find trainers and dancers who understand skating and the need for a specific training program. They generally do not market themselves as specialists for skaters. However, the time is coming when they will. For the time being, the selection of appropriate trainers must be carried out by the coach and the skater through a process of search and discussion. Telephone calls to ballet teachers and trainers in your area are a good starting point. Ballet schools, health clubs, and universities are places where such people may be found. If you are fortunate enough to live in a large urban area, theatrical organizations also merit a call. Next, a one-to-one meeting for discussing the dance teacher's and the trainer's approach and interest is an absolute must. The rest is simply pure judgment. No matter how much time is spent finding them, it will be worth it.

As with on-ice training, off-ice training should be pursued for ten months of the year. Obviously, there will be times when the thrust of the off-ice training will change to accommodate preparations for a particular event, a test or a competition. Always remember that the purpose of off-ice training is to improve on-ice performance.

TRAINING FOR GOALS

As mentioned previously, the structure of your training program will depend on what you are training for. It will also depend on when the goal is going to come up.

For example, if you have one month in which to prepare for a test, your training structure and time sheet should focus on the skills you absolutely have to have to pass that test. Less time should be spent on the foundations of skating technique. If, on the other hand, you are doing a spring and summer training program, with no tests or competitions in the near future, your primary concern will be improving fundamentals, perfecting old techniques, learning new moves and techniques, and increasing fitness and versatility.

Training during the winter months in preparation for a competition changes the approach again. In this case the emphasis shifts to perfecting relatively consistent moves, increasing the level of fitness, and improving finesse. What this boils down to is "peaking," getting into the best possible condition at just the right time.

The following are two sample training schedules with corresponding points of emphasis.

Competitor's Schedule

June, July, August
- Work on fundamentals.
- Work on techniques for new moves.
- Work on artistic versatility on the ice.
- Choreograph new programs.
- Increase strength, speed, and stamina in moderate increments.

September, October, November
- Perfect new techniques.
- Aim for greater consistency.
- Perfect choreography.
- Enlarge increments for greater strength, speed, and stamina.

December, January, February
- Aim for 100 percent consistency.
- Repeat technical moves many times.
- Peak for strength, speed, and stamina.

March, April

If you must skate exhibitions, maintain your present level of technical ability and a moderately high level of fitness. If not, rest and work on off-ice exercises.

May

REST!
VACATION!

Test Skater's Schedule

Six-month Program Leading to a Test
First and second months
- Work on the basics and the general techniques required for the test.
- Begin strength, speed, stamina, and control work.

Third and fourth months
- Work on specific techniques for the test.
- Perfect basics.
- Enlarge increments for strength, speed, and stamina.

Fifth month
- If figures, begin layouts.
- If dance, begin partnering.
- If pairs or free skating, begin program run-throughs.
- Perfect specific techniques.
- Continue to enlarge increments for strength, speed, and stamina.

Sixth month
- If figures, bring layouts and technique together.
- If dance, bring technique, partnering, and unison together.
- If pairs and free skating, perfect program run-throughs.
- Peak in strength, speed, and stamina.

Even the casual or recreational skater will find it very useful to work up a training schedule like those above. The basic principles are these:

- Start by improving foundational techniques and learning new ones. Correlated off-ice exercises should consist of small increments of stress and challenge.
- At the next stage, perfect the basics, concentrate on specific techniques, and increase stress increments for improved athletic and artistic capability.
- Perfect the new techniques and confront greater increments of stress during off-ice training.
- In the final stage, aim for 100 percent consistency in technical work and in performance. Off-ice training should help to bring your athletic and artistic prowess to its peak.

Following these principles will help you to pursue your goals in a methodical and persevering manner. When you have achieved your goals, you will be spurred on to greater challenges that will bring you even greater satisfaction.

METHODS OF TRAINING

Training must address four areas of athletic development: stamina, strength, speed, and flexibility. The best way to improve in these areas, with steady progress and the least risk, is to add small increments of stress. Large increments increase the risk of injury and can burn you out.

Ideally, training methods should be designed specifically for figure skating and should, if possible, take place on the ice. Incorporating technical training with fitness training reduces the amount of time required to achieve a particular goal. Furthermore, the muscles used in skating can be easily exercised over their range of motion. It will, nonetheless, be necessary to supplement on-ice fitness training with specific off-ice exercises. Stamina and speed exercises can be carried out to a large extent on the ice, while strength and flexibility training require some off-ice work.

Stamina

Stamina, or endurance, is the ability to exercise for extended periods of time, and it involves both the cardiovascular and the muscular systems. Stroking exercises on the ice can improve stamina: you would gradually increase the number of repetitions, increase the pace, and decrease the rest periods. Both endurance stroking (for long periods at a relatively fast pace) and sprint stroking (short bursts at full speed) should be done; an ideal ratio between the two might be three to one in favor of sprint stroking. If you do these exercises, you would probably not need to do any off-ice training for endurance.

The only time that off-ice endurance training might be useful is when a skater is without ice for an extended period. In this case, jumping exercises and cycling are good substitutes.

Running has often been suggested as an endurance training method. I do not recommend it for figure skaters for several reasons: it strengthens muscles not used in skating; the principles governing running are different from those governing skating; and strengthening occurs over a very limited range of motion. As far as I'm concerned, running is a last-resort training method.

For top-level skaters, a rigorous free skating program of four to five minutes should not be difficult to execute strongly. The sprint stroking mentioned above along with repetitions of timed segments of a skating program can improve stamina. In place of these short bursts of exercise, skaters can also stroke without stopping for an extended period once or twice each week.

Strength

Strength is the ability to exert a force or pressure against resistance. It is important for jumps, spins, and speed across the ice. Properly strength-

ened muscles make it easier to learn new techniques and to increase speed and flexibility; they also help reduce injuries.

The areas of the body requiring special attention are the legs, back, stomach, and shoulders. For pairs, the arms and neck might be added. Although the lower legs and ankles are important, they have a lesser priority.

Appropriate on-ice strengthening exercises include repeated jump sequences, particularly those done on one foot (loops and one-foot Salchows), stroking (one-foot sculling and turning), and repeated one-foot spins (continuous change-foot sit spins).

For off-ice exercising, weight training is an excellent way to increase strength. It is vitally important to ensure that the exercises are specific to skating and that the muscles are strengthened over their complete range of motion; discuss this with both your coach and your off-ice trainer. Consultations with a doctor specializing in sports medicine can also be very valuable.

Speed

Speed is the quickness with which work is performed. It is important in jumps, spins, footwork, and lifts. Although it is an essential element of skating, it is all too often neglected in training.

There are a number of on-ice methods for improving speed. Jumping repeatedly to maximum height, increasing the speed at which single and double jumps are executed, and sprint stroking are just a few of them. You should also work on increasing the speed at which you perform the footwork in your program.

Flexibility

Flexibility describes the range of motion within a joint. Being flexible without being strong is useless and can be injurious. In skating, stress is often applied to muscles when there is full extension. If there is no strength to control the stress, torn muscles, tendons, and ligaments can result. All flexibility exercises should be executed slowly and with a controlled muscular action. Mentally controlled muscular contraction should create the stress for stretch—it should not be produced by outside forces such as gravity or swinging motions. Even body weight gently lowered on an inadequately supported joint can result in an injury, although the damage may not be immediately apparent.

Most flexibility exercises are carried out off-ice, although there is no reason why some carefully devised, slowly executed ones could not be accomplished on the ice. It doesn't hurt to be flexible in all the joints. This increases the horizons for new moves and choreography. Traditionally, the main areas of the body stretched are the hips and the back. The best way to establish a routine of flexibility exercises is to consult with your coach, your trainer, and an expert in ballet.

I cannot state too often how important it is that training methods be tailored specifically for the figure skater's needs. This results in economies of time, efficient progress, and maximum performance. The principle of specificity is not yet widely accepted in figure skating, as it is in other sports. The more skaters and coaches emphasize it, however, the more progress will be made in this area, and one day it will be commonplace to consult trainers and dance instructors who specialize in the skater's unique requirements.

WARM-UP

One of the most frequent causes of injury in skating is inadequate warm-up. Some skaters hop on the ice and, after stroking around the rink a couple of times, immediately start working on jumps. The danger of this procedure is mind-boggling. Imagine a football player running the length of the field and then starting the game. Or put an Olympic track athlete in the hundred-meter race after he or she has taken a couple of hops. It makes no sense.

There are three purposes to the warm-up: (1) to increase body temperature by increasing heart rate, respiratory rate, and muscular activity; (2) to get the joints moving for greater flexibility; and (3) to prepare the body and mind for performance. The average warm-up consists of slow and gentle exercising of all the joints through their entire range of motion, of small hops and jumps, and of unstressed but continuous movements such as moderate-speed stroking around the rink. Further warm-up can be accomplished by executing basic spins several times over.

Only when the skater has warmed up sufficiently should he or she move into the hard practice session. Fifteen to thirty minutes of warm-up is usually enough.

The author performing a waltz jump during his warm-up prior to the freestyle phase of the 1971 North American Championships, which he won. The North American event was terminated after 1971. Thomas Parry

COOL-DOWN

Cool-down is nearly as important as warm-up, but for different reasons. A slow cool-down permits body temperature to drop gradually, ensures a sufficient blood supply to the brain, and enhances the breakdown of the lactic acid that has built up in the muscles during the workout.

When you are exercising, your heart beats faster, pushing blood into the vessels just under your skin. This has a cooling effect on the body. If exercise is stopped abruptly, the trained athlete's pulse will drop precipitously, and blood will not be circulating out to the skin. The body temperature remains high and may even increase to dangerous levels.

Leg muscle contractions and relaxations during exercise help push the blood back to the heart from the lower extremities. From the heart, the blood is pumped to the brain. A sudden end to muscular activity can result in a pooling of blood in the legs, diminishing the blood supply to the brain. You can become dizzy and light-headed.

Anaerobic exercise, that which does not use oxygen to supply the energy for muscular contractions, results in a buildup of lactic acid in the muscles, which slows muscle response and causes stiffness. (Anaerobic exercises include short bursts of intense activity, such as sprint stroking and weight-lifting.) During exercise, the fresh supply of oxygen in the blood flows to the muscles, and when this oxygen reacts with the lactic acid, the acid is broken down. When you stop exercising suddenly, your pulse rate declines, the supply of blood to your muscles declines, and less oxygen is available to break down the lactic acid, leaving the muscles stiff and therefore more vulnerable to injury.

Consequently, a cooling-down period of ten to fifteen minutes is essential. Do the same sort of exercises you did in the warm-up to accomplish your cool-down.

NUTRITION

The area of nutrition is the subject of much debate, with theories about the average person's nutritional needs constantly changing. It is no surprise to find that nutrition for athletes is even more heatedly discussed.

Because of this uncertainty, it is essential to design a diet in consultation with a trainer, a nutritionist, or a sports physician. I shall outline some basic considerations and urge you to consult the experts for details.

There are four essential food groups, and a nutritionally balanced diet incorporates servings from each of them. How much of each food and how many calories from each group make up your diet will depend to a large extent on your age and energy expenditure.

> Dairy products: whole milk and skim milk, yogurt, cheese, cottage cheese
>
> Meats and other proteins: beef, lamb, pork, veal, poultry, fish, eggs, legumes (e.g. peanut butter, lentils, soybeans)
>
> Vegetables and fruits: dark green and deep yellow vegetables, such as broccoli and squash; citrus fruits and fruit juices; other vegetables and fruits
>
> Breads and cereals: whole-grain and other breads, muffins, rolls; hot and cold cereals; rice, pasta

Other foods that serve as dietary supplements are oils and fats, including margarines, vegetable oils, salad dressings, and mayonnaise, and sugary foods.

A skater's diet should consist of the following caloric distribution: 15 percent of total calories consumed from protein, 30–35 percent from fats, and 50–55 percent from carbohydrates. Athletes must consume a high percentage of carbohydrates because they supply muscle glycogen, the most efficient source of energy.

Foods that tend to form gas, such as beans, onions, cabbage, and carbonated drinks, should be avoided prior to workouts and competitions. The precompetition meal should be bland, nongreasy, high in carbohydrate content, and contain moderate levels of fats and proteins. It should be eaten approximately three hours before skating. A sample meal would consist of a serving of roasted or broiled meat, one baked potato, one serving of vegetables, one glass of skim milk, a serving of fruit, and a serving of plain cake. At all other times, balance is the key.

INJURIES

Although figure skating is not a high-risk sport, injuries do occasionally occur. Skaters are very mobile athletes and are therefore particularly vulnerable to injuries to the ankles, knees, and groin. Dancers and pair skaters are more susceptible to back injuries than are singles skaters.

Many of the injuries that occur today are blamed on the increasing

number of skaters executing triple jumps. There is some truth to this, and yet it is not the jumps themselves that are the culprit. Skaters who have been injured doing triple jumps tend to fall into three categories:

1. Those who were simply not fit enough to attempt triples, lacking the necessary strength, speed, endurance, and/or flexibility.
2. Those who did not follow a routine warm-up that was both sound and sufficiently long.
3. Those who lacked the technical foundation to execute triples in the first place (poor coaching and insufficient experience on the ice may have been the problems).

Instead of making triple jumps the scapegoat of skating injuries, we would do better to take a good, hard look at present training methods and the extent of our skaters' preparation. The major causes of skating injuries are insufficient warm-up, poor technique, and, sometimes, an unfortunate landing, edge catch, or twisting motion. Overall fitness and good warm-up procedures can drastically reduce the already low risks in this sport.

8

THE COSTS
OF A SKATING CAREER

In the economic climate that exists today, the question of cost is all-important. At the recreational level, skating can be a very reasonably priced sport. At the competitive level, it is undeniably expensive. However, skaters can turn to sponsors and to the Memorial Fund of the United States Figure Skating Association to help defray a part of the total costs. If your desire to skate is strong, you can find a way to finance it.

THE CASUAL SKATER'S COSTS

If you are skating primarily for the fun of it, the costs will not be terribly high. In fact, they will be far less than those incurred by recreational downhill skiers or people who sail boats.

A casual skater practicing once a week for thirty weeks could expect to pay, on the average, a total of $50 to $70 for equipment and $50 to $70 for ice time (although in some pricey areas, such as New York City, ice time can run as high as $150). Travel costs to and from the rink, as well as additional clothing, would be figured in separately.

THE RECREATIONAL SKATER'S COSTS

The costs for a recreational skater, one who skates seriously for the fun of it, are somewhat more than they are for the casual skater. Recreational skaters spend more time on the ice and will want to own better equipment. Furthermore, instruction will more than likely be a part of the skating program. Additional costs might include attending ISIA competitions, having costumes made for competitions or shows, and paying dues as a member of an organized skating program.

A recreational skater taking eight one-hour practice sessions and one hour of instruction each week for thirty weeks a year would find the financial outlay to be something like the following.

Ice time	$ 450
Instruction	360
Equipment	200
Costumes and music	100
Dues and fees	15
Total	$1,125

Costs for travel to and from the rink would be extra. Also, if you decided to skate competitively, other expenses would enter into the scheme: travel, accommodation, food, entry fees, any extra ice time and lessons, and additional music or costumes. Extra costs associated with competitions could be as little as $50 or as much as $2,000, depending on the number of contests entered and how far you have to travel for them.

THE AMATEUR SKATER'S COSTS

There are two different types of amateur skaters, and they have different types of expenses. There is the skater who simply enjoys amateur skating and is training to pass tests; and there is the skater who is pursuing a competitive career. Costs borne by test skaters are substantially less than those borne by competitive skaters.

The variables in the test skater's budget are the amount of ice time used, the number of lessons taken, the number of tests tried each year, and the type of equipment purchased. Since there can be great variation

in any one of these factors, the following is an indication only of the average costs for a middle-level test skater.

Ice time (two hours per day, six days per week, forty weeks per year)	$2,400
Instruction (four lessons per week, forty weeks per year)	2,000
Equipment (two pairs of skates)	500
Equipment maintenance	50
Accessories	100
Costumes and music	300
Dues and fees (club fees, USFSA dues, test fees)	150
Total	$5,500

As before, travel costs to and from the rink and to test sessions are additional.

This figure may seem high, but costs for competitors are much higher. Here is a breakdown of the costs that a high-level competitor might expect to incur in one year of training.

Ice time (four hours per day, six days per week, forty weeks per year)	$4,800
Instruction (eight lessons per week)	4,800
Off-ice instruction (six hours per week, forty weeks per year)	1,200
Equipment (three pairs of skates per year)	1,200
Other equipment	100
Costumes and practice outfits	1,500
Music	200
Makeup and props	100
Publicity photographs	300
Dues and fees	500
Tutors (for classes in skills missed because of competitions, or because of preparation for competition)	500
Competition expenses: skater	2,000

Competition expenses: coach	1,500
Special foods and dietary supplements	1,000
Parents' expenses for travel (at this level of competition, the USFSA Memorial Fund generally takes care of the skater's travel expenses)	5,000
Miscellaneous expenses	1,000
Total	$25,700

There will be a good bit of variation in the costs for each particular case. It is safe to assume, however, that the costs for a competitive skater can range from $10,000 to as much as $50,000. The present regulations limiting amateurs from receiving financial remuneration for skating-related work makes this picture even more grim. Fortunately, the trend recently has been to loosen the restrictions related to amateur status. Skaters may one day be able to use their talents to defray some of the costs of competitive skating. And the limited funds and cash awards that are available will then be put to use helping younger skaters who are not in a position to use their reputations or their skating to earn money.

THE MEMORIAL FUND

The Memorial Fund was established in memory of the 1961 U.S. World Team, whose members lost their lives in a Brussels airplane crash on the way to the World Championships. It acts as an independent entity within the USFSA.

The purpose of the fund is twofold: to provide some financial support for competitive skaters, and to help defray some of the costs of higher education for competitors (generally, though not necessarily, these are skaters who have retired from skating competitively and want to develop new careers). The great majority of the monetary awards are given with the first purpose in mind.

To apply for Memorial Fund assistance, you need to have a sectional competition track record. If you are of National novice standing, it is worth applying.

On February 1 each year, the Memorial Fund sends applications to

all previous grant recipients and to all USFSA clubs for new applicants. The applications must be filed by June 1. The sectional chairman of the Memorial Fund examines the applications and rates the skaters from 1 to 5 on the basis of skating promise, motivation, financial need, and general character. The higher the total points, the more money a skater receives. For the 1981–82 skating season, the World Team members each received $2,500 and were able to take an additional $1,875 on a loan basis. Skaters with a lower national standing in competition generally receive less money since their promise has not yet been proven beyond a shadow of a doubt.

Educational grants, accounting for about 5 percent of the total monies awarded, are given on the basis of academic record and the skater's intention to continue in the sport.

More detailed information on the Memorial Fund can be obtained directly from the USFSA or its member clubs.

9

THE SPORT AND
THE ART OF SKATING

Over the decades, there has been much debate about the essence of figure skating: is it sport or is it art? The controversy seems rather pointless, because there have been ample examples of both throughout the history of skating. Why should it be limited to one or the other by a mere label?

Figure skating has all the ingredients of a sport. It requires technical expertise and precision, athletic agility and coordination, and physical endurance. It features specific moves and feats that can be objectively assessed. And there are many competitive skating events.

The lack of a continuous tradition in the art of figure skating does somewhat cloud its legitimacy as an art form. There have been many singular examples of artistic expression in skating, however. During the first part of the twentieth century, Charlotte performed in her own ice ballets. Sonja Henie started a touring ice show, the *Hollywood Ice Revue*, with overtones of dance. Barbara Ann Scott skated in the first musical on ice, *Rose Marie*, in England in 1950. Tenley Albright gave some artistic exhibition programs in the 1950s, and in the 1960s the Protopopovs perfected the classical line in pair skating; they have since gone on to skate narrative and theatrical programs. There is great beauty of movement in performances by skaters such as Peggy Fleming and Janet Lynn.

Toller Cranston created *The Ice Show*, a theatrical evening of drama and dynamic sculpture. And it was a direct line from classical ballet that brought John Curry's *Ice Dancing* troupe to the theater. Eventually, these diverse attempts to establish skating as an art form will lead to a continuous tradition, and the label "art" will be as unquestionable as the label "sport."

What the controversy really boils down to is not whether skating is an art or a sport, but how much of each element should be present in a given situation. It is the setting that dictates which must predominate. But this is not an important dilemma, for artistry without athletic expertise is not good skating, and athleticism without artistry is pointless.

THE SPORT

Throughout the course of this book, the athletic aspects of skating have been either directly discussed or implied. In the compulsory events (figures and dance), a skater needs discipline, precision, control, and absolute balance. For the freestyle events (short and long singles and pairs programs, and the original set-pattern and free dances), a skater must demonstrate numerous athletic abilities. Stamina, strength, speed, flexibility, agility, balance—all these qualities must be present. Skaters must also have the ability to execute both basic and difficult moves with grace, consistency, and power. It's imperative that they have enough self-confidence to pit their abilities against those of other skaters.

All these qualities indicate in one way or another the athleticism of a given skater. If any one of them is missing, the skater has not reached his or her peak. Without technical athletic achievement, skating becomes mere recreation.

THE ART

It is very difficult to define what is "art" in skating. Certainly, there are characteristics common to all good art. As always, however, taste and aesthetic judgments play a major role. As the nature of taste and aesthetics is far beyond the scope of this book, we will restrict ourselves here to identifiable characteristics.

Perhaps the most obvious aspect of figure-skating art is musical

Toller Cranston in one of his original positions, demonstrating a departure from the usual style of free skating. The attention to detail is notable: the angularity of the arms and the position of the wrists and fingers are all consciously conceived and executed. David Street

expression. It is fairly easy to tell if a skater is or is not skating to the music. All too often, skaters ignore the fact that music is an integral part of a freestyle program. When the music and the skater are one, observers will immediately recognize that it is an interesting program whether or not they find that skater particularly appealing. The meaningful interpretation of music can turn a movement into a gesture.

Another fairly obvious aspect of artistic expression is the completeness of each gesture. If a movement is executed only halfway, it loses strength, conviction, meaning. The audience's response to a completed gesture is subconscious and spontaneous.

Dramatic intent is a third important ingredient. Every program as a whole must communicate some purpose. The purpose may be as nihilistic as the communication of nothing at all, or it may be abstract, intending only to treat the observer to a visual feast of forms. Some programs intend to communicate quite literally some story; such presentations might be termed narrative. Whatever the intent, it must be clear.

A program or performance must above all have dramatic coherence. This does not mean that the whole program must be on one level— completely sad, completely abstract, completely ethereal. It means that the program should begin at some point and follow a course of action through time that is aesthetically reasonable. It should not, for example, start as a takeoff of a musical and change in the middle to an interpretation of *Sleeping Beauty*, for no apparent reason. At the 1983 World Championships, World ice dance champions Jayne Torvill and Christopher Dean presented a "*Barnum* on Ice" program that had wonderfully coherent, dramatic expression, as they mimed the elements of a circus while skating to music from the Broadway hit *Barnum*. Another excellent program at the same competition was presented by the American ice dancing champions Judy Blumberg and Michael Seibert. Their freedance program evoked the era of Fred Astaire and Ginger Rogers.

When all the above-mentioned elements are carried through, the result is a very special demonstration of art and beauty. Art gives variety, depth, and meaning to what would otherwise merely be a display of technical feats, spectacular though they might be.

Music

It should be clear that the choice of music must not be left to chance. Music is the foundation of a successful artistic performance. Although most skaters are constantly searching for new and different music to

express their dramatic intent, there is still insufficient emphasis placed on the choice of music and its arrangement in a program.

Here are some considerations to keep in mind as you select your music.

- Almost any piece of nonvocal music can be used in amateur competition; in exhibitions and professional competitions all types of music are permissible.
- The music should be suitable for the fulfillment of a dramatic intent. This is easier to accomplish with certain types of music. Unless you consider yourself a master of musical interpretation, it is best to stick to something that can be easily translated into movement. Music with an obvious rhythm or a distinct melodic line, for example, is good. Stravinsky's *Firebird* and Bartok's *Concerto for Orchestra* have been used quite successfully by a number of top skaters. I skated to *On the Waterfront* by Bernstein in 1970, and to the Piano Concerto no. 2 by Rachmaninoff in 1971.
- The dramatic intent and design of the program should harmonize with the music selected. Don't combine classical balletic choreography with a score from a Broadway musical.
- Music containing climaxes and resolutions is more easily rendered dramatic than music with numerous repetitions and subtle changes.
- Dramatic coherence is more easily accomplished with music that comes from one source: from one particular symphony, from one Broadway musical, from one genre of popular music. Blending rock music with Schubert is not likely to work unless there is a *very* well-defined artistic reason for the combination.
- If the kind of music you are interested in skating to defines a particular era or genre, listen extensively to selections from that era or genre.

There is no easy way to pick music, except, perhaps, by chance inspiration. Once the specific piece has been chosen, identify the parts you intend to use. Make every effort to create a total composition that is coherent and has some dramatic contours. The splicing and arranging should always be done with harmony and rhythm, as well as pitch and tone, in mind. When the completed music is ready, take it to the ice and create a program to match it.

Choreography

The purpose of choreography is to crystallize the dramatic intent you have conceived in response to your choice of music. All the aspects of artistry mentioned above apply here. The realization of an idea through movement to music is one of the most exciting experiences there is.

The quest for greater artistic breadth and new creative horizons has prompted skaters to turn to choreographers from diverse backgrounds. Finding an appropriate choreographer is just about as difficult as finding the right coach. It is safe to assume, however, that any choreographer with a respectable background is going to bring some new dimension to your work.

Whether you are a beginner or already have some experience as a choreographer, there are several considerations in choreographing that it would be useful to mention here.

1976 Olympic Champion John Curry took the classical line of the Proto-popovs and developed it into a school of skating that was manifested that year in an ice ballet show, Ice Dancing. Margaret S. Williamson

1. Be sure that you make your movements in response to the music.

2. Jumps, spins, and other technical feats are usually done at points in the music that call for such movements. A sudden, loud crescendo is a particularly good opportunity to show off your jumps, while a phrase of music covering several measures seems to call for a spin. Fast, choppy music is well suited to fast footwork. At the World Championships in 1962, Donald Jackson began his program with a triple lutz on the opening crescendo of his music, which was Bizet's *Carmen.* To a long phrase from Rachmaninoff's Piano Concerto no. 2, I glided on one foot down the entire length of the ice, using only slow, deliberate arm movements.

3. There is no reason you have to fit the mold. Often a jump is very effective during a lull in the music, though unfortunately this strategy is rarely used. The Protopopovs have used it through-out their career, putting pair lifts to very minor climaxes in the music and extended spirals at points of dramatic crescendo. In his 1983 World Championships program, Scott Hamilton per-formed a triple toe loop at a very quiet, lyrical interlude, and he landed a beautiful double Axel during a pause in the music—a most effective presentation.

4. The choreography, like the music, should have dramatic con-tours, climaxes, and resolutions. This means that both the speed of the skater across the ice and the rapidity and breadth of the movement should not be constant throughout the program. The right kind of pacing, always fresh and satisfying, was particularly apparent in Scott Hamilton's program, mentioned above. The first part of the program was flashy, jazzy, and upbeat. Then he slowed down for a reflective and lyrical section, still maintain-ing the jazz theme. A waltz section followed, which lent itself well to a fast, go-get-'em ending. It was a program with great variety, yet the parts were all smoothly joined together.

5. Movements other than technical maneuvers should be consis-tent with the dramatic intent, the genre of the music, and/or the cultural period that the music suggests.

6. It is not necessary to restrict your movements to those that have already been performed. Toller Cranston, Allen Schramm, and Gary Beacon are among the skaters who are expanding the vocabulary of movement on ice today. Cranston has incorporat-ed footwork that consists of running sideways on his toes;

The author executing a Bourkey, a side stag flip jump he invented and named after his coach, Arthur Bourque. William Udell

Schramm is known for his two-footed footwork and edges involving velvety, slinking upper body movements; and Beacon has recently done such unusual things as landing Axels on forward outside edges, and skating forward crossovers with his arms in the reversed position.

7. The layout of the program on the surface of the ice should be consciously conceived, and it should accentuate the drama unfolding in the music and the movements. In other words, a particularly powerful moment in the music should not come with a movement buried in the corner of the rink.

Peggy Fleming, 1968 Olympic Champion, is known for her exquisite grace on the ice. Here she wears a "fishy" costume decorated with sequins and scale-like glitter for the 1982 Strawberry Ice *television special.* Courtesy Toller Cranston

8. Finally, choreography is dynamic and constantly changing. Experimenting with new ideas is well worth the trouble.

Costumes

As mentioned in Chapter 3, the skater's costume should be designed to be harmonious with the music, the choreography, and the dramatic purpose of the program. The costume, and the appropriate makeup when necessary, are the final touches to theatrical presentation.

In designing a costume, it is always useful to refer to what others have worn in similar dramatic circumstances. Costumes for all the dramatic arts are an invaluable source of ideas, and there are many books on theatrical costume design you can consult.

A number of considerations accompany the designing of a costume.

- The design must allow for complete movement. Stretch fabrics or costumes that are loosely designed at the joints are two solutions to the motion problem.
- It should ideally enhance the form of the body and not accentuate or magnify figure problems.
- Harmony with the music, choreography, and dramatic intent of the program is all-important. The fiery red costume with hanging tendrils of cloth that Toller Cranston wore for his *Firebird* number in the 1982 World Professional Championships was a perfect complement to the music. In that same competition, JoJo Starbuck and Ken Shelley skated to Debussy's *Claire de Lune* in beautifully flowing beige costumes. This element of artistic presentation in skating cannot be overemphasized.

Presentation

A figure skating program should be presented as a living art form. It requires movement, drama, and musical expression. The entire body, including the face, should work to realize the dramatic intent. Your heart, soul, and mind must be focused on that singular end. If they are not, it will be obvious to your audience. Only in this way can the carefully structured plans for music, choreography, costume, and dramatic purpose come together in a unified, powerful work.

10

PARENTS, COACH, AND SKATER: THE TRIANGULAR RELATIONSHIP

The triangle of parent, athlete, and coach is a delicate and vital one. In degree, certainly, it is unique to the sport of figure skating. In most other athletic endeavors, the important relationship is between the coach and the athlete; the role of the parents is relatively minor. In skating, parents play a very significant role.

There are a number of reasons for this unique situation. At the head of the list is the monetary investment required in skating. Competitive skating is expensive. People who invest large sums of money usually take a keen and critical interest in what they have invested.

Second, the daily life of a skater demands the involvement of the parents. Skaters frequently must commute long distances to rinks, and parents consequently end up remaining at the rink during the training sessions. Rink proximity is the only way to circumvent this problem. Even so, the responsibility for the transportation more often than not falls upon the parents' shoulders. With older teenagers, this becomes less of an issue, particularly after they've obtained driver's licenses.

Third, skating is not a team sport. It is a sport of individuals, and its creative aspects make it even more individualistic. No matter how self-motivated a skater is, parental support is very helpful.

Lastly, parents rightly perceive that figure skating has an element of the subjective in it, and thus of the political. The "skating mother" is not unlike the "stage mother," who deals in similar currency. The term is not necessarily derogatory, nor is the role restricted to mothers. With the proper spirit and intent, a skating mother or father can be one of the most valuable friends the skater has—and one of the most valuable boosters of the sport in general.

From this, it is not difficult to see why parents have become such an integral part of a skater's life, and why the relationship must be a triangular one. Every member of the triangle is important, and every member must be strong if the relationship is to work. The goals are the same, but the responsibilities of each differ somewhat. There are, however, four common denominators.

Honesty

To establish realistic goals, all three members of the triangle must be honest about the skater's capabilities. All three should participate in an assessment of the skater's weaknesses and strengths. From this, short-term and long-range goals can be agreed upon. The training program can then be designed to convert weaknesses into strengths. The outcome will be a sense of team effort, a sense of excitement each time another step is taken toward the final goal, and a satisfaction upon achieving goals. Honesty brings a realism that is the basis for trust and commitment.

Trust

The relationship must be built on trust. Without trust, the members of the triangle will not be able to withstand the pressures of training and competition.

In simplest terms, trust is the recognition and acceptance that each member will fulfill his or her responsibilities. The coach must believe that the skater is sincere in the intention to pursue his or her goals, and that the parents will be candid and live up to their commitment to the coach. The skater must believe that the coach is committed to the skater's progress and is capable of guiding the skater to achieve his or her goals. The parents and the skater must have a sound, healthy, familial relationship based on love. From the coach, parents must believe that commitment to their child will persist and that the instruction will be of the standard expected.

The author with his coach during a private lesson in 1970. They are working on a long, gliding edge performed to a phrase of Rachmaninoff's Piano Concerto no. 2 (see page 107). Ruth Silverman

Commitment

There must be commitment to achieve goals, meaning that nothing can deter the skater from following through. The training program that has been designed to achieve those goals must be faithfully adhered to. Perseverance, determination, and mental discipline are integral parts of the commitment. No sacrifice from any member of the triangle can be too great.

Positivism

Honesty and achievement lead to self-confidence, and self-confidence leads to a positive attitude. Much has been said in recent years about taking an optimistic approach to oneself and one's activities. It is true that one cannot succeed without believing in oneself and one's abilities. The

formula is simple: a positive, confident attitude helps skaters perform without harmful tension. Some form of tension necessarily accompanies most performances—tension from the excitement of the event, from the desire to excel, which is healthy—but tension aroused by lack of confidence and uncertainty is unhealthy. With realistic goals derived through honest appraisal, with trust among the members of the triangle, and with an unwavering commitment, positivism should evolve naturally.

SPECIAL ROLES

Parents

In addition to all the qualities described above, parents must provide the skater with support, guidance, and a healthy family life. Parental support gives the skater the psychological sustenance he or she needs to carry through. Every champion remembers rough times that were endured more easily because of a sense of emotional strength. Parents can help a young skater to face a crisis, to understand problems, and to grow stronger as a result. It has been said that parents should neither encourage nor discourage, but *give* courage.

Parents should also be available to provide guidance whenever the need arises. Most issues should be discussed by all three members of the triangle. If an outside expert must be consulted, parents should participate in the choice of that expert. If the issue is very personal, it may be best for only the parents and the skater to discuss it.

A healthy family life is the most important factor. It is there that personal strength and confidence first blossom and develop. It is the single most important source of strength for a young skater.

Whether or not parents should push a child to skate is a problem that almost always arises in the course of a skater's career. One element of the answer is quite simple—never should a child be *forced* to skate. More often than not, however, the pushing that one sees at rinks across the country stops just short of force, and the issue becomes clouded.

There is certainly nothing wrong with encouragement and guidance. Very few people, even adults, are capable of persevering without encouragement through all the storms that accompany an important activity. The line between persuasion and encouragement is fine, however. Persuasion does not allow the skater to formulate a firm and unremitting personal commitment; encouragement, on the other hand, serves to

Tenley Albright Gardiner and her daughter, Elin, skating in the 1974 Superskates *at Madison Square Garden.* Margaret S. Williamson

reinforce a decision that the skater has already made. Children who simply follow commands will not be able to think a problem through on their own—their creativity and independence will be stifled. Parents must provide guidance through suggestion and advice, to allow their child to develop important decision-making capabilities and to teach the child how to live with his or her own decisions.

The Coach

The coach has many areas of responsibility. On the professional level, he or she must provide expert instruction, devise a plan of attack for short-term and long-range goals, provide the skater with guidance on training,

The author skating figures in the 1968 Olympics in Grenoble. Great precision and intense concentration are required for the successful execution of figures—which is only one of the areas in which a championship singles skater must excel.

artistry, music, costumes, and diet, foster positivism in the skater, ensure an attitude of good sportsmanship, and see to it that the training program does not interfere with the skater's other long-term goals, such as education.

On the personal level, the coach can be a very important influence in the skater's life. Often there is a great spirit of camaraderie. At the same time, the coach must let his or her authority and experience be felt and insist that it be recognized. The skater should know that when the coach speaks, it is with deliberation and wisdom. A coach is obliged to be a teacher, a guide, and a friend.

The Skater

In the final analysis, of course, it is the skater who achieves the goals. It is the skater who steps on the ice to perform, alone; and the road there is paved with many responsibilities. The skater must

- be willing to learn
- possess a burning desire to excel, backed up by commitment
- be willing to accept advice and criticism
- accept and acknowledge the parents' contribution to his or her effort
- respect the coach
- be willing to place personal pleasure second to personal achievement
- possess an enduring love for the sport and the art of figure skating
- resolve to be a model of good sportsmanship.

In addition, there is one responsibility that is too often neglected, because many coaches and skaters see it as an impediment to achievement in skating. This responsibility is education. In no way does education interfere with skating; if anything, the mental discipline required is a benefit to the skater, particularly at the secondary school level. Generally, when a skater finds that he or she cannot pursue both, it is because time is being used poorly, not because the two endeavors are mutually exclusive. The scholar-athlete is a model worth emulating.

When all this effort comes together, we might see a champion in the making. We have seen it again and again throughout skating history. Figure skating may be a sport for the individualist, but it requires the commitment and participation of three distinct entities before one of them, the athlete, can excel.

11

PROFESSIONAL CAREERS

Until very recently, there were realistically only two professional careers a skater could pursue: coaching and performing in a skating show. Certainly, there have been the occasional superstars who could command large fees for endorsements, appearances on television or in person, and movie roles. But these were and are the exceptions. Even the increasing number of television shows that feature skaters generally do not afford enough work or money to be a full-time occupation.

There is, however, another avenue that is just beginning to open up. In 1980 Dick Button, a stellar figure in the world of figure skating, started an annual World Professional Championship, which sought to bring together the top professionals in a team competition. Although there has been a World Professional competition since 1931, it has generally not attracted the top stars. As a result of this new team championship, there are now moves to develop a professional competition circuit. Several groups, including the Pro Skate Company, are developing ideas to promote such a circuit. The eventual aim is to include head-to-head contests as well as team competitions.

This development, coupled with the increasing number of entertainment opportunities involving skating, has transformed the professional skating horizon from bleak to bright. In this chapter we shall examine the various opportunities for today's professional skaters.

TEACHING

In figure skating, a teacher is called a coach or a pro. Once you receive money for instruction, you are considered a professional and you lose your amateur status under the present regulations.

Becoming a pro is not simply a matter of making up your mind to do so. Many rinks and clubs throughout the world insist that their pros be members of the appropriate professional skaters' guild. In some countries in which the professional union has a rating system, rinks may even insist that the newly hired pro be rated.

In the United States, the professional union is the Professional Skaters Guild of America (PSGA). The international body is the International Professional Skaters Union. Several other countries have national organizations; see Appendix A for a complete list of names and addresses.

The *PSGA Rating System Requirements Manual*, which is available at no charge to PSGA members, gives all the details about the rating

Belita during her performance in the 1981 Superskates. *Belita was a great show skater during the 1940s and later became a movie star on the strength of her acting ability.* Margaret S. Williamson

Lynn-Holly Johnson, shown here rehearsing with Robby Benson for the movie Ice Castles, *has used her skating talent to break into an acting career.* Courtesy Lynn-Holly Johnson

system. In general, ratings depend on the pro's test record, on the test and competition record of the pro's pupils, and on an oral examination. To prepare for rating exams, young professionals are encouraged to attend educational seminars and conventions. It is also possible to arrange private conferences with master-rated professionals.

PSGA RATINGS
AVAILABLE IN EACH CATEGORY

Figure and Free Skating Instructor: Master, Senior, Certified, Registered
Dance and Free Dance Instructor: Master
Dance Instructor: Master, Senior, Certified
Pair Skating Instructor: Master, Senior, Certified
Administrator: Master, Senior, Certified
Program Director: Master
Group Instructor: Master, Senior, Certified

The professional unions in Canada, West Germany, and Austria also have rating systems. Unlike the PSGA system, which is based solely on knowledge of skating, these countries require knowledge in several related areas. For example, Austria calls for six months of schooling on general knowledge, basic physiology, anatomy, first aid, and the science of teaching. After pros pass a standard exam in these areas, they are required to demonstrate their knowledge of skating, the practical side. Both teaching ability and demonstrating ability are assessed. Even former Olympians must follow this procedure.

Professional skaters' unions provide a number of services. For example, for an annual membership fee of $65, plus a $15 initiation charge for new members, the PSGA makes available group liability insurance and group medical insurance; members also receive the PSGA newsletter, which contains information about skating regulations, events, and educational opportunities. The bottom line, however, is that the PSGA provides teachers with a vehicle for taking concerted stands on issues of vital concern to the growth of the sport. For most of those involved in the amateur organizations, figure skating is a hobby, possibly even a consuming interest; but it does not provide them with a living. Skating *is* the pros' living, and issues affecting it should certainly be subject to their ideas and opinions.

The Qualities of a Good Coach

As we mentioned in the last chapter, a coach must be a very special person. Aside from infinite patience, a coach must frequently have nerves of steel. He or she must brave the cold on a daily basis, must cope with an irregular and often lengthy work schedule, and must enjoy working with young people. Above all, a coach must love skating.

There are three specific areas in which coaches who reach the top of the profession excel. The first is in knowledge and understanding. Coaches must know the technical and artistic aspects of skating inside out. To identify the source of difficulty on a particular maneuver, you must understand both body movement and the principles governing a mass in motion on the ice. It is relatively easy to discern an imbalance, but it is difficult to pinpoint the source of the error, which may have occurred four or five steps before the problem itself showed up. The coach must also have some aesthetic sensibility, and be able to identify beautiful movements that make artistic sense and possess dramatic intent.

The second area of coaching is the ability to apply this knowledge in a practical way, to convey principles of skating to the pupil. It helps to know a bit about psychology—often, teaching entails making something very dull seem very interesting. Aural, visual, and sensory aids often help the learning process. The coach will have succeeded when the skater understands the principles and is able to analyze errors, when he or she approaches skating with enthusiasm, interest, and curiosity.

Finally, a coach must have an excellent eye. Jumps take about 1.5 seconds from the step onto the takeoff edge to the landing. Film and videotape can help pinpoint problems, but who can use these all the time? By concentrating hard on the movements during a technical maneuver, the eye can be trained to pick up errors quickly.

Schools and Apprenticeships

A new development throughout the skating world is the formation of skating schools, which have a head coach and/or a group of individual coaches with similar approaches working together. This heralds a significant and fortuitous change from the individualistic style of coaching, which was formerly the only style. A unified approach taken by several coaches with many pupils encourages a more scientific attitude to training and technique, and it makes possible extended trial periods in a more controlled environment. It permits specialization and thus engenders

The author as an amateur skater demonstrating a spin to two young aspiring champions. Robert E. Crosby

expertise on the staff. The fact that resources are centralized helps keep the cost down. Finally, it provides the young coach with an opportunity to apprentice him- or herself to a head coach or to a school.

Apprenticeship has many advantages. For one thing, a new pro joins a staff with an established clientele. This eliminates that barren year while you are building up your business. The pro's learning process can also be dramatically expedited—what would otherwise take several years to absorb can be learned in a few months. Many skating schools are very prestigious, since they have developed around the best coaches in the skating world. At the very least, schools provide an on-the-spot forum for the airing and discussion of new ideas.

In the United States, most of the better-known skating schools can be found in Seattle, Los Angeles, Colorado Springs, Denver, Lake Placid, Atlanta, Wilmington, Del., and New York City. There are also a number of less well-known schools, many of which are not schools per se but rather occasional team efforts.

The Coach's Education

A figure skating coach's education is an ongoing process. With the many new technical breakthroughs resulting from research in biomechanics and sports medicine, it is essential to keep informed. At the annual PSGA meetings, there are almost always sessions on technique, training, and medicine. Coaches should also read books and journals on biomechanics, training, and other sports to gain new insights.

The multidimensional nature of figure skating necessitates journeys into even more diverse subject areas than those already mentioned. To expand creative horizons, coaches should attend the theater, ballet, both popular and classical concerts, and films. Fashion shows and makeup demonstrations nourish a sense of design and style—even hairstyling shows help create an awareness of the importance of the head in the overall impression. Art exhibits can call forth new insights into form and movement. Any visual, emotional, or aural experience is a valuable addition to a coach's education.

Coaching Ethics

In most professions there is a code of ethics, and skating is no exception. When it is followed, it paves the way for smooth day-to-day running of the sport in a spirit of camaraderie and mutual accomplishment. The standards of conduct are simple and are dictated by common sense.

Elaborate costumes and ingenious choreography helped make Sonja Henie a great artist and an indisputable star. Her Hollywood Ice Revue *reigned for twenty-one years.* Courtesy USFSA

- In dealing with young people, it is essential to be discreet yet candid.
- Professional candor should govern all dealings with other coaches; this is particularly important when a student is in the process of changing pros.
- Pros should always relay the true state of the skater's progress to his or her parents. Tell it like it is.
- Pros should respect other pros' technical innovations. Imitation may be the sincerest form of flattery, but this is small comfort when the creator does not receive the recognition he or she deserves.
- Every coach should possess a professional bearing and should meet each new crisis with maturity and equanimity.

Dorothy Hamill (center), *shown here receiving her 1976 Olympic Gold Medal, has had a multi-faceted professional skating career that has included appearances in the Ice Capades and various television shows and specials.* Courtesy ABC Television Public Relations

When the coach observes these ethical considerations, the only remaining concern is the production of great skating.

PROFESSIONAL SHOWS

The many varieties of professional shows include dinner theater, night-club acts, large variety entertainment productions, theme shows, exhibitions, and ice-ballet shows. Dinner theater shows and nightclub acts tend to be found in resort areas such as Lake George, New York, and Knotts Berry Farm in Los Angeles, or in Las Vegas and Atlantic City. They usually come and go as the demand arises. It is not easy to keep informed about them; occasionally, the producers will advertise in *Recreational Ice*

MAJOR PROFESSIONAL SHOWS

Buddy LaLonde Ice Classics
3777 Quinlan Lane
San Jose, CA 95118

Holiday On Ice (Europe)
10 Sheen Road
Richmond, Surrey
England

Ice Follies-Holiday on Ice
3201 New Mexico Avenue, N.W.
Washington, DC 20016

Ice Capades
6121 Santa Monica Boulevard
Hollywood, CA 90038

Skating, the journal of the ISIA, or in the PSGA newsletter. Often, the skating grapevine is the only source of such information.

Ice Capades and *Holiday on Ice* in Europe are large variety entertainment shows, featuring major production numbers interspersed with solo or pair performances by the stars of the show. Frequently, circus-type acts are also included. Although both these shows have been around for more than forty years, their format has not changed significantly. Of course, the style of skating in the shows has evolved along with the changes in skating in general.

A close relative of the large variety show is the single-theme show, such as *Ice Follies-Holiday on Ice (USA)* and, most recently, a part of the *Ice Capades. Ice Follies-Holiday on Ice* has evolved into *Walt Disney's World on Ice* and *Disney's Great Ice Odyssey,* and *Ice Capades* is adopting the Smurf theme. These shows used to have precisely the same format as the large variety entertainment productions, and the major change is in the addition of some thematic unity.

There are several exhibitions given by professionals. These are shows consisting almost exclusively of individual performances, unconnected with each other. The performers bring their own costumes and music.

Generally, these exhibitions are tied to some other event, such as a professional competition or club show (carnival).

Ice ballet troupes have existed from time to time, but at present there are none. One hopes that they will rise again. Surely, the time has come for skating to develop a dramatic and artistic tradition separate from its athletic heritage.

The Audition

Unless you are a superstar, you will have to audition for a place in a skating show. For those in the dramatic arts, this is an everyday occurrence; but it is rare in skating. You are not, for example, called upon to audition to gain a place in a skating school, or for a part in a local club show. In some respects, this is unfortunate, as it would be good experience.

A group of skaters in strawberry costume for the television special Strawberry Ice. *Courtesy Toller Cranston*

There are a number of points to remember when preparing for an audition. First, there is no better preparation than a history of hard work. If your skating technique is sound and your artistry is thoughtfully conceived, there is little to worry about.

Second, go to the audition with an image conceived in its totality. The costume, the hairstyle, the makeup, the music, the choreography, and the presentation should all be considered. Every element should emphasize your strengths and accentuate the drama you intend to unleash during your presentation.

Third, the audition should be done with personality and enthusiasm. Shows want soloists who will capture an audience, and corps members who will make an audience feel welcome. Knowing how to play to those in the stands and give them what they want is an invaluable asset in show business.

Finally, skate an audition with supreme confidence, as though there is no doubt that they will offer you a spot in the show.

PROFESSIONAL COMPETITIONS

The rise of professional competitions has been welcomed by both the public and the skaters. As I mentioned at the beginning of this chapter, the choices for a career were rather limited until these competitions came along. Television and a few creative people have broadened the spectrum and helped make skaters visible. More and more skaters are ranked in celebrity along with movie stars—Peggy Fleming and Dorothy Hamill, to name only two. Not only do professional competitions give the public more opportunity to see skaters in different guises, but they also will have a definite, positive effect on the evolution of figure skating.

The prize money offered is not insubstantial. At the 1982 World Professional Championships in Landover, Maryland, each solo or pair on the winning team received a prize of $20,000. The head-to-head competitions produced by the Pro Skate Company awarded $8,000 first prizes, with additional fees for the appearances of certain skaters.

Because the concept of professional competitions and a professional circuit is still in its earliest stages, it is not possible to delineate the whos, hows, and wheres at this time. The next few years will certainly see the establishment of some sort of professional circuit.

Another World Professional Competition, in Jaca, Spain, has been in existence since 1931. It originated in England and moved to Spain in the 1960s. The prize money at this event is $2,500 for the winner in the

JoJo Starbuck and Ken Shelley, 1971–72 World Bronze Medalists in the pairs event, have had very successful professional careers in ice shows, competitions, and television shows. Courtesy JoJo Starbuck and Ken Shelley

singles events and $3,000 for the pair and dance team winners.

With the exception of the championships held in Spain, professional competitions are by invitation only, although applications by the top skaters are generally reviewed, particularly by the Pro Skate Company. This review, however, does not necessarily lead to acceptance.

ALIGNED CAREERS

There are a number of other career options less well-defined than those described above. These include:

- product endorsements—for the superstar, nationally and internationally; for others, in local areas where their names are known
- spots on television specials—obtained through an agent or by publicizing one's interest in doing such work

David Jenkins, 1960 Olympic Gold Medalist, is now a physician. He was the 1983 U.S. World Team physician. Courtesy David Jenkins

- commentating—usually available only to the superstars
- production teams—television, large shows, and small dinner theaters; the organizational end of things
- rink management—available through the ISIA in the United States
- equipment design or sales—fashion, skates, rink equipment, accessories.

A WORD ABOUT AGENTS AND MANAGERS

Agents and managers are different things to different people. The mere mention of the word "manager" can send some producers into a fury. To the skaters, the "talent," they are either lifesavers or crooks. When you

link up with a reliable agent or manager, however, he or she can be a valuable person to have on your team.

Many professional skaters who want to focus their attention on developing their talents entrust the details of their careers to a third party. There are several categories of people who might deal with a professional skater's affairs; sometimes the management is a large organization that handles everything.

The personal manager is responsible for the day-to-day affairs of a star's life. The attorney negotiates contracts, while the agent seeks out employment opportunities. The business manager usually runs the personal fiscal program. Some professionals employ only one of these individuals, others all four.

If there is one thing to look for in an agent or manager, it is that he or she will always take care of your interests honestly and will sincerely pursue opportunities for you.

GLOSSARY
OF SKATING TERMS

Arabian A flying spin with a takeoff from two feet; in the air, the arms and legs are stretched out with the body parallel to the ice.

Artistic impression The part of the judge's mark given for the artistic merit of a performer's program.

Axel An edge jump of one-and-a-half revolutions in the air taken off from a forward outside edge and landed on the other foot on a back outside edge; invented by Axel Paulsen.

    Multiple revolutions Both double and triple axels have been done in competition; a double is two-and-a-half revolutions; a triple, three-and-a-half revolutions.

    Inside Axel The takeoff and landing are on the same foot; the takeoff is from a forward inside edge; the landing is on a back outside edge.

Axis An imaginary line that (a) bisects a circle, (b) bisects a figure eight at the point where the two circles are tangent, or (c) bisects the pattern of a dance.

Bielmann spin One-foot spin in which the free foot is behind the skater and is pulled above the head, making the free leg almost straight.

Bourkey A side stag jump of one revolution from a flip takeoff; invented by John Misha Petkevich and named after his coach, Arthur Bourque.

Bracket A turn on one foot from forward to backward or backward to

135

forward during which the edge is changed; the turn points away from the circle.

Camel A spin in an arabesque position; invented by Cecilia Colledge.

Choctaw A turn from forward to backward, entailing a change of foot and a change of edge.

Compulsory dance A set-pattern dance with specified steps, timing, rhythm, partner positions, and musical mood.

Counter A turn that is a bracket going in and a three-turn coming out; the skater remains on the same edge through the turn but changes from one circle to another.

Cranston camel A back camel in which the free leg is bent and the hips are open; the free hand holds the free knee; invented by Toller Cranston.

Crossfoot spin A two-foot spin on outside edges in which one foot is crossed over the other.

Crossovers The bread-and-butter of forward and backward stroking; the foot crossing over is set on the inside edge while the one crossed over is on the outside edge.

Dance An area of pair skating concentrating on intricate footwork married to body expression, both conveying the rhythm and mood of the music; unison between the members of the couple is of great importance.

Deathdrop An arabian with a one-foot takeoff and a landing into a back sit spin; when well executed, it is one of the most suspenseful moves in skating.

Death spiral A pair move in which the man does a pivot while holding the woman's arm and pulling her in a circle; the woman is on one foot and arches her back while leaning toward the man, bringing her head near the ice.

Double Any jump consisting of two revolutions or, in the case of the axel, two-and-a-half revolutions.

Edge The two razor-sharp sides of the hollow of the blade; when skaters lean, they "take an edge"; edges and radius make skating a circle possible; there are forward and backward inside and outside edges; a skater spends 99.9 percent of the time on edges.

Edge jump A jump in which the takeoff is from an edge on one foot.

Ena Bauer A spread-eagle in which the leading leg is bent with the corresponding foot on the forward outside edge, and the trailing leg is straight with the corresponding foot on a back outside edge.

Figures The figure eight and variations on the figure eight combining to make up the compulsory school figures.

Flip A toe-assisted, one-revolution jump; the takeoff is from two feet (one foot on a back inside edge and the other foot on the toe pick), while the landing is on a back outside edge on the toe-assisting foot.

Flying camel A flying spin that is landed in a back camel.

Flying sit spin A flying spin that is landed in a sit spin.

Flying spin A combination of a jump or a step with a spin; the takeoff is generally from a forward outside edge; the position in the air generally approximates the final spinning position; in a flying sit spin, for example, the position at the height of the jump portion of the move is similar to the position in the sit-spin portion.

Footwork A sequence of steps, turns, hops, and positions.

Free dance An aspect of dance in which the couple skates for a specified length of time to music of their own choice, with their own choreography of moves suitable for dance as stipulated by the ISU.

Freestyle That part of singles skating that pertains to jumps, spins, and footwork to music; it is sometimes referred to as free skating; that part of singles skating that is generally viewed on television.

Gold medalist Someone who has passed all the tests in a particular area of skating.

Grafstrom spiral An arabesque with both knees bent; a forerunner of the spiral.

Guards Rubber, wooden, or plastic holders that are put on blades when walking on skates off the ice.

Hamill camel A back camel with a turned body position, during which the skater collapses into a back sit spin; invented by Dorothy Hamill along with Gustav Lussi.

Hollow The groove that runs the length of the blade and creates the edges.

Hydrant lift A pair lift in which the man, skating backward, throws the forward-skating woman over his head in a straddle position, turning to catch her; invented by Ron Ludington.

Jump A move consisting of a lift off the ice with some form of revolution; when there is no rotation, a lift off the ice is usually referred to as a hop.

Landing The part of the jump or hop when the skater touches the ice after being in the air.

Lateral twist A pair move in which the man throws the woman into the air horizontally; while she is free of his hands and horizontal, she rotates.

Layout To skate a figure on clean ice.

Layover camel A camel or back camel in which the torso of the body is turned upward.

Lean The position of the body when it forms an angle that is less than 90 degrees relative to the ice.

Long program The freestyle program in the singles event counting for 50 percent of the total mark in a competition; the freestyle program of the pairs event counts for 71 percent of the total mark.

Loop jump An edge jump of one revolution, taken off from a back outside edge and landed on a back outside edge on the same foot.

Loops Small oval-shaped figures skated at the top of a reduced-size circle.

Lutz A toe-assisted jump taken off a back outside edge and landed on a back outside edge on the toe-assisting foot; it is a one-revolution jump.

Mohawk A turn from front to back involving a change of foot with no change of edge.

One-foot jump A jump in which the takeoff leg and landing leg are the same and the landing is on a back inside edge.

Original set-pattern dance A set-pattern dance with a prescribed rhythm created by the couple performing the dance.

Overhead lift A pair lift in which the man lifts the woman straight up in a hand-to-hand position, while the woman spreads her legs and arches her back.

Pair sit spin A man and a woman face each other in a position of an embrace while executing a sit spin.

Patch Time on the ice used for practicing figures; the terminology developed from the fact that each skater has his or her own "patch" of ice to practice on.

Pattern The path followed by a skater as manifested by the resulting marks or tracings on the ice.

Pivot A two-foot spin with one toe in the ice.

Radius The curvature of the blade from heel to toe as seen from the side.

Reverse lutz A half lutz landing on a forward outside edge on the toe-assisting foot and the toe pick of the takeoff foot; instead of being a counterlike jump, it is a bracketlike jump; invented by John Misha Petkevich.

Revolution Turning, particularly in the air.

Rocker A turn from forward to backward, the first part of which is a three-turn and the second part is a bracket; at the top of the turn, the skater changes from one circle to the other without changing edges.

Roll A deep outside edge.

Rotation The process of turning; also refers to the position of the torso relative to the pelvis.

Russian split A split jump in which the skater touches his or her toes.

Salchow An edge jump off a back inside edge with one revolution in the

air, landing on a back outside edge on the opposite foot; invented by Ulrich Salchow.

Scribe A large compass used to draw circles on the ice for figures.

Serpentine A figure consisting of three circles, often referred to as a three-lobe figure; also refers to footwork that winds back and forth across the rink.

Short program A freestyle program for single and pair skaters that contains required elements; of the total mark in competitions, it accounts for 20 percent in the singles event and 29 percent in the pairs event.

Single A one-revolution jump; in the case of the axel, a one-and-a-half-revolution jump.

Singles Events in which the skater skates alone.

Spin A move in which the skater turns rapidly in one spot on the ice; forward spins are on back inside edges, or, as in the case of the outside forward camel, on the forward outside edge; back spins are on a back outside edge.

Spiral An arabesque position held while gliding across the ice.

Split A half-revolution jump in which the legs are in a split position while airborne.

Split twist A pair lift in which the man lifts the woman from a lutz takeoff; as she is lifted, she splits her legs; he lets her go, and she turns with her legs now close together; just before she lands, he grabs her.

Spread-eagle A two-foot gliding position in which the leading foot is on a forward edge while the trailing foot is on the same edge but backward.

Stag A split jump with the leading leg bent.

Strike-off The initial push-off from a stationary position.

Stroking The act of gliding on the ice propelled by repeated thrusts.

Takeoff The lift-off edge on a jump.

Technical merit The part of a judge's mark given for the athletic achievement of the performer.

Three-turn A turn from forward to backward in which there is a change of edge; the turn faces into the circle being skated.

Throw lift A pair move in which the woman sets up on a jump takeoff edge; the man essentially throws the woman as she lifts off.

Thrust A pushing motion designed to propel the skater across the ice.

Toe-assisted jumps Jumps in which the free toe is placed in the ice at the beginning of lift-off; it acts as a pole vault.

Toe Axel An Axel in which the free foot reaches forward and its toe pick is placed in the ice, acting in part as a pole vault and in part as a lifting mechanism; invented by John Misha Petkevich.

Toe loop A toe-assisted loop jump.

Toe picks The teeth on the front of a skate blade.

Toe walley A toe-assisted walley.

Tracings The marks left on the ice by the skate as it glides across the ice.

Triple A three-revolution jump; in the case of the axel, three-and-a-half revolutions.

Walley A one-revolution edge jump off a back inside edge with a landing on a back outside edge on the same foot; the revolution is opposite the natural rotation of the takeoff edge in the same way as in the lutz.

Zamboni The machine that cuts the ice and lays fresh water, providing a clean surface.

Appendix A
SKATING ORGANIZATIONS

AMATEUR AND RECREATIONAL

International

International Skating Union (ISU)
Haus Schöneck
Promenade 73
Postfach CH-7270
Davos Platz
Switzerland

United States

The United States Figure Skating
  Association
20 First Street
Colorado Springs, CO 80906
(303)635-5200

Ice Skating Institute of America (not an
  NGB)
1000 Skokie Boulevard
Wilmette, IL 60091
(312)256-5060

Australia

National Ice Skating Association of
  Australia
1016 Doncaster Road, P.O. Box 23
Doncaster East
3109 Victoria

Austria

Österreichischer Eislaufverband
Prinz Eugen Strasse 12 (Haus des Sports)
A-1040 Vienna

Belgium

Fédération Royale Belge de Patinage
  Artistique
Fl. Pauwelslei 2 B4
2100 Deurne

Bulgaria
Bulgarian Skating and Ice-Hockey
  Federation
18 Tolboukhin Bulvd.
Sofia 1000

Canada
The Canadian Figure Skating Association
333 River Road
Ottawa, ON K1L 8B9

China
Skating Association of the People's
  Republic of China
9 Tiyukuan Road
Peking

Czechoslovakia
Czechoslovak Skating Association
Na porici 12
115 30 Prague 1

Denmark
Dansk Skøjte Union
Idraettens Hus
Brøndby Stadion 20
DK 2600 Gastrup

Finland
Suomen Taitoluistelulotto
Topeliuksenkatu 41a
Box 202
SF 00251 Helsinki 25

France
Fédération Française des Sports de Glace
42 rue du Louvre
75001 Paris

East Germany
Deutscher Eislauf-Verband der Deutschen
  Demokratischen Republik
Storkower Strasse 118
1055 Berlin

West Germany
Deutsche Eislauf-Union
Betzenweg 34
8000 Munich 60

Great Britian
National Skating Association of Great
  Britian
117 Charterhouse Street
London EC1M-6AT

Hungary
Hungarian Icesport Federation
Istvánmezei ut ⅓
Kisstadion
1146 Budapest

Italy
Federazione Italiana Sport del Ghiaccio
Via Piranesi 44/B
20137 Milan

Japan
National Skating Union of Japan
Kishi Memorial Hall, Room 413
1-1-1 Jinnan
Shibuya-ku, Tokyo

Korea
Skating Association of the Democratic
  People's Republic of Korea
Munsin-dong 2
Dongdaiwon District
Pyongyang

Republic of Korea
Korean Amateur Skating Association
19 Mukyo-dong
Chung-ku
Room No. 709, Sports Building
Seoul

Luxembourg
Union Luxembourgeoise de Patinage
9 rue Frantz Seimetz
L-2531 Luxembourg-City

Mongolia
Skating Union of the Mongolian People's
  Republic
Baga Toirog 55
Ulan Bator

Netherlands
Koninklijke Nederlandsche
  Schaatsenrijders Bond
Stadsring 103
3811 HP Amersfoort

New Zealand
New Zealand Ice Skating Association
P.O. Box 2755
Christchurch

Norway
Norges Skøyteforbund
Hauger skolevei 1
N-1351 Rud

Poland
Polish Skating Association
Stadion X-lecia
03-904 Warsaw

Romania
Federatia Romana de Patinaj
Str. Vasile Conta 16
70139 Bucharest

South Africa
South African Ice Skating Association
21 Callevera
461 Windermere Road
Durban
Natal 4001

Spain
Federacion Española Deportes de
  Invierno
Claoudio Coello 32
Madrid 1

Sweden
Svenska Konstakningsförbundet
Idrottens Hus
123 87 Farsta

Switzerland
Schweizer Eislauf-Verband
7 chemin des Sylvains
CH-1227 Veyrier-Geneva

USSR
USSR Skating Federation
Luzhnetskaya naberezhnaya 8
Moscow

Yugoslavia
Savez Klizackil I Koturaljkaskih Sportova
  Jugoslavije
Celovska 25
61000 Ljubljana

PROFESSIONAL UNIONS

United States
Professional Skaters Guild of America
1552 Hertel Avenue
Buffalo, NY 14216
(716)834-9431

Australia
Professional Skating Association of
  Australia
241 Toorak Road
South Yarra, Victoria 3141

Austria
Professional Skaters Association of Austria
Thea Visser-Wittman
Aderklaaerstrasse 9
1210 Vienna
 and
Günter Anderl
Postfach 161
7000 Eisenstadt

Canada
Figure Skating Coaches of Canada
P.O. Box 93
Agincourt, ON M1S 3B4
(416)438-2871

Denmark
Professional Skaters Association of
 Denmark
Harry Glick
Skoldborg Alle 23
2860 Soborg
Copenhagen

France
Fédération Nationale des Professionals de
 Patinage sur Glace
1 rue Victor Grifuelhes
92100 Boulogne Billancourt

West Germany
Deutscher Sportlehrerverband
 Landesverband Bayern
Fachgruppe Eiskunstlauf

Müllerstrasse 41/II
8000 Munich 5

International Professional Skating Union
Luess Strasse 5
Garmisch-Partenkirchen

Italy
Associatione Maestri Istuttori Pattinaggio
Marina d'Agata
Via Ripamonti 66
20141 Milan

Japan
Figure Skating Instructors Association of
 Japan
Shinagawa Sports Land
4-10-30 Takanawa Manato-ku
Tokyo

Republic of Korea
Professional Skaters Association of Korea
Hunjoo Lee
210 Samil Building
400-4 Changshin-dong
Tongro-ku Seoul 110

Switzerland
Professional Skating Association of
 Switzerland
Christine Szakas
Brüggackerstrasse 38
3303 Jegenstorf

Appendix B
EQUIPMENT DIRECTORY

BOOT MANUFACTURERS

United States

Harlick & Co., Inc.
893 American Street
San Carlos, CA 94070
(415)593-2093

Hyde Athletic Industries
432 Columbia Street
Cambridge, MA 02138
(617)547-9210

Klingbeil Shoe Labs Inc.
145-01 Jamaica Avenue
Queens, NY 11427
(516)297-6864

Micron USA
50 Jonergin Drive
Swanton, VT 05488
(800)868-7337
(800)451-5120 (out of state)

Oberhamer Shoe Co.
425 Minnehaha Avenue
St. Paul, MN 55103
(612)488-6629

Riedell Shoes Inc.
P.O. Box 21
Red Wing, MN 55066
(612)388-8251

S.P. Teri Inc.
2490 San Bruno Avenue
San Francisco, CA 94134
(415)467-7620

Canada

Don Jackson's Skating Products
14-1080 Brock Road
Pickering, ON L1W 3H3
(416)831-2400

John Knebli Ltd.
32 Camden Street
Toronto, ON
(416)368-5565

Lange Inc.
5972 Ambler Drive
Mississauga, ON L4W 2N3

Micron Sports Products, Inc.
5790 Ferrier Street
Montreal, PQ H4P 1M7
(514)735-2255

SK Sport Shoes Ltd.
280 Donlands Avenue
Toronto, ON M4J 3R4
(416)465-2784

COTTAGE INDUSTRIES AND REBUILDERS

F. A. Cooke
250 Middlesex Avenue
Wilmington, MA 01887
(617)657-7586
(617)657-4087

Sunseri
9 Demarest Road
West Haverstraw, NY 10927
(914)429-4060

BLADE MANUFACTURERS

Daoust Lalonde Inc.
4343 Hochelaga Street
Montreal, PQ H1V 1C3
Canada
(514)259-4664

Mitchel and King Skates Ltd.
216–219 Bedford Avenue
Slough, Berkshire SL1 4SA
England

St. Lawrence Manufacturing Co., Inc.
3030 Ste. Anne Blvd.
Beauport, ON G1E 6N1
Canada
(416)661-3721

John Wilson Blades
Wilson Marsden Brothers & Co.
Sheffield S8 DSR
England

SCRIBES

Marko Machine Co., Inc.
1064 Main Street
Hanson, MA 02341
(617)293-3627
(617)293-2988

Martin and Company
P.O. Box 18174
Cleveland, OH 44118

Perfect Circle
Frank Davenport
Box 43
Orinda, CA 94563
(415)254-5067

Sports Products Ltd.
8027 Steilacoom Boulevard S.W.
Tacoma, WA 98498
(206)582-8187

SHARPENING EQUIPMENT

CCM
Executive Drive
Hudson, NH 03051
(603)883-2880

Custom Radius Corp.
249 Boston Street
Topsfield, MA 01983
(617)887-8531

Fleming Grey Ltd.
690 Bishop Street
Cambridge, ON N3H 4S6
Canada
(519)653-2400

DISTRIBUTORS—SKATES AND ACCESSORIES

United States
California
Damschroder Sales and Distributing Co.,
  Inc.
6850 Vineland Avenue
Units 1 and 2
North Hollywood, CA 91605
(213)766-6115

Western Skates Sales
P.O. Box 2766
Menlo Park, CA 94025
(415)592-6767

Colorado
Cass's Pro Shop
Memorial Park Ice Arena
1766 E. Pike's Peak
Colorado Springs, CO 80909
(303)578-6883

Cass's Sports Center
802 Cheyenne Boulevard
Colorado Springs, CO 80906
(303)634-1418

Illinois
Presto's Skate Shop
Stadium Ice Arena
9300 N. Bronx
Skokie, IL 60077
(312)673-0011

Rainbow Sport Shop
4836 N. Clark Street
Chicago, IL 60640
(312)275-5500

The Riverview Pro Shop
324 N. Madison Street
Rockford, IL 61107
(815)962-0808

Massachusetts
Lubins Rink Supply
1455 Concord Street
Framingham, MA 01701
(617)877-5551
(800)225-3228 (out of state)
(800)852-3068

Murray Sandler Skate and Sport Supply
60 Concord Avenue
P.O. Box 301
Belmont, MA 02178
(617)484-5100

Michigan
Midwest Skater Co.
24370 Indoplex Circle
P.O. Box 87
Farmington Hills, MI 48024
(800)482-8399
(800)521-3325 (out of state)

Montana
The Skate Stop
P.O. Box 950
Great Falls, MT 59403

New Jersey
USA Sports Supply, Inc.
134 Ridge Avenue
P.O. Box 73
East Hanover, NJ 07936
(201)887-6112

New York
Bauer Canadian Skate, Inc.
75 Isabelle
Buffalo, NY 14207
(217)243-6464

Stan Belliveau
662 Bay Sixth Street
West Islip, NY 11795
(517)587-1658

Corona & Liebenow Skate Shops, Inc.
450 W. 33rd Street
New York, NY 10001
(212)868-9788

Jesse Halpern Skate & Tennis Shop
99 Cutter Mill Road
Great Neck, NY 11022
(516)487-6978

Nassau Skate Shop
Nassau County Arena
Magnolia Boulevard and Bay Drive
Long Beach, NY 11561
(516)889-3838

Omnitrade Industrial Co. Ltd.
135 Dupont Street
Plainview, NY 11803

Princeton Skate and Ski Chalet
379 Fifth Avenue
New York, NY 10001
(212)684-0100

Roll 'n' Ice
1128 Sunrise Highway
Copiaque, NY 11726
(516)842-6919
(516)842-8510

Skater's Patch
Lake Placid Olympic Arena
Lake Placid, NY 12946
(518)523-3325

Ohio
Nicholls Sports
3422 Lee Road
Shaker Heights, OH 44120
(216)921-4300

Virginia
Skater's Paradise
1508-A Belleview Boulevard
Alexandria, VA 22307
(703)660-6525

Canada

Alberta
Les Visser Ltd.
47 Dradburn Crescent
St. Albert, AB T8N 2J8
(403)458-9293

British Columbia
Can Alpine Agencies Ltd.
1314 S.W. Marine Drive
Vancouver, BC V6P 5Z6
(604)266-4490

Manitoba
Brian Sippel Ltd.
55 Kushner Crescent
Winnipeg, MB R2P OP2
(204)633-3036

New Brunswick
Colin Thompson Ltd.
P.O. Box 22
St. Stephen, NB E3L 2W9
(506)466-4761

Ontario
David Bournes & Associates Ltd.
138 Spruce Street
Aurora, ON L4G 3P3
(416)727-4742

Harcon Skating Products
41 Dormington Drive
Scarborough, ON M1G 3N1
(416)439-3862
(416)495-1217

Don Jackson's Skating Products
14-1080 Brock Road

Pickering, ON
(416)831-2400

McCrea Agencies
230 Lakeside Drive
Kitchener, ON N2M 4C5
(519)745-6529
(519)578-8104

Quebec
Manapar
3605 Berne
Brossard, PQ
(514)462-0670

Omnitrade Ltd.
750 McArthur Boulevard
St. Laurent, PQ H4T 1W2
(514)739-7781

CLOTHING AND FASHION

United States

California
Figures
2623 Ashby Avenue, #2
Berkeley, CA 94705

Inga Creations
11684 Ventura Boulevard
Studio City, CA 91604
(213)982-0616

J. P. Designs, Inc.
220 LaEspiral
P.O. Box 446
Orinda, CA 94563
(415)254-2322

Lucky "S" Fashions
1145 W. Fremont
Stockton, CA 95203
(209)946-0458

Colorado
Freestyles by Carolyn
5150 Bluestem Drive
Colorado Springs, CO 80917

Skate-Stag
8212 Ammons Crescent
Arvada, CO 80005
(303)423-7098

Vonita
1627 S. Tejon
Colorado Springs, CO 80906

Illinois
Centre Ice Figure Skating Boutique
1730 Pfingsten Road
Northbrook, IL 60062
(312)272-4330

Kansas
Action Skate Wear
623 Lakeshore Drive
Wichita, KS 67230
(316)522-1845

New York
Polar Sport Ltd.
264 W. 35th Street
New York, NY 10001
(212)736-5477

Protogs
55 Ludy Street
Hicksville, NY 11801
(516)935-8830

Tennessee
Unicorn Sport
505 Lovenia Avenue
Knoxville, TN 37917
(615)523-3343

Canada

Alberta
Skaters Boutique Ltd.
6551-111 Street
Edmonton, AB T6H 4R5
(403)437-4874

Ontario
Glynn and Webb
41 Attwood Crescent
Ottawa, ON K2E 5B1

Motions 1
Windsor Theatrical Supplies, Inc.
3041 Dougall Avenue
Hampton Plaza
Windsor, ON N9E 1S3
(519)969-4055

Appendix C
DIRECTORY OF RINKS AND SKATING CLUBS

United States

Alabama

†*Oxmoor Ice Lodge
 Birmingham Figure Skating Club, Inc.
 160 Oxmoor Road
 Birmingham, AL 35209
 (205)942-0223

†*Point Mallard Ice Rink
 Decatur Figure Skating Club
 Mallard Drive
 Decatur, AL 35601
 (205)350-1616

†*Ice Palace
 Huntsville Figure Skating Club
 402 Governors Drive S.W.
 Huntsville, AL 35801
 (205)539-3571

Von Braun Civic Center Arena
 700 Monroe Street S.W.
 Huntsville, AL 35801
 (205)533-1953

*Affiliated with the USFSA.
†Affiliated with the ISIA.

†Eastdale Mall Ice Rink
Eastdale Mall
Montgomery, AL 36117
(205)277-2088

Alaska
*ACC/UAA Ice Rink
Anchorage Community College
(Associate Member)
Anchorage Figure Skating Club
2801 Providence Avenue
Anchorage, AK 99504
(907)786-1233

†Ben Boeke Ice Arena
334 E. 16th Avenue
Anchorage, AK 99501
(907)274-2767

†*University of Alaska Ice Arena
Fairbanks Figure Skating Club
1824 Kennedy
Fairbanks, AK 99701
(907)456-7840

Arizona
Flagstaff Municipal Ice Rink
1850 N. Turquoise Drive
Flagstaff, AZ 86001
(602)774-1051

Arizona Veterans' Memorial Coliseum
1826 W. McDowell Road
Phoenix, AZ 85201
(602)252-6771

†*Ice Capades Chalet–Metrocenter
Arizona Figure Skating Club
9637 Metro Parkway West
Phoenix, AZ 85021
(602)997-6158

*The Ice Palace
Skating Club of Phoenix
Tower Plaza
3853 E. Thomas Road
Phoenix, AZ 85018
(602)267-0591

*Oceanside Ice Arena
Saguaro Vista Figure Skating Club, Inc.
1520 N. Hayden Road
Tempe, AZ 85281
(602)947-2470

*Iceland Skating Rink
Tucson Figure Skating Club
5915 E. Speedway Boulevard
Tucson, AZ 85712
(602)886-4076

Arkansas
†Royal Ice Palace
1311 Bowman Road
Little Rock, AR 72211
(501)227-4333

California
Bakersfield Civic Auditorium
1001 Truxtun Avenue
Bakersfield, CA 93302
(805)327-7553

†*Belmont Iceland
El Camino Ice Skating Club
815 Old County Road
Belmont, CA 94002
(415)592-0532

†*Berkeley Iceland
St. Moritz Ice Skating Club, Inc.
2727 Milvia Street
Berkeley, CA 94703
(415)843-8800

*Big Bear Ice Chalet
14605 Lakeview Drive
Big Bear Lake, CA 92315
(714)866-3535

Blue Jay Outdoor Ice Rink
Daley Canyon Road
Blue Jay, CA 92317
(714)337-1511

†*Ice Capades Chalet
Brea Canyon Figure Skating Club
400 Brea Mall
Brea, CA 92621
(714)990-4445

†*Pickwick Ice Arena
Los Angeles Figure Skating Club
1001 Riverside Drive
Burbank, CA 91506
(213)846-0032

†*Ice Capades Chalet
Gold & Silver Blades Figure Skating Club
6600 Topanga Canyon Boulevard
Canoga Park, CA 91303
(213)348-9121

*Bird Cage Walk Arena
Skating Club of Sacramento
5961 Sunrise Boulevard
Citrus Heights, CA 95610
(916)966-2874

†*Sun Valley Ice Arena
Diablo Figure Skating Club
185 Sun Valley Mall
Concord, CA 94521
(415)687-3690

†*Raydines Ice Skating Rink
Marin Figure Skating Club
10 Fifer Avenue
Corte Madera, CA 94925
(415)924-2050

†*Ice Capades Chalet
Mesa Verde Figure Skating Club
2701 Harbor Boulevard
Costa Mesa, CA 92626
(714)979-8880

*Culver Ice Arena
All Year Figure Skating Club
4545 Sepulveda Boulevard
Culver City, CA 90230
(213)398-5718

†*Ice Capades Chalet
Vallco Skating Club
101–23 N. Wolfe Road
Cupertino, CA 95014
(408)446-2906

†Dublin Iceland
7212 San Ramon Road
Dublin, CA 94566
(415)829-4444

*Icelandia
Ice Skating Club of Fresno
Marks and Clinton
Fresno, CA 93705
(209)275-1118

†*Olympic Ice Rink
South Bay Figure Skating Club, Inc.
23770 S. Western Avenue
Harbor City, CA 90710
(213)325-4474

†*Southland Ice Arena
Palomares Figure Skating Club
661 Southland Mall
Hayward, CA 94545
(415)785-7750

The Forum
3900 W. Manchester Boulevard
Inglewood, CA 90306
(213)674-6000

*Ice Capades Chalet
La Jolla Figure Skating Club
4545 La Jolla Village Drive
La Jolla, CA 92037
(619)452-9110

†*House of Ice
Harbor Figure Skating Club
5333 Lake Murray Boulevard
La Mesa, CA 92041
(714)461-0800

†*Melody Ice Gardens
Desert Blades Figure Skating Club, Inc.
45044 N. Trevor Street
Lancaster, CA 93534
(805)942-8127

Long Beach Arena
300 E. Ocean Boulevard
Long Beach, CA 90801
(213)437-2771

Los Angeles Memorial Sports Arena
3939 S. Figueroa Street
Los Angeles, CA 90053
(213)748-6131

*The Ice Pond
Monterey Bay Figure Skating Club
280 Reservation Road
Marina, CA 93933

*Scott-Ellis Lake Arena
1525 C Street
Marysville, CA 95901
(916)743-6939

†*Conejo Valley Ice Center
Conejo Valley Figure Skating Club
510 Ventu Park Road
Newbury Park, CA 91320
(805)498-6669

†*Ice Capades Chalet
Nordic Figure Skating Club
6100 Laurel Canyon Boulevard
North Hollywood, CA 91607
(213)985-5555

†*Zero Temp Ice Arena
Glacier Falls Figure Skating Club
14100 Shoemaker Avenue
Norwalk, CA 90650
(213)921-5391

Oakland-Alameda County Coliseum
Nimitz Freeway and Hegenberger
Road
Oakland, CA 94623
(415)569-2121

*Blyth Arena
Squaw Valley Figure Skating Club,
Inc.
P.O. Box 2067
Olympic Valley, CA 95730
(916)583-1617

*Ontario Ice Bowl
Arrowhead Figure Skating Club
1225 W. Holt Boulevard
Ontario, CA 91762
(714)986-0793

†The Winter Club of Palo Alto
3009 Middlefield Road
Palo Alto, CA 94306
(415)493-4566

†*Arctic Blades Figure Skating Club
Iceland Arena
8041 Jackson Street
Paramount, CA 90723
(213)633-1171

†*Ice Capades Chalet
Pasadena Figure Skating Club

300 E. Green Street
Pasadena, CA 91101
(213)578-0800

*Redwood City Ice Lodge
Crystal Springs Ice Skating Club
3140 Bay Road
Redwood City, CA 94063
(415)364-8767

†*Hilltop Ice Arena
Hilltop Ice Skating Club
2125 Hilltop Mall Road
Richmond, CA 94806
(415)223-7011

†Ice Capades Chalet
550 Deep Valley Drive
Rolling Hills Estates, CA 90274
(213)541-6630

*Iceland Ice Skating Rink
Capital City Figure Skating Club, Inc.
1430 Del Paso Boulevard
Sacramento, CA 95815
(916)925-3121

*House of Ice
San Diego Figure Skating Club
11001 Black Mountain Road
San Diego, CA 92126
(619)271-4000

†Ice Capades Chalet
E23–4545 La Jolla
San Diego, CA 92122
(714)452-9110

San Diego Sports Arena
3500 Sports Arena Boulevard
San Diego, CA 92138
(714)224-4171

Cow Palace
Box 34206

Geneva Avenue
San Francisco, CA 94101
(415)584-2480

*San Francisco Ice Arena
Skating Club of San Francisco, Inc.
1557-48th Avenue
San Francisco, CA 94122
(415)664-1406

†*Eastridge Ice Arena
Mission Valley Ice Skating Club
2190-A Tully Road
San Jose, CA 95122
(408)238-0440

†Ice Capades Chalet
2248 San Mateo Fashion Island
San Mateo, CA 94404
(415)574-1616

†*The Ice Patch
Santa Barbara Figure Skating Club
1933 Cliff Drive
Santa Barbara, CA 93109
(805)963-0833

†*Ice Capades Chalet
Santa Monica Figure Skating Club
500 Broadway
Santa Monica, CA 90401
(213)451-1677

†*Redwood Empire Ice Arena
Santa Rosa Figure Skating Club
1667 W. Steele Lane
Santa Rosa, CA 95402
(707)546-7147

†*Oak Park Ice Arena
Stockton Figure Skating Club
3545 Alvarado
Stockton, CA 95204
(209)944-8432

*Ice Palace
Silver Edge Figure Skating Club
1155 Reed Avenue
Sunnyvale, CA 94086
(408)296-0601

†Ontario Ice Skating Center
600 N. Mountain D103
Upland, CA 91786
(714)986-0793

*Van Nuys Iceland
The Skating Club of Van Nuys
14318 Calvert Street
Van Nuys, CA 91401
(213)785-2171

*Icelandia
Mineral King Ice Skating Club
8474 Mineral King Avenue
Visalia, CA 93277
(209)732-5326

*West Covina Ice Arena
West Covina Figure Skating Club
2235 E. Garvey
West Covina, CA 91790
(213)966-8666

Colorado
†*North Jeffco Ice Arena
Alpine Skating Club
9101 Ralston Road
Arvada, CO 80002
(303)421-1786

†*Aspen Ice Garden
Aspen Skating Club
233 W. Hyman Avenue
Aspen, CO 81611
(303)925-7485

Campus Box 355
Boulder, CO 80309
(303)492-7255

†*Broadmoor World Arena
Broadmoor Skating Club, Inc.
Broadmoor Hotel
Colorado Springs, CO 80901
(303)634-7711

Honnen Ice Rink
Colorado College
Colorado Springs, CO 80905
(303)473-2233

†*Memorial Ice Center
Centennial Skating Club
1705 E. Pikes Peak
Colorado Springs, CO 80905
(303)471-6883

†*Colorado Ice Arena
Colorado Skating Club
5555 W. Evans Avenue
Denver, CO 80227
(303)986-9552

McNichols Sports Arena
1635 Clay Street
Denver, CO 80201
(303)575-3712

†University of Denver Arena
E. Jewell and S. Gaylord
Denver, CO 80208
(303)753-2253

Colorado State University Ice Rink
c/o Student Center
Fort Collins, CO 80521
(303)491-6916

†*University of Colorado Ice Arena   †*South Suburban Ice Arena
University of Colorado (Associate)   Denver Figure Skating Club

6580 S. Vine Street
Littleton, CO 80122
(303)798-7881

†*Pueblo Plaza Ice Arena
Pueblo Figure Skating Club
Pueblo, CO 81003
(303)542-8784

U.S. Air Force Academy
†Air Force Academy Ice Arena
AHSAH
USAF Academy, CO 80840
(303)472-4032

*John Dobson Arena
Skating Club of Vail, Inc.
Box 100
Vail, CO 81620
(303)476-1560

*Hyland Hills Ice Arena
Rocky Mountain Figure Skating Club
4201 W. 94th Avenue
Westminster, CO 80030
(303)426-8912

Connecticut
†*Bolton Ice Palace, Inc.
Skating Club of Hartford
Rt. 6, 145 Hop River Road
Bolton, CT 06040
(203)646-7851

†*Wonderland of Ice
Bridgeport Skating Club, Inc.
Glenwood Avenue
Bridgeport, CT 06606
(203)576-8110

†*Cheshire Skating Center
New Haven Skating Club, Inc.
150 Schoolhouse Road

Cheshire, CT 06410
(203)272-7788

†*Darien Ice Rink
Skating Club of Westchester
1201 Old King Highway North
Darien, CT 06820
(203)655-8251

†East Haven Veterans Memorial Rink
Hudson Street
East Haven, CT 06512
(203)468-3367

†*Enfield Twin Rinks
The Skating Club of Springfield
One Prior Road
Enfield, CT 06082
(203)741-2022

†*Dorothy Hamill Skating Rink
Windy Hill Skating Club
10 Western Junior Avenue
Greenwich, CT 06830
(203)531-8560

*Greenwich Skating Club, Inc.
P.O. Box 569
Cardinal Road
Greenwich, CT 06830
(203)622-9583

*Hamden Community Ice Rink
Hamden Figure Skating Association,
  Inc.
Mix Avenue
Hamden, CT 06514
(203)248-3461

Hartford Civic Center
One Civic Center Plaza
Hartford, CT 06101
(203)566-6588

*Nadal Rink
Kent School, Associate
Rt. 341
Kent, CT 06757
(203)927-3537

Schmidt Rink
Hotchkiss School
Lakeville, CT 06039
(203)435-2591

Wesleyan University Arena
Knowles Avenue
Middletown, CT 06457
(203)347-9411

†Milford Ice Pavilion
291 Bic Drive
Milford, CT 06460
(203)878-6516

*New Canaan Winter Club
P.O. Box 208
New Canaan, CT 06840
(203)966-2122

*Ingalls Rink
Yale Figure Skating Club
Yale University
Sachem Street
New Haven, CT 06520
(203)436-3685

New Haven Veterans Memorial
   Coliseum
New Haven Coliseum Figure
   Skating Club
275 S. Orange Street
New Haven, CT 06508
(203)722-4330

Crystal Ice Skating Rink
Crescent Street
Norwalk, CT 06856
(203)866-2918

The Brown Rink
Rt. 44
Pomfret, CT 06258
(203)928-2744

*Ridgefield Skating Center
Laurel Ridge Skating Club
111 Prospect Ridge Road
Ridgefield, CT 06877
(203)438-5277

†*Terry Connors Ice Rink
Southern Connecticut Figure
   Skating Club, Inc.
Cove Island Park
Stamford, CT 06904
(203)358-4513

*University of Connecticut
   Skating Rink
Storrs Figure Skating Club
University of Connecticut
   Student Skating Club
U 78
Storrs, CT 06268
(203)486-3808

Rensen Arena
Choate School
Christian Street
Wallingford, CT 06492
(203)269-7722

*Mays Rink
Watertown Skating Club, Inc.
Taft School
Watertown, CT 06795
(203)274-2516

†*Veterans Memorial Rink
Charter Oak Figure Skating Club
Buena Vista Drive
West Hartford, CT 06107
(203)521-1573

The Loomis-Chaffee School Rink
Island Road
Windsor, CT 06095
(203)688-4934

Delaware
†*University of Delaware Ice Arena
University of Delaware, Associate
Newark, DE 19711
(302)738-2868

*Skating Club of Wilmington, Inc.
Jct. US 202 and 195
Wilmington, DE 19803
(302)656-5005

District of Columbia
†Liberty Plaza Ice Rink
1700 G Street N.W.
Washington, DC 20552
(301)596-5817

Florida
†*Center Ice Country Side Mall
Suncoast Figure Skating Club of
Florida
2601 US Highway 19 North
Clearwater, FL 33515
(813)796-0586

Sportatorium
16661 Hollywood Boulevard
Box 7029
Hollywood, FL 33022
(305)431-5901

*Veterans Memorial Coliseum
Jacksonville Figure Skating Club
E. Adams Street
Jacksonville, FL 32211
(904)633-2105

†Miami Beach Youth Center Ice Rink
2700 Sheriden Avenue
Miami Beach, FL 33140
(305)673-7767

†The Orlando Ice Palace
3121 W. Colonial
Orlando, FL 32808
(305)299-5440

†*Sunrise Ice Skating Center
Skating Club of Sunrise
3363 Pine Island Road
Sunrise, FL 33321
(305)741-2366

*West Palm Beach Municipal
Auditorium
The Skating Club of Florida, Inc.
P.O. Box 1431
West Palm Beach, FL 33402
(305)683-6061

Georgia
*Omni International Ice Skating Rink
The Figure Skating Club of Georgia
Hotel Lobby
Atlanta, GA 30303
(404)681-2161

†*Parkaire Olympic Ice Rink
Atlanta Figure Skating Club and
Tara Figure Skating Club
4859 Lower Roswell
Marietta, GA 30067
(404)937-0753

*Solar Ice at Shenandoah Recreation
Center
Figure Skating Club at Shenandoah
Shenandoah, GA 30265
(404)253-2235

Hawaii
†The Ice Palace
4510 Salt Lake Boulevard
Honolulu, HI 96818
(808)422-9418

Idaho
*Valley Ice Arena
Boise Figure Skating Club
1771 Wildwood Avenue
Boise, ID 83704
(208)377-2001

†*Sun Valley Ice Arena
Sun Valley Figure Skating Club, Inc.
Box 351
Sun Valley, ID 83353
(208)622-3888

Illinois
†*Barrington Area Figure
   Skating Club, Inc.
1115 Pine Street
Barrington, IL 60021

Fox Valley Sports Arena
Rt. 14 and Pepper Road
Barrington, IL 60010
(312)381-1434

†Carol Stream Ice Rink
540 E. Gunderson Drive
Carol Stream, IL 60187
(312)682-4480

*University of Illinois Ice Rink
Illini Figure Skating Club
406 E. Armory
Champaign, IL 61614
(217)333-2081

Chicago Stadium
1800 W. Madison

Chicago, IL 60607
(312)733-5300

†Southwest Ice Arena
5505 W. 127th Street
Crestwood, IL 60445
(312)371-1344

†Danville Civic Center
100 W. Main
Danville, IL 61832
(217)431-2424

†Decatur Civic Center
One Civic Center Plaza
Box 1031
Decatur, IL 62525
(217)422-7300

†*Downers Grove Ice Arena
Dupage Figure Skating Club
5501 Walnut Street
Downers Grove, IL 60515
(312)971-3780

†Polar Dome Ice Arena
Routes 25 and 72
East Dundee, IL 60118
(312)426-6751

†Elmhurst YMCA Ice Rink
211 W. First Street
Elmhurst, IL 60126
(312)823-9200

†*Robert Crown Recreation Center
Evanston Figure Skating Club, Inc.
1701 Main Street
Evanston, IL 60202
(312)328-9401

†*Franklin Park Ice Arena
Oak Park Figure Skating Club, Inc.
9711 Waveland Avenue

Franklin Park, IL 60131
(312)671-4268

†Planerts Glen Ellyn Ice
  Skating School
19 North Park Boulevard
Glen Ellyn, IL 60137
(312)469-5770

†Watts Ice Rink
  305 Randolph Street
Glencoe, IL 60022
(312)835-4440

†*Glenview Ice Center
  Chicago Figure Skating Club
1851 Landwehr Road
Glenview, IL 60025
(312)724-2800

†Granite City Ice Rink
  Benton and Oregon Streets
Granite City, IL 62040
(618)877-2549

†Centennial Ice Rink Skating School
3100 Trailway
Highland Park, IL 60035
(312)432-4790

†*Homewood Flossmoor Arena
  Glenwood Figure Skating Club
777 Kedzie Avenue
Homewood, IL 60430
(312)957-0100

†Inwood Ice Arena
  3000 W. Jefferson Street
Joliet, IL 60435
(815)725-2603

†Kankakee Valley Park District Ice
  Arena
Sixth and Hickory

Kankakee, IL 60901
(815)939-1311

†All Seasons Ice Rink
31 W. 330 North Aurora
Naperville, IL 60540
(312)851-0680

†Niles Sports Complex
8435 Ballard Road
Niles, IL 60648
(312)297-8011

†Northbrook Sports Center
1730 Pfingsten Road
Northbrook, IL 60062
(312)291-2980

†Oak Lawn Ice Arena
9400 S. Kenton
Oak Lawn, IL 60453
(312)424-8980

†Ridgeland Common
451 Lake Street
Oak Park, IL 60302
(312)848-9661

†Oakton Ice Arena
2800 W. Oakton Street
Park Ridge, IL 60068
(312)692-3359

†Memorial Arena
1701 Court Street
Pekin, IL 61554
(309)346-1240

†*Owens Recreation Center
  Illinois Valley Figure Skating Club
1017 W. Lake
Peoria, IL 61614
(309)682-2020

†*Riverview Ice House
  Figure Skating Club of Rockford, Inc.
  324 Madison Street
  Rockford, IL 61107
  (815)963-7408

†*Rolling Meadows Park District Ice
    Arena
  Wagon Wheel Figure Skating Club
  3900 Owl Drive
  Rolling Meadows, IL 60008
  (312)392-8680

†Woodfield Ice Arena
  Woodfield Mall, Bldg. K
  Schaumburg, IL 60195
  (312)884-1171

†Skokie Stadium
  9300 N. Bronx
  Skokie, IL 60077
  (312)674-1500

†*Franklin Nelson Recreation Center
  Old Capitol Figure Skating Club
  1601 N. Fifth Street
  Springfield, IL 62702
  (217)753-2800

†*Ice Chateau
  Sangamon Valley Figure Skating Club
  2700 W. Lawrence Avenue
  Springfield, IL 62704
  (217)787-8301

†*Centennial Ice Rink
  Skokie Valley Skating Club
  2300 Old Glenview Road
  Wilmette, IL 60091
  (312)256-6100

†Winnetka Ice Arena
  490 Hibbard Road
  Winnetka, IL 60093
  (312)446-5398

†Zion Ice Arena
  2400 Dowie Memorial Drive
  Zion, IL 60099
  (312)746-5500

Indiana
†Frank Southern Ice Rink
  349 S. Walnut
  Bloomington, IN 47401
  (812)323-2971

†*Carmel Ice Skadium
  Ice Skating Club of Indianapolis, Inc.
  1040 Third Avenue S. W.
  Carmel, IN 46032
  (317)844-8889

†*Lincoln Center Ice Rink
  Lincoln Center Figure Skating Club,
    Inc.
  25th and Lincoln Park Drive
  Columbus, IN 47201
  (812)379-4144

†*Swonder Ice Rink
  Greater Evansville Figure Skating
    Club
  201 N. Boeke Road
  Evansville, IN 47711
  (812)479-0989

†Ice Rink on the Terrace
  4201 Coldwater Road
  Fort Wayne, IN 46805
  (219)483-2119

*McMillen Ice Arena
  Fort Wayne Ice Skating Club, Inc.
  McMillen Park
  Fort Wayne, IN 46806
  (219)744-0848

†*Indiana State Fair Coliseum
  Winter Club of Indianapolis, Inc.

Indiana State Fair Grounds
Indianapolis, IN 46205
(317)923-3431

Market Square Arena
300 East Market Square
Indianapolis, IN 46204
(317)639-6411

†*Notre Dame Ice Arena
Michigan Figure Skating Club, Inc.
Notre Dame Athletic and Conven-
   tion Center
Notre Dame, IN 46556
(219)239-5247

The Ice Box
1421 S. Walnut Street
South Bend, IN 46624
(219)282-3300

Purdue University Recreational
   Gymnasium
Purdue University
West Lafayette, IN 47906
(317)494-7110

Iowa
†Cyclone Area Community Center
Depot Annex
Ames, IA 50010
(515)292-6835

*Des Moines Ice Arena
Des Moines Figure Skating Club
7201 Hickman Road
Des Moines, IA 50322
(515)278-9757

†Siouxland Ice Arena
P.O. Box 1650
Sioux City, IA 51102

*McElroy Auditorium
Northeast Iowa Figure Skating Club

Waterloo, IA 50701
(319)291-4551

Kansas
†*Fox Hill Ice Arena
Kansas City Figure Skating Club
4401 W. 107th Street
Overland Park, KS 66221
(913)648-1123

†*Ice Chateau Of King Louie West
Silver Blades Figure Skating Club of
   Kansas City
87th at Metcalf
Overland Park, IA 66212
(913)648-0129

†*Frontier Ice Arena
Wichita Figure Skating Club, Inc.
13000 W. Highway 54
Wichita, KS 67235
(316)722-2171

Kansas Coliseum–Britt Brown Arena
Box 9112
Wichita, KS 67201
(316)755-1243

Kentucky
†Dixie Ice Bowl
1665 Dixie Highway
Covington, KY 41011
(606)261-2551

†*Gardiner Skate Rink
Louisville Figure Skating Club
1825 Gardiner Lane
Louisville, KY 40104
(502)451-9600

†Riverfront Ice Plaza
Riverfront Plaza
Louisville, KY 40270
(502)587-3689

†Owensboro Sports Center Ice Rink
12th at Hickman
Owensboro, KY 42301
(502)685-8290

Louisiana
 *Airway Iceland Arena
Baton Rouge Figure Skating Club
1717 Airway Drive
Baton Rouge, LA 70815
(504)924-9759

†*Chateau Village Ice Skating Rink
Figure Skating Club of New Orleans,
    Inc.
3501 Chateau Boulevard
Kenner, LA 70062
(504)469-7603

†*The Plaza Ice Rink
Dixieland Figure Skating Club
5700 Read Boulevard
New Orleans, LA 70127
(504)246-5402

Maine
 *Dayton Arena
Skating Club of Brunswick
Bowdoin College
Brunswick, ME 04011
(207)725-8731

†*Kennebec Ice Arena, Inc.
Kennebec Skating Club
Box 219
Whitten Road
Hallowell, ME 04347
(207)622-6354

Hebron Academy
Hebron, ME 04238
(207)966-2812

Alfond Ice Arena
University of Maine
College Avenue
Orono, ME 04473
(207)581-2287

*Ice Arena
Rocky Coast Figure Skating Club
121 Main Street
Yarmouth, ME 04096

*N.Y.A. Ice Arena
Portland Skating Club of Maine
Yarmouth, ME 04096

Maryland
†U.S. Naval Academy Ice Rink
Dahlgren Hall
Annapolis, MD 21402
(301)263-4527

Baltimore Civic Center Ice Rink
201 W. Baltimore
Baltimore, MD 21203
(301)837-0903

†*Northwest Family Sports Center
Ice Club of Baltimore, Inc.
Free State Figure Skating Club
5600 Cottonworth Avenue
Baltimore, MD 21209
(301)433-4970

†*Bowie Ice Arena
Bowie Figure Skating Club
3310 Mitchelville Road
Bowie, MD 20715
(301)262-6200

†*Chevy Chase Club, Inc.
6100 Connecticut Avenue
Chevy Chase, MD 20015
(301)652-4100

†*Herbert Wells Ice Rink
Suburban Skating Club of Maryland
5211 Calvert Road
College Park, MD 20740
(301)277-3717

†*Columbia Ice Rink
Columbia Figure Skating Club
5876 Thunder Hill Road
Columbia, MD 21045
(301)596-3817

†Tucker Road Ice Arena
1771 Tucker Road
Fort Washington, MD 20744
(301)248-3124

†*Lake Forest Ice Arena
The Skating Club of Gaithersburg
701 Russell Avenue
Gaithersburg, MD 20877
(301)840-1215

Capital Centre
Landover, MD 20786
(301)350-3400

†Benfield Pines Ice Rink
Rt. 3 and Benfield Boulevard
Millersville, MD 21108
(301)987-5100

†*Orchard Ice Rink
The Baltimore Figure Skating Club,
  Inc.
1530 E. Joppa Road
Towson, MD 21204
(301)825-4253

Massachusetts
*Orr Rink
Skating Club of Amherst, Inc.
Amherst College

Amherst, MA 01002
(413)542-2000

Summer Smith Hockey Rink
Phillips Academy
Andover, MA 01810
(617)475-3400

†Veterans Memorial Sports Center
422 Summer Street
Arlington, MA 02174
(617)643-4800

Keller Rink
Belmont Hill School
350 Prospect Street
Belmont, MA 02178
(617)484-3266

*Hallenborg Ice Pavilion
Twin State Figure Skating Club
Good Street
Billerica, MA 01821

Boston Garden
150 Causeway Street
Boston, MA 02101
(617)227-3206

*Brown Skating Arena
Boston University, Associate
275 Babcock Street
Boston, MA 02215
(617)353-4632

Steriti North End Skating Rink
Commercial Street
Boston, MA 02101
(617)523-9327

†John Gallo Ice Arena
231 Sandwich Road
Bourne, MA 02532
(617)759-7455

†*Nashoba Valley Olympia
Colonial Figure Skating Club
Rt. 111
Boxborough, MA 01719
(617)263-3020

Daly-Brighton Rink
Nonantum Road, Newton Line
Brighton, MA 02135
(617)527-1741

Reilly Memorial Rink
Cleveland Circle
Brighton, MA 02135
(617)277-7822

The Skating Club of Boston
1240 Soldiers Field Road
Brighton, MA 02135
(617)782-5900

†*ASIAF Skating Rink
Flagg Pond Skating Club
Forest Avenue
Brockton, MA 02401
(617)586-0900

†Metropolitan Figure Skating School
21 Regent Circle
Brookline, MA 02146
(617)566-1245

†*Burlington Ice Palace
Winchester Figure Skating Club
36 Ray Avenue
Burlington, MA 01807
(617)272-9517

*Bright Rink
Harvard University, Associate
60 Boylston Street
Cambridge, MA 02138
(617)495-2228

*Cambridge Skating Club
40 Willard Street
Cambridge, MA 02138
(617)354-9427

*MIT Figure Skating Club, Associate
Vassar Street
Cambridge, MA 02139
(617)253-4498

Simoni Rink
Gore Street
Cambridge, MA 02139
(617)354-9523

†Town of Canton Recreation Department
79 Pleasant Street
Canton, MA 02021
(617)828-0050

Emmons-Horrigan Rink
Rutherford Avenue
Charlestown, MA 02129
(617)242-9728

*McHugh Forum
Boston College, Associate
Skating Club of Chestnut Hill, Inc.
Boston College
Chestnut Hill, MA 02167
(617)969-0100, ext. 3030

†*Cohasset Winter Gardens, Inc.
Silver Blades Skating Club
Cushing Highway
Cohasset, MA 02025
(617)383-9447

Middlesex School Rink
Lowell Road
Concord, MA 01742
(617)469-7323

*Town Line Twin Rinks
North Shore Skating Club
58 Andover Street
Danvers, MA 01923
(617)774-6506

Deerfield Academy Rink
Albany Road
Deerfield, MA 01342
(413)772-0241

AKK Franklin Field Rink
Blue Hill Road and Talbot Avenue
Dorchester, MA 02122
(617)436-1460

Devine-Neponset Rink
Garvey Playground
Morrissey Boulevard
Dorchester, MA 02122
(617)436-4356

Levit Parrazzo Memorial Rink
Constitution Beach
East Boston, MA 02128
(617)567-9571

Lossone Rink
Williston Academy
Easthampton, MA 01027
(413)527-4012

*Chaval Skating Rink
Chaval Figure Skating Club, Inc.
Western Avenue
Essex, MA 01929
(617)768-6055

Allied Veterans Memorial Rink
65 Elm Street
Everett, MA 02149
(617)389-8684

*Driscoll Memorial Rink
Greater Fall River Figure Skating
  Club
Elsbree Street
Fall River, MA 02720
(617)679-0009

†Falmouth Ice Arena
Rt. 28
Falmouth, MA 02540
(617)548-9083

†George R. Wallace Jr. Civic Center
1000 John Fitch Highway
Fitchburg, MA 01420
(617)345-7300

†*Loring Arena
Bay Path Figure Skating Club
Dudley and Fountain Street
Framingham, MA 01701
(617)875-5939

*Veterans Memorial Arena
Symmetric Figure Skating Club
Oak Street
Franklin, MA 02038
(617)528-2333

†*Cape Ann Figure Skating Club
P.O. Box 1193
Gloucester, MA 01930
(617)283-8958

*Greenfield Area Ice Rink
Greenfield Area Figure Skating
  Club
Barr Avenue
Greenfield, MA 01301
(413)772-6891

Groton School Ice Rink
Farmers Row
Groton, MA 01450
(617)444-3369

†Pilgrim Skating Arena
75 Recreation Park
Hingham, MA 02043
(617)749-6660

Bajko Rink
Turtle Pond Parkway
Hyde Park, MA 02136
(617)364-9867

Kelly Rink
Jamaicaway, Willow Pond Road
Jamaica Plain, MA 02130
(617)522-8091

Steven's Sports Center Arena
Bible Speaks School
40 Kemble Street
Lenox, MA 02140
(413)637-2131

*Hayden Recreation Center, John P.
   Chase Rink
Hayden Recreation Center Figure
   Skating Club
24 Lincoln Street
Lexington, MA 02173
(617)862-5575

Connery Rink
Shepard Street
Lynn, MA 01904
(617)599-9474

†*North Shore Sports Center
Greater Lynn Skating Club
30 Boston Street
Lynn, MA 01904
(617)598-2550

*John J. Navin D.N.R. Rink
Glacier Figure Skating Club, Inc.
85 Bolton Street
Marlborough, MA 01752
(617)481-5252

John W. Flynn Rink
Woodland Road
Medford, MA 02155
(617)395-9700

Lo Comte Rink
Veterans Memorial Parkway
Medford, MA 02155
(617)395-9636

Max Ulin Memorial Rink
Unquity Road
Milton, MA 02186
(617)696-9869

McCollum Arena
Northfield-Mount Herman School
Box 35
Mount Herman, MA 01354
(413)498-5311

†*West Suburban Arena
Comet Figure Skating Club, Inc.
Windsor Avenue
Natick, MA 01760
(617)655-1014

*Stephen Hetland Memorial Skating
   Rink
The New Bedford Skating Club, Inc.
310 Hathaway Boulevard
New Bedford, MA 02740
(617)997-1416

*Henry Graf Rink
Newburyport Figure Skating Club
Low Street
Newburyport, MA 01950
(617)462-8112

*Charles River Ice Skating Club
125 Wells Avenue
Newton, MA 01259
(617)969-5560

*Vietnam Veterans Memorial Skating Rink
South Church Street
North Adams, MA 01247
(413)664-9474

†Lower Cape Sports Center
O'Connor Way
Orleans, MA 02653
(617)255-5902

†*Hobomock Arena
Pilgrim Skating Club
Hobomock Street
Pembroke, MA 02359
(617)294-0260

*Boys Club Ice Rink
Pittsfield Figure Skating Club
16 Melville Street
Pittsfield, MA 01201
(413)448-8258

Shea-Quincy Rink
Willard Street
Quincy, MA 02169
(617)472-9325

*Randolph Ice Arena
Commonwealth Figure Skating Club
240 North Street
Randolph, MA 02368
(617)963-4053

Paul W. Cronin Rink
Revere Beach Parkway
Revere, MA 02151
(617)284-9491

Cass Rink
Washington Street at Martin Luther
    King Boulevard
Roxbury, MA 02119
(617)445-9519

†O'Keefe Center Rink
Salem State College
225 Canal Street
Salem, MA 01970
(617)745-9556

Kasabuski Brothers Rink
Lynn Fells Parkway
Saugus, MA 01906
(617)233-9713

Veterans Memorial Rink
Somerville Avenue
Somerville, MA 02143
(617)623-3523

Murphy Ice Skating Rink
Day Boulevard
South Boston, MA 02127
(617)269-7060

*Cape Cod Coliseum
Yarmouth Ice Club, Inc.
Whites Path
South Yarmouth, MA 02664
(617)394-2131

St. Marks School Rink
St. Marks School
Southboro, MA 01772
(617)485-9729

*Smead Arena
Little Sun Valley Skating Club, Inc.
Roosevelt Avenue
Springfield, MA 01109
(413)733-8879

†*Stoneham Arena
Stoneham Figure Skating Club
101 Montvale Avenue
Stoneham, MA 02180

*Taunton Memorial Rink
Taunton Area Figure Skating Club, Inc.
Williams Street
Taunton, MA 02780
(617)824-4342

†Skate 3
Middlesex Road
Tyngsboro, MA 01879
(617)649-7913

*Turners Pond
Country Skating Club
397 Elm Street
Walpole, MA 02081

Veterans Memorial Ice Skating Rink
Totten Pond Road
Waltham, MA 02154
(617)893-9409

†Watertown Municipal Skating Arena
Paramount Place
Watertown, MA 02172
(617)923-0306

†*Babson Recreation Arena
Babson Skating Club, Inc.
150 Great Plain Avenue
Wellesley, MA 02181
(617)253-0627

*Valley Sports Arena
Leominster Figure Skating Club
Rt. 62, P.O. Box 1223
West Concord, MA 01742
(617)369-8100

Bryan Skating Rink
VFW Parkway
West Roxbury, MA 02132
(617)323-9512

†North Star Youth Forum
Bridle Lane

Westboro, MA 01581
(617)366-9373

Connell Rink
220 Broad Street
Weymouth, MA 02188
(617)335-2090

*Chapman Rink
Christmas Brook Figure Skating Club
Williams College
Williamstown, MA 01267
(413)597-2141

†Youth Ice Arena, Inc.
33 Upton Court
Wilmington, MA 01887
(617)658-4777

†*Clark Memorial Ice Palace
Skating Club of Clark Memorial
155 Central Street
Winchendon, MA 01475
(617)297-0869

*Universal Sports Arena
Universal Figure Skating Club of
   Winchester
7 Conant Road
Winchester, MA 01890
(617)729-9320

*Larsen Athletic Facility
Mass Bay Skating Club, Inc.
Pauline Street
Winthrop, MA 02152
(617)846-5770

†Worcester Arena, Inc.
1049 Main Street
Worcester, MA 01603
(617)757-6326

*Worcester Rink
Skating Club of Worcester, Inc.

284 Lake Avenue
Worcester, MA 01604
(617)755-0582

Michigan
Allen Park Civic Center
15800 White Street
Allen Park, MI 48101
(313)928-8303

†Fuller Park Rink
100 N. Fifth Avenue
Ann Arbor, MI 48103
(313)994-2783

*Veterans Ice Arena
Ann Arbor Figure Skating Club
2150 Jackson Road
Ann Arbor, MI 48101
(313)761-7240

Yost Ice Arena
University of Michigan
1016 S. State Street
Ann Arbor, MI 48101
(313)763-0064

†Kellogg Center
200 Hamblin Avenue
Battle Creek, MI 49017
(616)963-8540

Ferris State College Ice Arena
Big Rapids, MI 49307
(616)796-9971

†Berkley Arena
2300 Robina Avenue
Berkley, MI 48072
(313)545-6180

†*Detroit Skating Club
888 Denison Court
Bloomfield, MI 48013
(313)332-7133

*Academy Figure Skating Club
21902 Telegraph Road
Brownston Township, MI 48183
(313)676-6429

†Fairlane Ice Arena
Fairlane Town Center
Dearborn, MI 48126
(313)593-1551

†*Ford Woods Ice Arena and
Mike Adray Sports Arena
Great Lakes Figure Skating
Club
14900 Ford Road
Dearborn, MI 48126
(313)943-2364

†Dearborn Heights–John Canfield
Arena
2100 Kinloch
Dearborn Heights, MI 48127
(313)563-9700

*Grosse Pointe Community Rink
Grosse Pointe Skating Club
4831 Canyon
Detroit, MI 48224
(313)885-4100

Joe Louis Arena
600 Civic Center Drive
Detroit, MI 48226
(313)962-2000

Olympia Stadium
5920 Grand River
Detroit, MI 48224
(313)895-7000

Michigan State University Ice Arena
Chestnut Street
East Lansing, MI 48824
(517)353-7263

*Escanaba Area Figure Skating Club
Wells, MI 49829

†All Seasons Ice Arena
1160 S. Elms Road
Flint, MI 48504
(313)635-4979

†Flint Department of Parks and Recreation
1101 S. Saginaw Street
Flint, MI 48502
(313)766-7463

*IMA Ice Arena
Flint Skating Club
3501 Lapeer Road
Flint, MI 48503
(313)744-0580

†Fraser Hockeyland
34400 Utica Road
Fraser, MI 48026
(313)294-2400

*Garden City Civic Arena
Garden City Figure Skating Club
200 Log Cabin Road
Garden City, MI 48135
(313)261-3491

*Cascade Sports Arena
Grand Rapids Figure Skating Club,
Inc.
2845 Thornhill Drive, S. E.
Grand Rapids, MI 49508
(616)949-9451

†Jolly Roger Ice Club
2600 Village Drive, S. E.
Grand Rapids, MI 49506
(616)452-7516

Stadium Arena
2500 Turner Avenue, N. W.

Grand Rapids, MI 49508
(616)364-7017

Francis McCann Rink
University Liggett School
1045 Cook Road
Grosse Point, MI 48236
(313)884-4444

Hamtramck Ice Rink
3201 Roosevelt
Hamtramck Recreation Department
Hamtramck, MI 48212
(313)872-5561

†*Michigan Technological University
Ice Arena
Portage Lake Figure Skating Club
Sharon Avenue
Houghton, MI 49931
(906)487-2578

†Jackson Sports Arena, Inc.
1300 W. North Street
Jackson, MI 49202
(517)783-2664

†*Lawson Ice Arena
Kalamazoo Figure Skating Club
Western Michigan University
Howard and Stadium
Kalamazoo, MI 49008
(616)383-0421

†*Lansing Ice Arena
Lansing Skating Club
1475 Lake Lansing Road
Lansing, MI 48912
(517)482-1597

†Eddie Edgar Ice Arena
32025 Lyndon Avenue
Livonia, MI 48154
(313)261-2260

†*Lakeview Arena
Marquette Figure Skating Club
401 E. Fair Avenue
Marquette, MI 49855
(906)228-7530

†John K. Kessey Ice Arena
4300 S. Dearborn Street
Melvindale, MI 48122
(313)928-1201

*Midland Figure Skating Club
1601 George Street
Midland, MI 48640

L. C. Walker Sports Arena
470 W. Western Avenue
Muskegon, MI 49444
(616)726-4941

*Oak Park Multi-purpose Arena
North Suburban Figure Skating Club
13950 Oak Park Boulevard
Oak Park, MI 48237
(313)543-2338

†*Plymouth Community Cultural Center
Plymouth Figure Skating Club
525 Farmer Street
Plymouth, MI 48170
(313)455-6620

Waterford Lakeland Ice Arena
7330 Highland Road
Pontiac, MI 48054
(313)666-1910

Henry McMorran Memorial Sports
Arena
701 McMorran Boulevard
Port Huron, MI 48060
(313)985-6166

†Redford Ice Arena
12400 Beech Daly Road
Redford, MI 48239
(313)937-0913

River Rouge Veterans Memorial
Complex
141 E. Great Lakes Avenue
River Rouge, MI 48218
(313)842-4122

†John Lindell Memorial Ice Arena
1403 Lexington Avenue
Royal Oak, MI 48073
(313)435-7310

†Lee J. Verbeke Memorial Ice Arena
6129 Bay Road
Saginaw, MI 48604
(517)799-8950

*St. Clair Shores Civic Arena
St. Clair Shores Figure Skating
20000 Stephens Drive
St. Clair Shores, MI 48080
(313)779-4300

*Pullar Community Rink
Hiawatha Skating Club
435 E. Portage Avenue
Sault Ste. Marie, MI 49783
(906)632-6853

†Shelby Valley Figure Skating Club
837 Dumont Place
Rochester, MI 48063
(313)652-4913

†Southfield Sports Arena
26000 Evergreen Road
Southfield, MI 48076
(313)354-9357

†Taylor Community Center
12111 Pardee Road
Taylor, MI 48180
(313)287-2800

*Traverse City Civic Center
Twin Bays Skating Club
1125 W. Civic Center Drive
Traverse City, MI 49684
(616)941-2246

*Kennedy Park Ice Arena
Trenton Community Skating Club
2800 Third Street, West R
Trenton, MI 48183
(313)676-7172

†USA Arena
45300 Mound Road
Warren, MI 48092
(313)739-7313

†Wayne Community Center
4635 Howe Road
Wayne, MI 48184
(313)721-7400

†Westland Multi-Purpose Arena
6210 N. Wildwood
Westland, MI 48185
(313)729-4560

†*Benjamin Franklin Yack Arena
Wyandotte Figure Skating Club
3131 Second Avenue
Wyandotte, MI 48192
(313)285-0700

Minnesota
†Apple Valley Sports Facility
14200 Cedar Avenue South
Apple Valley, MN 55124
(612)432-3829

*Babbitt Arena
Independent School District
Babbitt Figure Skating Club
692 South Drive
Babbitt, MN 55706
(218)827-3101

Baudette Area Arena
Box 310
Baudette, MN 56623
(218)634-2735

John Glas Fieldhouse
Bemidji State University
Bemidji, MN 56601
(318)755-2940

*Neilsen-Riese Arena
Bemidji Figure Skating Club, Inc.
23rd and Ash
Bemidji, MN 56601
(218)751-4541

†*Bloomington Ice Garden
Figure Skating Club of Bloomington
3600 W. 98th Street
Bloomington, MN 55431
(612)887-9641

†*Brainerd Area Civic Center
Vacationland Figure Skating Club,
Inc.
Fifth and Jackson
Brainerd, MN 56401
(218)829-9901

†*Burnsville Ice Arena
Burnsville-Minnesota Valley Figure
Skating Club
251 Civic Center Parkway
Burnsville, MN 55337
(612)890-4100

*Chisholm Sports Arena
Chisholm Skating Club
Chisholm, MN 55719
(218)254-2635

†Cottage Grove Ice Arena
8020-80th Street South
Cottage Grove, MN 55016
(612)458-2845

*Pioneer Hall
Duluth Arena
Duluth Figure Skating Club
350 S. Fifth Avenue West
Duluth, MN 55807
(218)727-4434

Civic Recreation Center
300 N.E. 15th Street
East Grand Forks, MN 56721
(218)773-1181

*Hibbing Figure Skating Club
2620 16th Avenue
East Hibbing, MN 55746
(218)263-9852

†*Braemar Arena
Braemar-City of Lakes Figure Skating Club
5108 W. 74th Street
Edina, MN 55435
(612)941-1322

*Farmington Ice Arena
Tri-County Figure Skating Club
114 W. Spruce Street
Farmington, MN 55024
(612)463-2510

†*Columbia Arena
Columbia Figure Skating Club
7011 University Avenue, N.E.
Fridley, MN 55432
(218)757-3926

*Bronco Arena
International Falls Figure Skating Club
11th Street and 15th Avenue
International Falls, MN 56649
(218)283-2424

Lower St. Claire Valley Youth Center
Rt. 1
Lakeland, MN 55043
(612)436-9982

†Le Sueur Community Center
821 E. Ferry Street
Le Sueur, MN 56058
(612)665-3325

†*All Seasons Arena
Mankato Figure Skating Club
301 Monk Avenue
Mankato, MN 56001
(507)387-6552

*Augsburg College Arena
St. Paul Figure Skating Club, Inc.
2323 Riverside Avenue
Minneapolis, MN 55406
(612)330-1255

*Ice Center
Figure Skating Club of Minneapolis
5800 Wayzata Boulevard
Minneapolis, MN 55416

Minneapolis Auditorium
1403 Stevens Avenue
Minneapolis MN 55416
(612)870-4436

†Parade Ice Garden
600 Kenwood Parkway
Minneapolis, MN 55403
(612)377-7382

†Victory Memorial Ice Arena
1900 42nd Avenue North
Minneapolis, MN 55412
(612)521-2209

Williams Arena
University of Minnesota
Oak and Washington
Minneapolis, MN 55440
(612)373-4298

†*Minnetonka Ice Arena
Lake Minnetonka Figure Skating Club
3401 Williston Road
Minnetonka, MN 55343
(612)870-1545

†New Hope Ice Arena
4949 Louisiana
New Hope, MN 55428
(612)533-8442

*Municipal Sports Complex
St. Cloud Figure Skating Club
5001 Eighth Street
North St. Cloud, MN 56301
(612)253-6600

†Northfield Ice Arena
Highway 3 South
Northfield, MN 55057
(507)645-6556

*Four Seasons Arena
Owatonna Figure Skating Club
Owatonna, MN 55060
(507)451-1093

*Richfield Ice Arena
Richfield Figure Skating Club
636 E. 66th Street
Richfield, MN 55423
(612)861-2281

*Rochester-Olmsted Recreation
    Center

Rochester Figure Skating Club
21 Elton Hills Drive, N.W.
Rochester, MN 55901
(507)288-7536

†*Roseville Ice Arena
Roseville Figure Skating Club
1200 Woodhill Drive
Roseville, MN 55113
(612)484-0269

†*Aldrich Arena
Maplewood Figure Skating Club
Fun and Pleasure Skating School
1850 White Bear Avenue
St. Paul, MN 55109
(612)777-1361

Drake Arena
St. Paul Academy
1712 Randolph Avenue
St. Paul, MN 55165
(612)698-2451

Oscar Johnson Ice Rink
1039 Flynn Drive
St. Paul, MN 55165
(612)645-7203

Minnesota State Fair Coliseum
Fairgrounds
St. Paul, MN 55165
(612)645-2781

†St. Croix Valley Youth Center
3415 University Avenue
St. Paul, MN 55114
(612)436-9982

St. Paul Civic Center
I.A. O'Shaughnessy Plaza
St. Paul, MN 55165
(612)224-7361

Gustavus Adolphus College Ice Rink
St. Peter, MN 56082
(507)931-4300, ext. 343

Highland Arena Jump and Spin
  Skating School
142-Thirteenth Avenue
South St. Paul, MN 55075
(612)451-9336

*Wakota Civic Arena
Rivers Edge Figure Skating Club
1040 Villaume Avenue E.
South St. Paul, MN 55075
(612)451-1727

†*Lily Lake Ice Arena
  Stillwater Figure Skating Club
1208 S. Greeley
Stillwater, MN 55082
(612)439-1337

*Thief River Falls Arena
  Thief River Falls Skating Club
105 E. Second Street
Thief River Falls, MN 56701
(218)681-9990

†Cottonwood County Arena
  Fairgrounds Box 38
Windom, MN 56101
(507)831-1050

Mississippi
Mississippi Coliseum
Box 892
Jackson, MS 39205
(601)354-3558

Missouri
†*Brentwood Ice Arena
  Gateway/St. Louis Figure Skating Club
2505 S. Brentwood Boulevard

Brentwood, MO 63144
(314)962-4806

St. Louis Country Club Rink
400 Barnes
Clayton, MO 63105
(314)994-0011

*Creve Coeur Ice Arena
Creve Coeur Figure Skating Club
11400 Olde Cabin Road
Creve Coeur, MO 63141
(314)432-3960

†*Miracle Sports Complex
Rainbow Figure Skating Club of
  Greater Kansas City
12416 Grandview Road
Grandview, MO 64030
(816)966-9306

†*Carriage Figure Skating Club, Inc.
5301 State Line
Kansas City, MO 64112
(816)363-1310

†Crown Center Ice Terrace
2440 Pershing Road, #500
Kansas City, MO 64108
(816)274-5524

Kemper Arena
1800 Genesee Street
Kansas City, MO 64141
(816)421-6460

Greensfelder Recreation Complex
550 Weidman Road
Manchester, MO 63011
(314)391-0900

Marriots Tan-Tar-A Resort
State Road KK and Highway 54
Osage Beach, MO 65065
(314)348-3131

†*Bode Ice Arena
St. Joseph Figure Skating Club, Inc.
2500 Hyde Parkway
St. Joseph, MO 64503
(816)271-4673

†Checkerdome
5700 Oakland Avenue
St. Louis, MO 63166
(314)644-0900

†North County Recreation Complex
2577 Redman Road
St. Louis, MO 63136
(314)355-7373

†South County Recreation Complex
6050 Wells Road
St. Louis, MO 63122
(314)894-3088

Montana
Yellowstone Metra Rink
Box 1523
Billings, MT 59101
(406)245-6561

*Butte Civic Center
Butte Figure Skating Club
1370 Harrison Avenue
Butte, MT 59701
(406)723-8262

*Four Seasons Ice Arena
Great Falls Figure Skating Club
State Fairgrounds
Great Falls, MT 59401
(406)452-6401

Nebraska
Pershing Auditorium
15th and North
Lincoln, NE 68508
(402)471-7500

*Ak-Sar-Ben Coliseum
Figure Skating Club of Omaha
63rd and Shirley
Omaha, NE 68106
(402)556-2305

†Benson Ice Arena
7028 Military Avenue
Omaha, NE 68183
(402)444-5932

†*Hitchcock Ice Rink
Blade & Edge Figure Skating Club
of Omaha
43rd and P Street
Omaha, NE 68107
(402)731-5300

Nevada
*Iceland Inc.
Las Vegas Figure Skating Club
704 Sunset Road
Henderson, NV 89015
(702)565-6373

Centennial Coliseum
4590 S. Virginia Street
Reno, NV 89510
(702)825-5100

†*Meadowood Ice Arena
Sierra Nevada Figure Skating Club
5353 Meadowood Mall
Reno, NV 89502
(702)826-8990

New Hampshire
†*Cheshire Fair Ice Arena
Cheshire Figure Skating Club
Rt. 12 South, P.O. Box 76
Cheshire, NH
(603)357-4740

Malcolm Gordon Memorial Rink
St. Paul's School
Concord, NH 03301
(603)225-3341

*Dover Ice Arena
Great Bay Figure Skating Club, Inc.
Portland Avenue
Dover, NH 03820

Snively Arena
University of New Hampshire
Main Street
Durham, NH 03824
(603)862-1850, ext. 603

Phillips Exeter Academy Rink
Exeter, NH 03833
(603)772-4311, ext. 323

*Rupert C. Thompson Arena & The
Davis Rink
Dartmouth College
Skating Club at Dartmouth, Inc.
Hanover, NH 03755
(603)646-2463

†*John F. Kennedy Coliseum
Southern New Hampshire Skating Club
Maple Street
Manchester, NH 03103
(603)267-8183

Annie Duncan Memorial Hockey Rink
Kinball Union Academy
Meriden, NH 03770
(603)469-3211

New Jersey
†*Ocean Ice Palace
Garden State Skating Club
Laurelton Pines Skating Club
Chambers Bridge Road

Brick Town, NJ 08723
(201)477-4411

*East Brunswick Ice Palace
Raritan Valley Figure Skating Club,
Inc.
Sixth Street
East Brunswick, NJ 08816

Byrne Meadowlands Arena
East Rutherford, NJ 07073
(201)460-4370

*Warinanco Park Ice Center
Union County Figure Skating Club,
Inc.
Thompson Avenue
Elizabeth, NJ 07027
(201)241-3262

Englewood Field Club
341 Engle Street
Englewood, NJ 07631
(201)568-6360

†Mackay Park Arena
Englewood Avenue
Englewood, NJ 07631
(201)567-1800

Lawrenceville School
Lawrenceville, NJ 08648
(609)896-0123

*Navesink Country Club
Navesink Figure Skating Club
Luftburrow Lane
Middletown, NJ 07748
(201)842-0789

†*Montclair Arena
Skating Club of Montclair, Inc.
Chestnut Street
Montclair, NJ 07042
(201)774-6088

†*William G. Mennen Sports Arena
Skating Club of Morris, Inc.
161 E. Hanover Street
Morristown, NJ 07960
(201)267-0700

†Old Bridge Arena
One Old Bridge Plaza
Old Bridge, NJ 08857
(201)679-3100

Bergen Mall Ice Arena
601 Bergen Mall
Paramus, NJ 07652
(201)845-4649

†Essex Hunt Club
Holland Road
Peapack, NJ 07977
(201)234-0062

†*Baker Rink
Princeton Skating Club, Inc.
Princeton University, Box 260
Princeton, NJ 08540
(609)452-3511

Princeton Day School Rink
P.O. Box 75
Princeton, NJ 08540
(609)924-6700

†Beacon Hill Club
250 Hobart Avenue
Summit, NJ 07901
(201)277-6655

†*New Shrewsbury Ice Arena
Olde Monmouth Skating Club, Inc.
864 Shrewsbury Avenue
Tinton Falls, NJ 07724
(201)542-4947

†Winding River Skating Center
1211 Whitesville Road

Toms River, NJ 08753
(201)244-0720

†*Ice World
Ice World Figure Skating Club
670 Union Boulevard
Totowa, NJ 07512
(201)785-1111

†*Ventnor City Ice Rink
Atlantic City Figure Skating
Club, Inc.
New Haven and Atlantic
Ventnor City, NJ 08406
(609)823-1429

†*The Coliseum
Coliseum Figure Skating Club
333 Preston Avenue
Voorhees, NJ 08034
(609)429-6900

†*South Mountain Arena
Essex Skating Club of New Jersey, Inc.
560 Northfield Avenue
West Orange, NJ 07052
(201)731-3829

*South Mountain Figure Skating
Club, Inc.
560 Northfield Avenue
West Orange, NJ 07052
(201)731-3829

†Mercer County Skating Center
Old Trenton and South Post Roads
West Windsor, NJ 08611
(609)586-8092

†*Fritz Dietl Ice Rink
North Jersey Figure Skating
Club, Inc.
639 Broadway
Westwood, NJ 07675
(201)666-9883

New Mexico
†*Iceland Ice Arena
Albuquerque Figure Skating Club
5110 Copper N.E.
Albuquerque, NM 87108
(505)255-1628

Los Alamos Skating Rink
4475 West Road
Los Alamos Canyon, NM 87544

New York
*Albany Academy Field House
Skating Club of the Albany Academy
Hackett Boulevard
Albany, NY 12208
(518)465-1461

*Municipal Recreation Center
The Alexandria Bay Figure Skating
Club
Bolton Avenue
Alexandria Bay, NY 13607
(315)482-9360

†*Newbridge Road Park Ice Rink
Newbridge Road Park Figure Skating Club
2600 Newbridge Road
Bellmore, NY 11710
(516)826-5100

*Dann Memorial Rink
Buffalo Skating Club, Inc.
1250 Amherst Street
Buffalo, NY 14216
(716)875-1419

†Holiday Twin Rinks
3465 Broadway
Buffalo, NY 14227
(716)685-3660

†Skating Association for the Blind
and Handicapped
3236 Main Street
Buffalo, NY 14214
(716) 694-5583

*Shove Park Rink
Camillus Figure Skating Club
Slawson Drive
Camillus, NY 13031
(315)487-5085

*Appleton Arena
St. Lawrence Figure Skating Club,
Inc.
St. Lawrence University
Canton, NY 13617
(315)379-5011

*Clinton Arena
Clinton Figure Skating Club
Kirkland Avenue
Clinton, NY 13323
(315)853-5541

*Abe Stark Ice Rink
Interboro Figure Skating Club
W. 19th Street and Boardwalk
Coney Island, NY 11224
(212)266-7937

*All Weather Roll 'N' Ice
Paumanok Figure Skating Club
1128 Sunrise Highway
Copiague, NY 11726
(516)842-8264

†*P.E.R. Center Ice Arena
Cortland State University
Cortland College Community Figure
Skating Club
Cortland, NY 13045
(607)753-4964

†Homowack Ice Rink/Jon Newson
  Ice Skating Rink
Luerenkill Road
Ellenville, NY 12428
(914)647-5751

†Nevele C. C. Skating Rink
Nevele Hotel
Ellenville, NY 12428
(914)647-6000

Murray Athletic Education Center
Elmira Figure Skating Club, Inc.
Elmira College, Associate
Elmira, NY 14902
(607)739-8786

*Grippen Park Ice Rink
Binghamton Figure Skating Club
S. Grippen Avenue
Endicott, NY 13760
(607)748-9461

†*Flushing Meadow Rink
  Park Figure Skating Club, Inc.
Corona Park
Flushing, NY 11352
(212)271-1966

*Salmon River Central School Arena
Shamrock Figure Skating Club
Fort Covington, NY 12937
(518)358-9510

†Freeport Recreation Center
130 E. Merrick Road
Freeport, NY 11520
(516)223-8000

*Fulton Community Center
Fulton Figure Skating Club, Inc.
W. Broadway
Fulton, NY 13069
(315)598-9928

*Nassau Community College
Metropolitan Figure Skating Club, Inc.
Hangar 5, Stewart Avenue
Garden City, NY 11040
(516)222-7501

†*Low Tor Ice Arena
Bear Mountain Figure Skating Club, Inc.
205 Ramapo Road
Garnerville, NY 10923
(914)429-2805

*Ira S. Wilson Ice Arena
State University College, Associate
State University of New York
Geneseo, NY 14454
(716)245-5211

†Geneva Recreation Complex
666 S. Exchange Street
Geneva, NY 14456
(315)789-2277

*Civic Center
Glens Falls Figure Skating Club
Glens Falls, NY 12801
(518)761-3852

†*Parkwood Skating Rink
Great Neck Figure Skating Club,
  Inc.
65 Arrandale Road
Great Neck, NY 11023
(516)487-2976

Grossinger Ice Arena
Grossinger Hotel
Grossinger, NY 12734
(914)292-5000

*Starr Rink
Colgate Hamilton Skating Club
Colgate University
Broad Street

Hamilton, NY 13346
(315)824-1000

†*Cantiague Park Ice Rink
Cantiague Figure Skating Club, Inc.
W. John Street
Hicksville, NY 11801
(516)935-3501

*Huntington Country Club
The Winter Club
Rt. 25A
Huntington, NY 11743
(516)427-0876

†Cass Park Ice Rink
Taughannock Boulevard
Ithaca, NY 14850
(607)273-1090

*James Lynah Rink
Cornell Figure Skating Club of
Ithaca
Cornell University
Ithaca, NY 14853
(607)256-2312

*Allen Park Rink
Jamestown Skating Club
Jamestown, NY 14701
(716)661-2315

†*Harvey School Ice Rink
Hickory Hill Figure Skating Club
Rt. 22
Katonah, NY 10536
(914)232-3618

Concord Hotel
Kiamesha Lake, NY 12751
(914)794-4000

Superior Ice Rink
270 Indian Head Road

Kings Park, NY 11754
(516)269-3904

†*Lake Placid Olympic Complex
The Skating Club of Lake Placid
216 Main Street
Lake Placid, NY 12946
(518)523-3325

†Hommocks Park Ice Rink
Hommocks Road
Larchmont, NY 10538
(914)834-1069

†*Kenan Center Arena
Lockport Figure Skating Club
195 Beattie Avenue
Lockport, NY 14094
(716)433-6373

†*Sports Club
Beaver Dam Winter Sports Club
Kaintuck Lane
Locust Valley, NY 11560
(516)671-1923

†*Nassau County Arena
Nassau Figure Skating Club, Inc.
Long Island Figure Skating Club
Magnolia Boulevard and Bay Drive
Long Beach, NY 11561
(516)889-3839

*Massena Community Arena
Massena Figure Skating Club, Inc.
Hartel-Haven Plaza
Massena, NY 13662
(315)769-3161

†*Rockland Sport-O-Rama
Skating Club of Rockland New York
18 College Road
Monsey, NY 10952
(914)356-3919

*New Hartford Recreation Center
The Skating Club of New Hartford
Hill Street
New Hartford, NY 13413
(315)724-0600

†The Ice Studio
1034 Lexington Avenue
New York, NY 10021
(212)535-0304

Madison Square Garden
4 Pennsylvania Plaza
New York, NY 10001
(212)563-8150

†*Sky Rink, Midtown Skating Corporation
Manhattan Figure Skating Club, Inc.
450 W. 33rd Street
New York, NY 10001
(212)695-6556

*Hyde Park Ice Pavilion
Skating Club of Niagara Falls, Inc.
522 Memorial Parkway
Niagara Falls, NY 14301
(716)278-8231

*Tonawanda Sports Center
Grand Island Figure Skating Club
Ridge Road
North Tonawanda, NY 14120

*Ogdensburg Free Academy Golden Dome
Ogdensburg Figure Skating Club
Ogdensburg, NY 13669
(315)393-5320

*YMCA Ice Forum
South Towns YMCA Figure Skating Club
S-3636 Eggert Road
Orchard Park, NY 14127
(716)662-1222

*Golden Romney Field House
Oswego Figure Skating Club, Inc.
State University College
Oswego, NY 13126
(315)341-2500

Trinity Pawling School
Pawling, NY 12564
(914)855-3100

*Crete Memorial Civic Center
Skating Club of the Adirondacks, Inc.
Beach Road
Plattsburgh, NY 12901
(518)563-4431

*Maxcy Hall Ice Arena
Potsdam State University
Potsdam, NY 13676
(315)268-3762

Pine Street Arena
The Potsdam Figure Skating Club
Pine Street
Potsdam, NY 13676
(315)265-4030

Walker Arena
Clarkson College
Potsdam, NY 13676
(315)268-7750

†*Mid-Hudson Civic Center McCann
Arena
Dutchess Figure Skating Club
Hudson Valley Figure Skating Club
Civic Center Plaza
Poughkeepsie, NY 12601
(914)454-5800

Boys Club of Rochester, Inc.
One Boys Club Place
Rochester, NY 14206
(716)325-2216

†Lake Shore Rinks, Inc.
123 Ling Road
Rochester, NY 14612
(716)865-2800

†*Frank Ritter Memorial Arena
Genesee Figure Skating Club
Rochester Institute of Technology,
   Associate
Rochester Institute of Technogy
One Lomb Memorial Drive
Rochester, NY 14623
(716)475-2222

Rochester War Memorial
100 Exchange Street
Rochester, NY 14623
(716)546-2030

 *Rouses Point Recreation Center
North Country Skating Club
Lake Street
Rouses Point, NY 12979
(518)297-6776

†*Playland Ice Casino
Rye Figure Skating Club, Inc.
Playland Park
Rye, NY 10580
(914)967-2040

†*Rye Country Day School
Rye Country Day School Skating
   Club
Gerald Lagrange Field House
Cedar Street
Rye, NY 10580
(914)348-1932

 †Saratoga Springs Youth Commission
   Recreation Skating Rink
East and Excelsior Avenues
Saratoga Springs, NY 12866
(518)584-6590

†*Achilles Rink
Achilles Figure Skating Club, Inc.
Union College
Schenectady, NY 12308
(518)370-6133

†Center City Ice Skating
433 State Street
Schenectady, NY 12305
(518)370-5007

*Austin Park Ice Rink
Skaneateles Figure Skating Club
Austin Park
Skaneateles, NY 13152
(315)685-5607

Pines Hotel Ice Skating Rink
South Fallsburg, NY 12779
(914)434-6000

Raleigh Hotel Rink
Raleigh Hotel
South Fallsburg, NY 12779
(914)434-7000

*Clifton Fine Arena
Clifton Fine Figure Skating Association
Star Lake, NY 13690
(315)848-2578

War Memorial Rink
Victory Boulevard and Labau Street
Staten Island, NY 10314
(212)442-4409

Onandaga County War Memorial
515 Montgomery Street
Syracuse, NY 13202
(315)425-2650

*Sunnycrest Rink
Salt City Figure Skaters
Robinson Road
Syracuse, NY 13206

*Youth Arena Building
Syracuse Figure Skating Club, Inc.
New York State Fair Grounds
Syracuse, NY 13209
(315)487-6422

*Houston Field House
Hudson-Mohawk Figure Skating Club
Peoples Avenue
Troy, NY 12180
(518)270-6262

†Randall School of Ice Skating
200 Oakwood Avenue
Troy, NY 12182
(518)274-2392

*Fairground Ice Arena
Figure Skating Club of Watertown,
  Inc.
W.T. Field Drive
Watertown, NY 13601
(315)782-8870

†Smith Rink
USMA Bldg. 600
West Point, NY 10996
(914)938-3727

*Sabreland
Kenawan Skating Club
3385 Niagara Falls Boulevard
Wheatfield, NY 14220
(716)695-1055

†*Ebersole Ice Rink
White Plains Figure Skating Club
95 Lake Street
White Plains, NY 10605
(914)682-4348

†Westchester Skating School
150 N. Broadway
White Plains, NY 10603
(914)428-4976

*Amherst Skating Club
Scarbora Drive
Williamsville, NY 14221
(716)634-3887

†Edward J. Murray Memorial Skating
  Center
348 Tuckahoe Road
Yonkers, NY 10710
(914)779-5249

North Carolina
†*Polar Palace Ice Rink
Blue Ridge Figure Skating Club
Boone Heights Shopping Center
Boone, NC 28607
(704)264-4121

Charlotte Auditorium-Coliseum
2700 E. Independence Road
Charlotte, NC 28202
(704)372-3600

†*Ice Capades Chalet
Eastland Mall Ice Skating Club
5595 Central Avenue
Charlotte, NC 28212
(706)568-0772

†Holiday Ice Rink
638 Grandview Drive, N.E.
Concord, NC 28025
(706)782-9028

†Fort Bragg Ice Skating
Bldg. #3-1606, Reilly Road
Fort Bragg, NC 28307
(919)396-5127

†*Ice Chalet
Greensboro Ice Skating Club, Inc.
Carolina Circle Mall
Greensboro, NC 27405
(919)375-3010

†*Daniel Boone Ice Rink
Daniel Boone Ice Skating Club
Old Rt. 86
Hillsboro, NC 27278
(919)732-4647

†Beneath the Elms Ice Rink
450 N. Cherry Street
Winston-Salem, NC 27102
(919)727-2975

North Dakota
Bismark Civic Center
Sixth and Sweet
Bismark, ND 58501
(701)222-6487

*Winter Sports Building
Lake Region Skating Club
Devils Lake, ND 58301
(701)662-7488

*The Coliseum
Red River Valley Figure Skating
  Club
807-17th Avenue
Fargo, ND 58102
(701)232-8752

*Grand Forks Arena
Border Blades Figure Skating Club
1122 Seventh Avenue South
Grand Forks, ND 58201
(701)772-6881

Winter Sports Arena
University of North Dakota
Grand Forks, ND 58201
(701)777-2654

*John Wilson Arena
Jamesriver Figure Skating Club
7th Street and 12th Avenue

Jamestown, ND 58401
(701)252-3939

*All Seasons Arena
Magic City Figure Skating Club
State Fair Grounds
Minot, ND 58701
(701)852-3113

Ohio
Bird Arena
Ohio University
Athens, OH 45701
(614)594-5485

†*Bowling Green State University Ice
  Arena
Bowling Green Skating Club
Bowling Green State University, As-
  sociate
Bowling Green, OH 43403
(419)372-2264

*Multi-purpose Recreation Center
Brooklyn Figure Skating Club of Ohio
7600 Memphis Avenue
Brooklyn, OH 44144
(216)351-2111

Cincinnati Gardens
2250 Seymour Avenue
Cincinnati, OH 45202
(513)731-8300

†*Northland Ice Center/Queen City
  Figure Skating Club
Figure Skating Club of Cincinnati
10400 Reading Road
Cincinnati, OH 45241
(513)563-0001

*Cleveland Heights Recreation
   Pavilion
Pavilion Skating Club of Cleveland
   Heights and Cleveland Heights
   Skating Club
One Monticello Boulevard
Cleveland Heights, OH 44118
(216)371-6510

*Ohio State University Ice Rink
Columbus Figure Skating Club
Ohio State University, Associate
390 W. Woodruff Avenue
Columbus, OH 43210
(614)422-4153

†*Dayton Hara Sports Arena-Winterland
Dayton Figure Skating Club
1001 Shiloh Springs Road
Dayton, OH 45415
(513)278-4776

*Clifford E. Orr Arena
Euclid Blade and Edge Club, Inc.
22550 Milton Drive
Euclid, OH 44123
(216)731-8440

†Hancock Recreation Center
3430 N. Main Street
Findlay, OH 45840
(419)423-8534

*Garfield Heights Recreation Center
Garfield Heights Figure Skating Club
12001 Tonsing Drive
Garfield Heights, OH 44125
(216)475-7272

†Hamilton Sports Arena
1600 Peck Boulevard
Hamilton, OH 45011
(513)895-2168

†*Kent State University Ice Arena
Kent Skating Club
Kent State University, Associate
Kent, OH 44240
(216)672-2415

*Winterhurst Ice Rink
Winterhurst Figure Skating Club
14740 Lakewood Heights Boulevard
Lakewood, OH 44107
(216)521-0019

†City of Mentor Department of
   Parks, Recreation, and Public Lands
8500 Civic Center Boulevard
Mentor, OH 44060
(216)255-1100, ext. 260

Williams Ice Rink
Oberlin College
Woodland Avenue
Oberlin, OH 44074
(216)775-8149

†*Miami University Ice Arena
Oxford Skating Club
Miami University, Associate
Oxford, OH 45056
(513)529-6830

*Forestwood Ice Rink
Forestwood Figure Skating Club
5000 Forestwood Drive
Parma, OH 44129
(216)886-4994

†*Parma Heights Municipal Ice Rink
Greenbrier Figure Skating Club
6200 Pearl Road
Parma Heights, OH 44130
(216)842-5006

Coliseum
2329 Streetsboro Road

Richfield, OH 44286
(216)659-9100

†*Rocky River Recreation Center
West Shore Figure Skating Club
21018 Hilliard Boulevard
Rocky River, OH 44116
(216)331-0600

*Cleveland Skating Club
2500 Kemper Road
Shaker Heights, OH 44120
(216)791-2800

*Thornton Park Ice Rink
Shaker Figure Skating Club
20701 Farnsleigh Road
Shaker Heights, OH 44120
(216)751-0828

*Tam O'Shanter Sports Center, Inc.
Toledo Figure Skating Club
7060 Sylvania Avenue
Sylvania, OH 43560
(419)882-1612

*Hobart Arena
Troy Skating Club
Adams Street
Troy, OH 45373
(513)339-2911

Ice Chalet
560 Charring Cross Boulevard
Westerville, OH 43081
(614)891-5101

†Mill Creek Park Rink
816 Glenwood Avenue
Youngstown, OH 44502
(216)744-4171

Oklahoma
Myriad Convention Center
One Myriad Gardens

Oklahoma City, OK 73125
(405)232-8871

*Oklahoma City Figure Skating Club
P.O. Box 75644
Oklahoma City, OK 73147

Tulsa Assembly Center
100 Civic Center
Tulsa, OK 74101
(918)581-5521

†*Williams Center Forum
Tulsa Figure Skating Club, Inc.
One Williams Center
Tulsa, OK 74101
(918)585-1286

Oregon
Valley Ice Arena
Carousel Figure Skating Club
9300 S.W. Beaverton-Hillsdale Highway
Beaverton, OR 97005
(503)297-2521

†*Ice Capades Chalet
Portland Ice Skating Club
Clackamas Town Center
Portland, OR 97266
(503)654-7733

†Lloyd Center Ice Pavilion
2201 Lloyd Center
Portland, OR 97232
(503)288-6073

Memorial Coliseum Complex
1401 N. Wheeler Avenue
Box 2746
Portland, OR 97208
(503)235-8771

†*Silver Skate Ice Rink
   Silver Skate Figure Skating Club
   1210 N.E. 102nd Avenue
   Portland, OR 97220
   (503)255-4644

Pennsylvania
†*Ice Palace
   Penguin Figure Skating Club, Inc.
   623 Hanover Avenue
   Allentown, PA 18103
   (215)435-3031

†North Park Ice Rink
   303 Pearce Mill Road
   Allison Park, PA 15101
   (412)935-1971

†*Philadelphia Skating Club and Humane Society
   Holland Avenue and County Line
   Ardmore, PA 19003
   (215)642-8700

†Beaver County Ice Arena
   R.D. 1, Box 526
   Beaver Falls, PA 15010
   (412)846-5600

†Rostraver Gardens
   Rt. 51
   Belle Vernon, PA 15012
   (412)379-7100

†South Park Skating Rink
   Corrigan Drive
   Bethel Park, PA 15129
   (412)833-1199

†*Grundy Ice Center
   Colonial Skating Club
   700 Jefferson Avenue
   Bristol, PA 19007
   (215)788-3312

†*Melody Brook Ice Skating Rink
   Quaker City Figure Skating Club
   Rt. 309 and Lenhart Road
   Colmar, PA 18915
   (215)822-3613

*Old York Road Skating Club
   York and Church
   Elkins Park, PA 19117
   (215)635-0331

†*Glenwood Ice Skating Rink
   Westminster Figure Skating Club of
      Erie
   W. 37th and Cherry Streets
   Erie, PA 16508
   (814)868-3651

†*Kirk S. Nevin Skating Rink
   Greensburg Figure Skating Club
   Rt. 119 North, Box 967
   Greensburg, PA 15601
   (412)834-4880

†Haverford Township Skadium
   Darby and Manoa Roads
   Havertown, PA 19083
   (215)853-2226

*Hershey Park Arena
   Hershey Figure Skating Club
   W. Derry Road
   Hershey, PA 17033
   (717)534-3900

†Mack Park Ice Rink
   719 Philadelphia Street
   Indiana, PA 15701
   (412)463-3473

†*Cambria County War Memorial
      Arena
   Johnstown Figure Skating Club
   326 Napoleon Street

Johnstown, PA 13901
(814)536-5156

*Upper Marion YMCA
Skating Club of Radnor
431 W. Valley Forge Road
King of Prussia, PA 19406
(215)265-1910

*Meadville Recreation Complex
Meadville Figure Skating Club
Meadville, PA 16335
(814)724-6154

†*Cumberland Skateium
Keystone Figure Skating Club
860 Wesley Drive
Mechanicsburg, PA 17055
(717)697-9477

†Ice Palace, Inc.
Monroeville Mall
Monroeville, PA 15146
(412)372-2652

†Mt. Lebanon Recreation Center
900 Cedar Road
Mt. Lebanon, Pittsburgh, PA 15216
(412)561-4363

*Ramage Hasson Skating Rink
Oil City Figure Skating Club
Hasson Park
Oil City, PA 16301
(814)676-9070

†*Class of 23 Ice Rink
University of Pennsylvania Figure
Skating Club, Associate
3130 Walnut Street
Philadelphia, PA 19104
(215)387-9223

The Spectrum, Inc.
Broad Street and Pattison Avenue

Philadelphia, PA 19104
(215)336-3600

†*Wissahickon Skating Club
Willow Grove Avenue and Cherokee Street
Philadelphia, PA 19118
(215)247-1759

*Civic Arena
Pittsburgh Figure Skating Club, Inc.
300 Auditorium Place
Pittsburgh, PA 15219
(412)642-1800

The Hill School
Pottstown, PA 19464
(215)326-1000

†Springfield Township Ice Skating Club
50 Powell Road
Springfield, PA 19064
(215)544-1300

†*Penn State University Ice Pavilion
Penn State Figure Skating Club
Pennsylvania State University, Associate
University Park, PA 16802
(814)865-4102

†Lake Vue Ice Palace
Lakevue Drive
Valencia, PA 15059
(412)898-2440

Radnor Skating Rink
789 Lancaster Avenue
Villanova, PA 19085
(215)527-1230

†Face-Off Circle
1185 York Road
Warminster, PA 18974
(215)674-1345

*Greater Washington Ice Rink
Ice and Blades Club of Washington
Dunn Avenue
Washington, PA 15301
(412)222-9476

†Westtown Sports Center
1646 Westchester Pike
Westchester, PA 19380
(215)436-6791

†*Wilkes-Barre Ice-A-Rama
Wyoming Valley Ice Skating Club
Coal Street Park
Wilkes-Barre, PA 18702
(717)822-0891

Rhode Island
†Cranston Veterans Memorial Ice Rink
900 Phoenix Avenue
Cranston, RI 02920
(401)944-8690

†*Smithfield Municipal Rink
Smithfield Figure Skating Club
Smithfield High School, Associate
Pleasant View Avenue
Esmond, RI 02917
(401)231-7677

†Burrillville June Rockwell Community Rink
95 East Avenue
Harrisville, RI 02830
(401)568-8615

*Rhode Island Sports Center
Skating Club of Rhode Island, Inc.
Rt. 146
North Smithfield, RI 02895
(401)762-1588

*Dennis M. Lynch Arena
Providence Figure Skating Club

Beatty Street
Pawtucket, RI 02860
(401)728-7420

*Meehan Rink
Brown University, Associate
235 Hope Street
Providence, RI 02912
(401)863-2773

Providence Civic Center
One LaSalle Square
Providence, RI 02940
(401)331-0700

†Schneider Arena
Providence College
Providence, RI 02918
(401)865-2168

*William H. Thayer Memorial Arena
Warwick Figure Skaters
975 Sandy Lane
Warwick, RI 02886
(401-739-9000

†West Warwick High School Athletic Complex
Webster Knight Drive
West Warwick, RI 02893
(401)821-2567

†Mount Saint Charles Arena
800 Logee Street
Woonsocket, RI 02895
(401)769-7727

Tennessee
†Iceland of Chattanooga
Terminal Station
Chattanooga, TN 37402
(615)266-5000

†Ober Gatlinburg Ice Rink
Box 176, Ski Mountain Lodge

Gatlinburg, TN 37738
(615)436-4117

†Chalet Ice Rinks, Inc.
Box 10668, 100 Lebanon Street
Knoxville, TN 37919
(615)588-1858

†Ice Capades Chalet
Mall of Memphis
4440 American Way
Memphis, TN 38118
(901)362-8877

Mid-South Coliseum
Memphis, TN 38101
(901)274-3982

†*Ice Centennial
Nashville Figure Skating Club
23rd and Leslie Avenues
Nashville, TN 37203
(615)320-1401

Nashville Municipal Auditorium
417 Fourth Avenue North
Nashville, TN 37202
(615)259-6461

Texas
Amarillo Civic Center
Third and Buchanan
Amarillo, TX 79105
(806)378-3000

†*The Ice Rink
Northcross Figure Skating Club
Northcross Mall, 2525 W. Anderson
  Lane
Austin, TX 78766
(512)451-5102

Coliseum Ice Arena
Box 26010

Dallas, TX 75221
(214)821-1546

†*Ice Capades Chalet
Plaza of the Americas
Tri-Cities Figure Skating Club
Pearl at Bryon
Dallas, TX 76010
(214)748-4001

†*Ice Capades Chalet
Prestonwood Town Center
Dallas Figure Skating Club, Inc.
5301 Belt Line Road
Dallas, TX 75240
(214)980-8988

†Tandy Center Ice Rink
One Tandy Center
Fort Worth, TX 76102
(817)338-1300

Tarrant County Convention Center
1111 Houston Street
Fort Worth, TX 76101
(817)332-9222

†Will Rogers Ice Arena
One Amon Carter Square
Fort Worth, TX 76107
(817)870-8150

†*Ice Capades Chalet
Galeria Ice Skating Club
5015 Westheimer
Houston, TX 77056
(713)626-1292

†*Sharpstown Ice Center
Houston Figure Skating Club
Iceland Figure Skating Club, Inc.
7300 Bellerive Drive
Houston, TX 77036
(713)783-6171

†*Palace Ice Arena
Palace Figure Skating Club
1000 Hampshire Lane
Richardson, TX 75080
(214)234-5369

The Woodlands Ice Rink
2322 Buckthrone Place
Woodlands, TX 77380
(713)367-5154

Utah
†*Bountiful Recreation Center
Utah Figure Skating Club
150 W. 600 North
Bountiful, UT 84010
(801)292-0422

*Cottonwood Heights Figure Skating
Club of Utah
7500 S. 2700 East
Salt Lake City, UT 84121
(801)943-3160

†Hygeia Iceland
1208 E. 21st South
Salt Lake City, UT 84106
(801)466-8611

Salt Palace
100 Southwest Temple
Salt Lake City, UT 84125
(801)521-6920

Vermont
Nelson E. Withington Skating
Facility
Living Memorial Park, Box 513
Brattleboro Figure Figure Skating
Club, Inc., Box 665

Brattleboro, VT 05301
(802)254-6700

†*Burlington Municipal Arena
Champlain Valley Skating Club
Leddy Park, Box 3282
Burlington, VT 05401
(802)862-8869

Gutterson Rink
University of Vermont
Burlington, VT 05401
(802)656-2085

†Essex Junction Skating Facility
R.F.D. Marvin Heights
Essex Junction, VT 05452
(802)879-0871

Memorial Field House Arena
Middlebury College
Middlebury, VT 05753
(802)388-7923

Taylor Arena
Norwich University
Northfield, VT 05663
(802)485-5011

†St. Albans Skating Association
P.O. Box 855
St. Albans, VT 05478
(802)524-3728

Stowe Ice Rink
Stowe Skating Club, Inc.
Stowe, VT 05662

Virginia
†*Mt. Vernon Ice Rink
Ice Club of Washington
Washington Figure Skating Club

2017 Belleview Boulevard
Alexandria, VA 22307
(703)768-3223

†*Fairfax Ice Arena
Skating Club of Northern Virginia
3779 Pickett Road
Fairfax, VA 22031
(703)323-1133

*Hampton Coliseum
Tidewater Figure Skating Club
1000 Coliseum Drive
Hampton, VA 23666
(804)838-4203

Homestead Ice Skating Rink
Homestead Hotel
Hot Springs, VA 24445
(703)839-5500, ext. 2607

*Ice Unlimited
Skating Club of Richmond, Inc.
7801 W. Broad Street
Richmond, VA 23229
(804)222-5765

Skateland
Skating Club of Richmond, Inc.
Williamsburgh Road
Richmond, VA 23229
(804)222-5765

*Roanoke Civic Center
Roanoke Valley Figure Skating Club,
    Inc.
710 Williamson Road, N.E.
Roanoke, VA 24016
(703)981-1201

Washington
†*Burien Ice Chalet
Chalet Figure Skating Club

154 First Avenue South
Seattle, WA 98148
(206)243-4242

†*Highland Ice Arena
Highland Figure Skating Club
18005 Aurora Avenue North
Seattle, WA 98133
(206)546-2431

Seattle Center Coliseum and Arena
305 Harrison
Seattle, WA 98111
(206)625-4254

†*Lilac City Ice-A-Rena
Lilac City Figure Skating Club
N. 6321 Addison
Spokane, WA 99207
(509)489-9295

Riverside Park Ice Palace
Expo Site
Spokane, WA 99208
(509)456-3964

Spokane Coliseum
N. 1101 Howard Street
Spokane, WA 99210
(509)456-3204

†*YMCA Ice Chalet
Walla Walla Figure Skating Club, Inc.
First at Birch
Walla Walla, WA 99362
(509)525-9870

The City of Wenatchee Ice Rink
25 N. Worthen
Wenatchee, WA 98801
(509)662-3451

†*Sno-King Ice Arena
Overlake Skating Club
Seattle Skating Club
19803-68th Street West
West Lynnwood, WA 98036
(206)775-7511

West Virginia
*Civic Center Arena
Charleston Figure Skating Club
Reynolds Street
Charleston, WV 25301
(304)348-8077

†Monogalia County Recreation Commission Skating Rink
Mississippi Street
Morgantown, WV 26505
(304)292-6865

*Wheeling Park Ice Rink
Wheeling Figure Skating Club
1801 National Road
Wheeling, WV 26003
(304)242-3770

Wisconsin
*DePere Recreation Center
DePere Figure Skating Club, Inc.
1450 Ft. Howard Avenue
DePere, WI 54115
(414)336-1568

*Eagle Sports Arena
Eagle River Figure Skating Club
Highway 70 East
Eagle, WI 54521
(715)479-8804

*Hobbs Ice Arena
Eau Claire Figure Skating Club
1000 Menomonie

Eau Claire, WI 54701
(715)839-5040

Brown County Arena
1901 S. Oneida Street
Green Bay, WI 54305
(414)494-3401

†*Janesville Ice Arena
Janesville Figure Skating Club
821 Beloit Avenue
Janesville, WI 53545
(608)756-4445

†*Kenosha County Ice Arena
Southport Skating Club
7727-60th Avenue
Kenosha, WI 53140
(414)694-8010

Camp Randall Memorial Sports Center
University of Wisconsin
1430 Monroe Street
Madison, WI 53710
(608)233-3321

Dane County Exposition Center
1881 Expo Mall East
Madison, WI 53710
(608)257-5681

†*Madison Ice Arena
Figure Skating Club of Madison, Inc.
725 Forward Drive
Madison, WI 53711
(608)266-5500

Milwaukee Exposition and Convention Center and Arena
500 W. Kilbourn Avenue
Milwaukee, WI 53201
(414)271-4000

University School of Milwaukee
6401 N. Santa Monica

Milwaukee, WI 53201
(414)352-6000

*Wilson Park Recreation Center
Greater Milwaukee Figure Skating Club
4001 S. 20th Street
Milwaukee, WI 53221
(414)384-4748

†Tri County Ice Arena
700 E. Shady Lane
Neenah, WI 54956
(414)731-9731

†K. B. Willett Arena
1000 Minnesota Avenue
Stevens Point, WI 54481
(715)346-1576

*Superior Municipal Rink
Superior Figure Skating Club
1513 Oakes Avenue
Superior, WI 54880
(715)394-9822

Wessman Ice Arena
University of Wisconsin
2600 Catlin Avenue
Superior, WI 54880
(715)392-8101

*Hart Park Indoor Ice Arena
Wisconsin Figure Skating Club, Inc.
P.O. Box 13341, 7300 Chestnut
Wauwatosa, WI 53226
(414)258-3000

†Mayfair Mall Ice Chalet
2500 N. Mayfair Road
Wauwatosa, WI 53226
(414)257-3111

Wyoming
*Caspar Ice House
Caspar Figure Skating Club
1700 Fairgrounds Road
Caspar, WY 82601
(307)265-9706; 235-5775

CANADIAN FIGURE SKATING ASSOCIATION

1983–84 SECTION CHAIRMEN

Alberta
Mr. Bill Petrunik
2018-20th Avenue S.
Lethbridge, Alberta.
T1G 1G5
(403) 327-0683 (Res)

Central Ontario
Mr. Larry Simpson
93 Stone Street
Elmvale, Ontario.
LOL 1PO
(705) 322-1814 (Res)
(416) 752-4444 ext. 270 (Bus)

British Columbia
Mrs. Carole Skuta
2495 Paulsen Place, Kamloops, B.C.
V2B 5A2
(604) 376-9977

Eastern Ontario
Mrs. Marilyn Dunwoodie
Century Road, R.R. #3,
North Gower, Ont.
KOA 2TO
(613) 489-3455 (Res)
(613) 749-6811 (Bus)

Manitoba
Mr. Jim Teeple
856 Charleswood Road,
Winnipeg, Manitoba.
R3R 1K6
(204) 895-0884 (Res)
(204) 946-2421 (Bus)

New Brunswick
Mrs. Betty Bouma
R. R. #1, Box 78,
Robertville, N.B.
EOB 2KO
(506) 783-4995 (Res)
(506) 548-8821 (Bus)

Newfoundland
Mr. Andy Joy
81 Golf Avenue,
St. John's, NFLD.
A1C 5E1
(709) 579-2294 (Res)
(709) 726-7880 (Bus)

Northern Ontario
Mr. Dave Campbell
135 Birchwood Drive,
Sault Ste. Marie, Ont.
P6A 5R9
(705) 949-5921

Nova Scotia
Mrs. Helen Pate
1214 Prince Street,
Truro, N.S.
B2N 1J4
(902) 895-3062

Prince Edward Island
Mrs. Heather Howatt
R.R. #6,
Kensington, P.E.I.
COB 1MO
(902) 836-3614 (Res)

Quebec
Mr. Jean Dussault
1415 Jarry Street,
Montréal, Québec
H2E 2Z7
(514) 688-0314 (Res)
(514) 374-4700 ext 375 (Res)

Saskatchewan
Mr. Dave Balon
173 Tucker Crescent, Saskatoon, Saskatche-
wan
S7H 3J1
(306) 374-9479

Western Ontario
Mr. Jack Hodges
8 Wardell Crescent,
P.O. Box 8,
Hagersville, Ont.
NOA 1HO

Executive Director and Secretary-Treasurer
Mr. Lou Lefaive
333 River Road, 11th floor tower A,
Ottawa, Ontario
K1L 8H9
(613) 746-5953 (Bus)

BIBLIOGRAPHY

JOURNALS

United States

American Skating World
1216 Grandview Avenue
Pittsburgh, PA 15211
(412)488-3400
(800)245-6280
12 issues/year: $12.95/year, continental USA; $24.95/year, Canada; $50/year
  overseas

Professional Skaters Guild of America Newsletter
1552 Hertel Avenue
Buffalo, N.Y. 14216
(716)834-9431
Bimonthly: $10/year

Recreational Ice Skating
Ice Skating Institute of America
1000 Skokie Boulevard

Wilmette, IL 60091
(312)256-5060
Quarterly: $5/year

Skating
United States Figure Skating Association
20 First Street
Colorado Springs, CO 80906
(303)635-5200
10 issues/year: $12/year, USA; $27/year, Canada and overseas

Canada

Canadian Skater
Canadian Figure Skating Association
333 River Road
Ottawa, ON K1L 8B9
(613)746-5953
Bimonthly: $11/year, Canada; $13/year, USA and overseas by sea mail;
    $16/year, overseas by airmail

Denmark

Skøjtesport
Ole B. Thomson
Lindtoften 39
DK 2630 Taastrup

West Germany

Pirouette
Neue Weinsteige 48
Postfach 542
7 Stuttgart 1

Finland

Suomen Taitoluistel
Topeliuksenkatu 41a
00250 Helsinki 25

Great Britain

Ice and Roller Skate
One Strathmore Close
Caterham, Surrey CR3 5EQ

Netherlands

Schaatskroniek
Postbox 1120
3800 BC Amersfoort and J. Kleine
Heemskerklaan 73
6881 EN Velp

Norway

Skøytesport
Aage Johansen
Ensjøveien 30 B
Oslo 6

South Africa

The Outside Edge
21 Callavera
461 Windermere Road
Durban 4001

Sweden

Konstakningsnytt
Svenska Konstakningsförbundet
Idrottens Hus
123 87 Farsta

Switerzland

Le Patinage Suisse
Bannhalden 28
CH-8307 Effretikon

BOOKS

On Skating

Bass, Howard. *Skating: Elegance on Ice.* Secaucus, N.J.: Chartwell Books, 1980.
———. *Tackle Skating.* Lawrence, Mass.: Hutchinson, Merrimack Book Service, 1979.
Bird, Dennis L. *Our Skating Heritage, 1879–1979.* London: National Skating Association of Great Britain, Oyez Press, 1979.
Burchard, S. H. *Dorothy Hamill.* New York: Harcourt Brace Jovanovich, 1978.
Burka, Ellen. *Figure Skating.* Don Mills, Ont.: Collier-Macmillan Canada, 1974.
Butterworth, Carol, and Cloran, Rosemary. *Step by Step Ice Skating Guide.* Montpelier, Vt.: The Leahy Press, 1978.
Button, Dick. *Dick Button on Skates.* Englewood Cliffs, N.J.: Prentice-Hall, 1955.
———. *Instant Skating.* New York: Grosset & Dunlap, 1964.
Canadian Figure Skating Association. *Figure Skating Coaching Certification Program, Level I Manual.* Ottawa, Ont.: Canadian Figure Skating Association, 1980.
———. *Happier Figure Skating.* Ottawa, Ont.: Canadian Figure Skating Association, 1981.
Dedic, Josef. *Single Figure Skating for Beginners and Champions.* Prague: International Skating Union, Olympia, 1974.
De Leeuw, Dianne. *Figure Skating.* New York: Atheneum, 1978.
Diagram Group. *Enjoying Skating.* South Hackensack, N.J.: Stoeger Publishing, 1978.
Fassi, Carlo. *Figure Skating with Carlo Fassi.* New York: Scribners, 1980.
Faulkner, Margaret. *I Skate.* Boston: Little, Brown, 1979.
Goodfellow, Arthur. *Wonderful World of Skates.* Wilmette, Ill.: Ice Skating Institute of America, 1972.
Gross, George. *Donald Jackson: King of Blades.* Toronto: Queen City Publishing, 1977.
Harris, Ricky. *Choreography and Style for Ice Skaters.* New York: St. Martin's Press, 1980.
Krementz, Jill. *A Very Young Skater.* New York: Knopf, 1979.
Lussi, Gustave, and Richards, Maurice. *Championship Figure Skating.* New York: Ronald Press, 1951.
Lynn, Janet. *Peace and Love.* Carol Stream, Ill.: Creation House, 1973.
Merriam, Robert L. *The Ancient Art of Skating.* Deerfield, Mass.: Deerfield Academy, 1957
Money, Keith. *John Curry.* New York: Knopf, 1978.
Noyes, Tina, and Alexander, Freda. *I Can Teach You to Figure Skate.* New York: Elsevier Dutton, 1979.

Ogilvie, Robert S. *Basic Ice Skating Skills*. New York: Harper & Row, 1968.

Oglanby, Elva. *Toller*. Agincourt, Ont.: Gage Publishing, 1975.

Proctor, Marion. *Figure Skating*. Dubuque, Iowa: Wm. C. Brown, 1969.

Richardson, T. D. *Modern Figure Skating*. New York: Gordon Press, 1980.

————. *Your Book of Skating*. Central Islip, N.Y.: Transatlantic Arts, 1980.

Schaefer, Karl. *Living Pictures of My Figure Skating*. Vienna: Gerold's Sohn, 1937.

Scott, Barbara Ann, and Kirby, Michael. *Skating for Beginners*. New York: Knopf, 1953.

Soanes, Sydney V. *Ice Dancing*. Toronto, Queen City Publishing, 1981.

Sullivan, George. *Better Ice Skating*. New York: Dodd, Mead, 1976.

Turner, Roger F. *Edges*. Mansfield Press, 1973.

United States Figure Skating Association. *Evaluation of Errors in Figures*. Colorado Springs, Colo.: United States Figure Skating Association, n.d. Updated periodically.

Wright, Benjamin T. *Reader's Guide to Figure Skating's Hall of Fame*. Colorado Springs, Colo.: United States Figure Skating Association, 1977. Updated periodically.

Training-Related

American Alliance for Health, Physical Education. Recreation, and Dance. *Nutrition for Athletes*. Reston, Va.: AAHPERD Publications, 1971.

Anderson, Bob. *Stretching*. Bolinas, Calif.: Shelter Publications, 1980.

Dominguez, Richard H. *The Complete Book of Sports Medicine*. New York: Scribners, 1979.

————, and Gajda, Robert S. *Total Body Training*. New York: Scribners, 1982.

Featherstone, Donald, and Allen Rona. *Dancing without Danger: The Prevention and Treatment of Ballet Dancing Injuries*. San Diego, Calif.: A. S. Barnes, 1970.

Holt, Laurence E. *Scientific Stretching for Sport*. Halifax, Nova Scotia: Sport Research Limited, n.d.

Mason, Anne Keohane, ed. *A Conditioning Manual for Figure Skaters*. Ottawa, Ont.: Canadian Figure Skating Association, 1980.

Sports in General

Brown, Gene, and Keylin, Arlene. *Sports as Reported by The New York Times.* New York: Arno Press, 1976.

Campbell, J. W. *The Snow Lover's Guide to Winter Sports.* Englewood Cliffs, N.J.: Prentice-Hall, 1979.

Grombach, John V. *The Official Olympic Guide.* Scranton, Pa.: Times Books, 1980.

Kaplan, Janice. *Women and Sports.* New York: Viking, 1979.

Kilinan, Lord, and Rodda, John. *The Olympic Games: 80 Years of People, Events, and Records.* New York: Macmillan, 1976.

Leonard, George. *The Ultimate Athlete.* New York: Viking, 1975.

Menke, Frank G. *Encyclopedia of Sports.* New York, Doubleday, 1977.

Michener, James A. *Sports in America.* New York, Fawcett, 1977.

Salak, John S. *Dictionary of American Sports.* New York: Philosophical Library, 1961.

A few of the preceding books are no longer in print but are often available in bookstores specializing in sports books or from NGBs.

In the United States, there is a substantial collection of references at the United States Figure Skating Hall of Fame and Museum, 20 First Street, Colorado Springs, CO 80906; (303)635-5200

INDEX